Using Research to Lead School Improvement

Turning Evidence Into Action

SCOTT C. BAUER

S. DAVID BRAZER

George Mason University

SAGE

Los Angeles | London | New Delhi
Singapore | Washington DC

For information:

SAGE Publications, Inc.
2455 Teller Road
Thousand Oaks,
   California 91320
E-mail: order@sagepub.com

SAGE Publications Ltd.
1 Oliver's Yard
55 City Road
London EC1Y 1SP
United Kingdom

SAGE Publications India Pvt. Ltd.
B 1/I 1 Mohan Cooperative
   Industrial Area
Mathura Road, New Delhi 110 044
India

SAGE Publications Asia-Pacific Pte. Ltd.
33 Pekin Street #02-01
Far East Square
Singapore 048763

Printed in the United States of America

Library of Congress Cataloging-in-Publication Data

Bauer, Scott C. (Scott Charles)
Using research to lead school improvement: turning evidence into action / Scott C. Bauer and S. David Brazer.
       p. cm.
Includes bibliographical references and index.
ISBN 978-1-4129-7405-9 (pbk.)

   1. School improvement programs—Research—United States. 2. Educational change—United States. I. Brazer, S. David. II. Title.

LB2822.82.B38 2012
371.2′07072—dc22   2010038674

This book is printed on acid-free paper.

11   12   13   14   15   10   9   8   7   6   5   4   3   2   1

Acquisitions Editor:	Diane McDaniel
Editorial Assistant:	Theresa Accomazzo
Production Editor:	Jane Haenel
Copy Editor:	Megan Speer
Typesetter:	C&M Digitals (P) Ltd.
Proofreader:	Sarah J. Duffy
Indexer:	Terri Corry
Cover Designer:	Candice Harman
Marketing Manager:	Katherine Winter
Permissions Editor:	Adele Hutchinson

BRIEF CONTENTS

Detailed Contents

PREFACE

*U*sing *Research to Lead School Improvement* requires some explanation because it is considerably different from most traditional education research texts. Springing from our work to create a unique course that couples research with action, this book is intended to meet the needs of prospective school leaders who aspire to promote continuous improvement in teaching and learning in their schools. But it is not just for novices. We believe this book will stimulate the thinking and inform the practice of veteran administrators as well. The role of the school principal continues to evolve from competent manager to inspiring instructional leader. This book supports that transition and would serve well any course or professional development activity designed to help leaders develop new insights and perspectives as they strive to work with their faculty to solve knotty instructional challenges. The purpose of this book is to engage you, the reader, in action planning for instructional leadership with research elements supporting development and implementation of school improvement projects.

This book is our attempt to slay at least two dragons: (a) the confusion that prospective and practicing leaders are likely to face with respect to learning about, conducting, and using research and (b) the notion that education leadership programs are not rigorous or relevant enough in today's complex world. Our belief is that this book helps readers meet and exceed expectations of data-informed decision making, and it can be a toolbox to help education leadership programs remain current and lead the way toward more thoughtful and effective use of research.

A NEED FOR CHANGE

Improvement requires change, and we—probably similar to you—needed the motivation to change before we began to improve the research offering in our master's and licensure program in education leadership. Motivation came from our own examination of program needs and feedback we received from students and school district partners. Deeper inquiry suggested that we faced a problem of curricular relevance. In our former program of study, to the extent that students developed skills in the use of research, they did it in the context of the traditional, collegewide research class. Typically, such a class was taught by a member of the foundations faculty—often a statistician—and the focus was on teachers becoming good consumers of research. In some cases, depending on the instructor, students may have been asked to write a grant or action research proposal as a performance-based activity, but more typically, assessment involved paper-and-pencil tests. Connections to leading schools and districts were largely or entirely absent.

Data collected from students and administrators in school systems throughout the region we serve further suggested that there was a wide chasm between what students learned about research and their needs as novice school leaders. Many school districts espouse an emphasis on the use of research to inform decision making. We found ourselves out of sync with our students' professional needs because our program lacked significant experience in applying the use of research to decision making associated with school improvement. Students typically took their research course at the very end of their program of study and often reported that what they learned in the research course was largely irrelevant.

As students of organizational theory, we appreciate that effective change requires a balance of pressure and support. Responding to productive pressure, we changed the traditional research course in our leadership preparation program, with its focus on administrators becoming good consumers of research, into a course that emphasizes using research literature, school-site data, and leadership skills to engage school colleagues in change processes that are directed squarely at improving the performance of an identified portion of their school's student body. We supported one another through collegial design and planning of the new research course. Three principles guided our work. First, we agreed that the course must emphasize how leaders use research to improve student achievement. Second, the performances embedded in the course should afford students the opportunity to work collaboratively with teachers and leaders in their schools to apply research to design instructional changes. Third, students ought to be active leaders in a change process that will ultimately be implemented and evaluated in their schools. In short, course experiences are focused on data- and research-informed instructional leadership.

The process embedded in this book also has its genesis, in part, in years of field work with school principals and their leadership teams. One of us (Bauer), in his role as research director of the School Leadership Center of Greater New Orleans, helped create the center's Learning Initiatives program, which involves cohorts of schools each year in a process of continuous improvement that mirrors in broad strokes the steps we lay out in this book. These experiences provided opportunities to learn about and improve our understanding of how research and school improvement intersect. They also convinced us that the process we present can be critical to the school improvement efforts of in-service school leaders.

Using Research to Lead School Improvement fills a gap in both the leadership preparation literature and the libraries of practicing school and district administrators. It is a unique guide through the instructional improvement process that begins with focusing on a well-articulated program and cycles through data collection and analysis, gleaning information from relevant literature to build a thorough understanding of the causes of the problem, implementing a solution, evaluating the effort, and modifying actions for greater effectiveness. In short, this book provides clear steps in an evidence-based process of continuous improvement.

DEVELOPING MORE EFFECTIVE INSTRUCTIONAL LEADERSHIP

Leaders will thrive if they can bring school-based action research and published research to bear in debates about both root causes of student achievement problems and potential solutions for addressing them. Thus, we take the lessons learned from our teaching and seek to combine leadership, research, and action. In the current policy context of No Child Left Behind and all the accountability pressures that come with it, a practical approach to using research to help solve problems makes sense.

Reading about how to conduct research, create new knowledge, and formulate action plans may be helpful, but we wish to go beyond mere "book learning" so that readers can practice the steps involved in using research to lead school improvement. We foster a bias for action through a series of performances that engage you in leadership learning in the context of creating a research-based plan for improving instruction in your school. Our approach involves your accessing research knowledge and using the research process to diagnose, plan, enact, and assess improvement efforts. The experiences included in the book prepare readers to launch school improvement ventures focused on student achievement; along the way, the learning journey will include introduction to concepts and processes of research and tools that support the actions leaders take to improve their schools. Our hope is that readers will implement the school improvement projects they design—either in-service administrators leading improvement planning and implementation processes or aspiring school leaders designing and nurturing instructional improvement. In our graduate program, for example, students enact school improvement projects they design in the research class as a key part of their internship experiences.

BECOMING A RESEARCH-INFORMED LEADER: THE LAYOUT OF THIS BOOK

This book has two major objectives. The first is to learn a process that provides a firm research foundation for readers. Steps include

- working collaboratively to develop an improvement focus area,

- reading published literature to glean pertinent information, and

- understanding the basic elements of quantitative and qualitative research.

The second major objective of the book is to teach readers how to produce diagnoses, plans, and evaluations that are crucial products of the school improvement planning cycle. Specific strategies for doing so are

- gathering and analyzing standardized test data and additional evidence at the school site;

- engaging in problem identification, problem articulation, and root cause analysis;

- setting objectives and engaging in action planning; and

- implementing and evaluating school improvement efforts.

Conceptually, we include material to help students understand the larger picture of making change and all the challenges that come with it—understanding the broader organizational context, change theory, and the role of leaders in school change. Practically, we include activities and discussions for in-class work, worksheets to be completed at students' school sites and/or at home, and detailed assignments with rubrics that professors may use and adapt for authentic assessment purposes. All these materials are designed to help professors, students, and practitioners apply the kinds of approaches to school improvement planning that we endorse.

AUDIENCE

We intend to speak to a broad audience—aspiring leaders, practicing leaders, university faculty, and others. Our point is that we believe that instructional leadership can come from many different quarters and that this book has value for all involved in the effort to improve student achievement. We want you, the reader, to understand that we intend this book for a variety of educators, yet for the sake of simplicity and economy of language, we address ourselves primarily to students in education leadership preparation programs and their instructors.

STRUCTURE AND RATIONALE

Topics are organized to prepare readers for the creation, implementation, and evaluation of a school improvement project plan. Consequently, our path goes from more conceptual to more practical as the book progresses from foundational theory through understanding published research to action planning and evaluation. Students revisit big-picture issues such as organization theory, change theory, and epistemology that we assume they have already encountered in their leadership preparation programs, as they relate to the development of a personal perspective on making change that makes a difference. At the same time, we offer practical approaches to understanding research methods embedded in published literature. Research tools are discussed at a relatively elementary level that takes into account the analytical experience and amount of time most likely to be available to practicing school leaders. This is not a text for an advanced or doctoral-level course; it is designed specifically for aspiring and practicing school leaders (teachers and administrators). Yet we understand that no leader works alone; so we advocate an organizational learning model that involves leading change in collaboration with colleagues and supervisors.

Our pedagogical approach is aligned with national trends in leadership preparation and professional development programming, focusing on embedding opportunities for authentic leadership experiences into coursework. This is consistent with our belief that students must have numerous opportunities to practice the kinds of strategies and techniques we are promoting to enhance their probability of success as they engage in change efforts concentrated on improving student achievement.

The book also incorporates what we know about effectively leading instructional change. In contrast to books that spotlight action research for teachers, we assume that students in leadership preparation programs need to learn to lead outside their own classrooms and begin to think about engaging others in change that affects larger units, ideally the whole school. As change leaders, students who engage in the learning activities embedded in this book will need to do so in consultation with administrators as well as other teachers in their school. We provide material and exercises to support that work.

Faculty who facilitate learning in leadership preparation programs should find this book helpful. The key performance-based activities that are provided to focus learning are accompanied by guidelines suitable for inclusion in course syllabi, along with assessment rubrics that are aligned with national standards. All activities and products are carefully scaffolded so that, across an entire semester, student engagement mirrors steps leaders would typically take in the real-world setting of schools. Learning activities fold together systematically, ending in the creation of a coherent, research-based school improvement plan that can be implemented and will have impact on the student's school.

THE PATH AHEAD

The chapters that follow engage the reader in a specific logic of action that says if our goal is student achievement, we must (1) understand an important instructional problem thoroughly, (2) learn how published literature informs the problem, (3) use literature and action research to articulate the problem clearly, (4) identify root causes of the problem, (5) engage in action planning, (6) implement a specific plan, and (7) evaluate the implementation both formatively and summatively. Not everything happens in schools and districts in a sequence as neat as this, but we make every effort to be neat and logical in our explanations that follow.

The chapters are organized into four larger parts that correspond to this book's broadly defined leadership themes—theoretical foundations, problem articulation, using research, and action planning. The introduction to Part I provides a brief rationale and overview of the first three chapters. The introductions to Parts II through IV also signal to the reader material contained in their chapters but in a different way. These part descriptions contain learning goals for the whole part—what we refer to as the Big Ideas. Each one also focuses the reader's attention on a student performance—an assignment—that we suggest instructors use to demonstrate understanding and build a student's school improvement project. We provide a graphic that shows where the reader is in the development of the project and a detailed description of the assignment, along with a corresponding assessment rubric. Each assessment rubric references the appropriate Educational Leadership Constituent Council (ELCC) standards to help both students and instructors place coursework into the framework of what prospective leaders are expected to know and be able to do. The complete list of ELCC standards is reprinted following the Preface. The introductions to Parts II through IV serve as road maps for both students and instructors.

Chapter 1 introduces the reader to the general context for conducting research in and about schools. We explain the tensions that exist regarding research—for both leadership and leadership preparation—and how they relate to the current context for school improvement. It is with this environment in mind that we provide the rationale for the research and action stages laid out in the rest of the book. This chapter is a conceptual road map for the process of improving student achievement and school performance.

Chapter 2 deals directly with leadership by explaining our perspective on the intersection among schools, research, and instructional leadership in the pursuit of improved student performance. Beginning with an explanation of our conceptual framework—or road map—for leading school improvement, we elaborate how research can enhance the quality of instructional leadership and decision making. We also explain specific leadership qualities and foci. We emphasize that leadership must be understood in the context of schools and districts as organizations with specific characteristics and environments. We provide a basic device for perceiving what happens in schools from multiple perspectives.

Chapter 3 broadens the conception of leadership to include facilitating collaboration and distributing leadership. We take the perspective that it is crucial to involve others—both within and beyond a core group that you choose—in your school improvement planning and implementation as a means to achieving higher-quality results. Many people throughout your school and district can assist you both conceptually and practically. More intensive involvement of others through a high-functioning team makes the work more feasible and encourages deeper roots for the change effort.

Chapter 4 emphasizes what is happening in readers' own schools. Improving student performance must begin with problem diagnosis in a specific area of student achievement. This chapter helps readers see their schools and the students and adults in them from a research perspective that will help them achieve a more accurate and useful problem diagnosis. By the end of the chapter, readers will understand how to look at their schools through a research lens, how to think more broadly about sources of evidence, and how to focus on a specific problem, challenge, or gap.

Chapter 5 is a practical guide to disseminating the knowledge you created in the process of problem diagnosis and articulation. We focus on organizing and displaying data effectively and clearly articulating what you conclude from data both orally and in writing.

With the instructional problem clearly identified, Chapter 6 takes up the discussion of root-cause analysis to understand why the problem exists and why it has persisted. Digging deeper into the problem in this fashion is critical to ensure that the reader's ultimate project embraces a compelling link between the causes of the problem the school faces and suggested solutions.

Chapter 7 presents strategies for conducting library research in support of the instructional challenge, problem, or gap the reader has identified. We provide readers with systematic ways of thinking about the kinds of sources they should pursue and how to go about finding them. By the end of the chapter, readers will know simple tactics to unearth the literature that will help them diagnose and articulate the achievement challenge they have identified.

Understanding published literature and conducting high-quality action research requires basic understanding of research methodology. Chapter 8 presents elements of research design and quantitative and qualitative data analysis. The purpose of this chapter is to help readers comprehend what they read in greater depth and acquire new tools to work with the data readily available at their school sites.

Chapter 9 follows with action planning. Readers learn in this chapter how to involve their teams in development of a clear, realistic proposal for improving student achievement. By the end of this chapter, readers will have considered the central elements of a viable action plan and will be ready to think about implementation and evaluation of what they have planned.

Chapter 10 concludes the book by taking readers into the process of enacting the plans they have made and determining if what they have done is meaningful to K–12 students. Planning implementation and evaluation helps readers understand what works and how to improve on their efforts in the future. Evaluation also nurtures inquiry habits of mind and keeps readers focused on continuous research to lead school improvement.

We have made every effort to write this book so that it is thorough, clear, and practical. We believe that the school improvement process is the most exciting and rewarding work in education. Our aspiration—our espoused theory—is that this book will help readers come to a similar conclusion as they feel empowered to make a meaningful difference in the lives of students, faculty, and administrators who look to them for leadership.

ACKNOWLEDGMENTS

We would like to thank the reviewers who put in the time and effort to give us insightful feedback:

Thomas L. Alsbury, North Carolina State University

Marilyn Jean Dono-Koulouris, St. John's University

Suzanne Franco, Wright State University

Lora Knutson, Governors State University

Lydia Kyei-Blankson, Illinois State University

We would also like to thank members of our writing group—Becky Fox, Julie Kidd, and Joe Maxwell—as well as doctoral student Rachel Charlton, for their patience and gracious criticism of early drafts. We are indebted beyond measure to both the staff of the School Leadership Center of Greater New Orleans and the principals and leadership teams who engaged with the center for sharing their learning as they improve their schools in the Learning Initiatives program. Most of all, we wish to thank our faculty colleagues and the licensure and master's students in the George Mason University College of Education and Human Development Education Leadership Program. We truly benefit from being members of the kind of collaborative team we describe in Chapter 3—the kind that we hope our students can assemble in their schools to support their work. The questions, contributions, and feedback our faculty colleagues provide as we implement and continue to reflect on our curricular redesign continue to shape our thinking. Our students have been willing guinea pigs, as they used various manuscript versions of *Using Research to Lead School Improvement* in their classes. Their responses to chapters provided both gratification and direction for revision. The feedback from all these sources has helped strengthen the book, yet we own any weaknesses that remain.

LIST OF TABLES AND FIGURES

TABLES

FIGURES

ELCC STANDARDS

Standards for Advanced Programs in Educational Leadership for Principals, Superintendents, Curriculum Directors, and Supervisors (January 2002)

Standard 1.0: Candidates who complete the program are educational leaders who have the knowledge and ability to promote the success of all students by facilitating the development, articulation, implementation, and stewardship of a school or district vision of learning supported by the school community.

- Develop a Vision
- Articulate a Vision
- Implement a Vision
- Steward a Vision
- Promote Community Involvement in the Vision

Standard 2.0: Candidates who complete the program are educational leaders who have the knowledge and ability to promote the success of all students by promoting a positive school culture, providing an effective instructional program, applying best practice to student learning, and designing comprehensive professional growth plans for staff.

- Promote Positive School Culture
- Provide Effective Instructional Program
- Apply Best Practice to Student Learning
- Design Comprehensive Professional Growth Plans

Standard 3.0: Candidates who complete the program are educational leaders who have the knowledge and ability to promote the success of all students by managing the organization, operations, and resources in a way that promotes a safe, efficient, and effective learning environment.

- Manage the Organization
- Manage Operations
- Manage Resources

Standard 4.0: Candidates who complete the program are educational leaders who have the knowledge and ability to promote the success of all students by collaborating with families and other community members, responding to diverse community interests and needs, and mobilizing community resources.

- Collaborate with Families and Other Community Members
- Respond to Community Interests and Needs
- Mobilize Community Resources

Standard 5.0: Candidates who complete the program are educational leaders who have the knowledge and ability to promote the success of all students by acting with integrity, fairly, and in an ethical manner.

- Act with Integrity
- Act Fairly
- Act Ethically

Standard 6.0: Candidates who complete the program are educational leaders who have the knowledge and ability to promote the success of all students by understanding, responding to, and influencing the larger political, social, economic, legal, and cultural context.

- Understand the Larger Context
- Respond to the Larger Context
- Influence the Larger Context

Standard 7.0: The internship provides significant opportunities for candidates to synthesize and apply the knowledge and practice and develop the skills identified in Standards 1 through 6 through substantial, sustained, standards-based work in real settings, planned and guided cooperatively by the institution and school district personnel for graduate credit.

- Substantial
- Sustained
- Standards-based
- Real Settings
- Planned and Guided Cooperatively
- Credit

To read the full standards, go to http://www.npbea.org/ELCC/ELCCStandards%20_5-02.pdf.

Source: Reprinted with permission from the National Policy Board for Educational Administration.

PART I

RESEARCH AND LEADERSHIP

The basic belief underlying this book is that prospective and practicing leaders who understand how to apply research to their local school's instructional challenges will experience greater success in their efforts to improve student performance. We understand that many readers could be skeptical about this basic premise. Therefore, Part I consists of three chapters that discuss our dual emphasis on research and leadership. These three initial chapters provide the conceptual foundation we use for instructional leadership and are therefore fundamental to understanding how we expect you to act in various leadership roles as you go through the process of using research to improve student achievement and overall school performance. We emphasize four broad areas in Part I: (1) the process of school improvement planning, (2) instructional leadership and what that means for school improvement work, (3) how research and leadership combine to inform a focus on instruction, and (4) how to involve others in the school improvement planning process.

Students in leadership preparation programs may find much of the material in Part I familiar if they have had courses that focus on organization, leadership, and/or decision theories. Others may have less experience with the concepts in this part of the book. Our goal is to provide just enough discussion of leadership to come to a shared understanding with readers. Those who wish to learn more about the various theoretical and empirical strands that provide the foundation for Part I are encouraged to mine the references. There is far more to say about instructional leadership than we can provide in these first few chapters.

CHAPTER 1

A STRUCTURED APPROACH TO LEADING SCHOOL IMPROVEMENT

LEARNING OUTCOMES

Readers who grasp the most important ideas from this chapter will be able to

- understand the logic of action that informs school improvement as explained in this book;
- explain some of the pressures on leadership preparation programs, leaders, and schools that lead to superficial uses of data; and
- perceive differences among problems, root causes, and solutions.

Most readers will easily agree on the need to improve student achievement, particularly in schools struggling to make adequate yearly progress (AYP). More difficult is reaching consensus on a wide variety of issues, from the nature of the most important problem(s) to how to implement good ideas in the classroom. This is a hurry-up society that demands answers now, but the problem with a fast-moving approach is that schools often experience a great deal of change that never really makes a difference for students (Schlechty, 2001). We advocate slowing the process down and carefully considering the general environment, or context, in which leaders aspire to make positive change. In this chapter, we will consider the context for school improvement and lay out the broad action stages we embed in the school improvement process described in the remainder of this book. The first contextual factor to consider is how leaders are prepared for service.

CONTEXT: LEADERSHIP PREPARATION PROGRAMS AND THE LEADERS THEY PREPARE

Two strong crosscurrents roil the waters of education leadership preparation programs today. First, there is a growing recognition that leadership is vital to school improvement (Leithwood & Riehl, 2003; Waters, Marzano, & McNulty, 2003) and that this is especially true in challenging schools (Leithwood & Steinbach, 2004). The notion that high-quality school leadership is associated with school effectiveness is certainly not a new idea, and there is a growing body of evidence that suggests that school leadership is a potent contributor to student learning (Leithwood, Seashore-Louis, Anderson, & Wahlstrom, 2004; Robinson, Lloyd, & Rowe, 2008). In their extensive review of the literature, Leithwood and Riehl conclude that leadership is second only to quality teaching as a school-related cause of student achievement.

A second major stream of thought is the claim that leadership preparation programs do a poor job preparing leaders to assume their critical role in helping all K–12 students achieve at a higher level (Levine, 2005; Southern Regional Education Board, 2006). Reading the criticisms of leadership programs suggests that professors are either asleep at the wheel or incapable of meeting the challenges of the contemporary policy climate and the needs of 21st-century students. The problem is more subtle than that, of course. To address the press for higher test scores for students who traditionally challenge schools and districts requires leadership preparation program pedagogy and curriculum that focuses on leading instructional improvement. But engaging pedagogy and worthwhile curriculum are not enough. To achieve better rigor and relevance, leadership preparation must put candidates into instructional leadership situations with the means to help them succeed. Learning occurs both on the job and in later reflection. We respond to the critics of education leadership programs with an action-oriented pedagogy that provides tools prospective leaders can use in their workplaces.

From Managers to Instructional Leaders

The impetus to reform leadership education stems in part from increased pressure on K–12 schools from high-stakes accountability policies and the realization that demands on principals have shifted from mostly managerial responsibilities to instructional leadership (Kochan, Jackson, & Duke, 1999). One of the most often mentioned changes to principals' roles involves using assessment data and educational research to inform decision making and enlisting stakeholders in research-based school improvement efforts (Fullan, 2001; Leithwood & Riehl, 2003). Creighton's (2007) comment summarizes the gist of this change:

> For too long, many school leaders have made decisions about instructional leadership by using "intuition" and "shooting from the hip." All too often, school leaders do not include data collection and data analysis in the decision-making process. We are realizing that meaningful information can be gained only from a proper analysis of data and that good decisions are based on this thoughtful process of inquiry and analysis. (p. ix)

By showing the way toward more open and deeper inquiry and analysis, we are able to help school leaders do more than follow hunches about what works or blindly adopt canned programs in an effort to improve student performance.

Producers of Research Knowledge

In recent years, the U.S. Department of Education has sought to place educational decision making on a more "scientific" footing and to provide resources for district and school leaders to use as they address instructional challenges. Through No Child Left Behind (NCLB) and a variety of other programs, the federal government calls on school leaders to make decisions informed by scientifically based evidence. Various tools such as the What Works Clearinghouse (and more recently, the Doing What Works web resource) have been made available to disseminate results pertaining to rigorous research on best practices. Justifying change efforts with intuitional expertise alone is no longer adequate.

Slavin (2007) observes, "In education today, teachers and administrators must not only know their craft. In addition, they must know the evidence that supports decisions they make, and they must be able to demonstrate that their students are learning" (p. 2). Preuss (2007) calls this the "most recent fundamental shift" (p. 2) in education, noting that the requirements of NCLB have resulted in the increased use of data to measure student learning, the use of data-based decision making, public accountability for student learning through the publication of student performance data, and the imposition of consequences for student failure. To receive federal funding, NCLB requires that leaders "be able to demonstrate that the instructional strategies, instructional materials, and staff development opportunities they choose to use have been proven effective" through the use of "scientifically based research" (Educational Research Service, 2003, p. 9). Research thus assumes a more prominent status among the proficiencies future educational leaders are expected to develop—school leaders must be both sophisticated critics of research to sort the good from the bad and, increasingly, producers of research knowledge to enhance their search for good solutions to the problems they face. Yet it is no longer enough merely to inform decision making with research knowledge; school leaders are also expected to amass evidence of the efficacy of educational programs and practice in terms of their impact on student learning. This implies that leaders themselves become researchers—they conduct action research, they work the findings into new knowledge, they act on that new knowledge in an effort to improve instruction and achievement, and they evaluate their improvement efforts.

One tack taken to help prospective principals in leadership preparation programs become more effective researchers, as reflected in many recent research texts, involves focusing on the collection and use of data. Similarly, in-service school leaders are increasingly exposed to workshops related to the use of various kinds of data to guide their practice. This appears to be a response to high-stakes accountability pressures and an effort to help aspiring and in-service school leaders learn how to use testing data in particular to guide decision making. We believe that this results in an extremely limited perspective on how to use research to lead school improvement efforts. As an analogy, imagine trying to teach someone a language by introducing only vocabulary. Data may be thought of as the building blocks of research knowledge in the same sense that words are the building blocks of language. But knowing how to read and interpret data gets you only so far.

To create knowledge about the instructional challenges principals and their faculty face, leaders must go beyond understanding data. We advocate shifting the logic of action toward using research knowledge *along with* analysis of school data to engage in a systematic action planning and implementation process focused on improving instruction. Thus, principals and their collaborative teams use their own analysis and analyses published by others to create their own justifiable logics of action to address instructional problems, challenges, or gaps.

FOSTERING POSITIVE CHANGE: THE LEADER'S JOURNEY

As should be abundantly clear by now, this book is intended to provide a guide for applying research to leading instructional change in schools. In this section, we introduce you to the journey we propose you undertake to develop your proficiency as a leader who effectively applies research to improve schools. This journey is embedded in some assumptions about the change process, as well as the leader's role in change.

It is tempting to teach leadership from a mostly technocratic perspective—improve research skills and administrators become instructional leaders. The impression may be of a major in-service effort that creates more effective leaders. We understand that leadership development is much more subtle than that, which is why we use the metaphor of a journey.

> **Typical Steps in Action Research**
>
> - Conducting some assessment of "where the school is" in terms of indicators of success (needs assessment)
> - Determining priority areas/goals for the year
> - Setting change objectives for these issues (defining "where we want to be")
> - Researching alternative action possibilities
> - Developing and implementing action plans
> - Evaluating progress on action plans in terms of the indicators of success

Action Research at the Core

Overall, the journey we propose involves steps similar to the action research process typically associated with school improvement planning (see sidebar). Initially, an assessment is made to determine "where the school is" in relation to agreed-on goals and objectives (presumably related to student learning). Performance gaps are identified as the difference between "where we are" and "where we want to be," and some number of performance objectives are crafted to define how the school will improve in terms of some specific, measurable outcomes. Research is conducted to identify alternative actions that may help achieve the stated objectives, an action or set of actions is adopted, and plans are developed to describe how these will be implemented. The plans are put into effect and possibly evaluated based on defined indicators of progress on specific performance objectives. In theory, the process is renewed annually and becomes a generator of continuous improvement.

The change process embedded in this book intentionally mirrors these steps for a number of reasons. Ideally, in-service leaders and aspirants using this book will be able to situate their learning into existing school improvement processes and thus begin to develop and demonstrate their research proficiencies while assisting in promoting significant improvements in their schools. The performance-based activities included can be shared with colleagues to augment decision making and planning processes in real time. In fact, our perspective on leading change *requires* engaging others collaboratively. Working with a team to improve instruction is not only politically wise, but it is a functional necessity—stakeholders have critical information necessary to the improvement process.

Persistent Problems Have Multiple Causes

The Mathematics Department met with the principal during one department meeting to discuss the disconcerting fact that 30% to 40% of students in Algebra I were earning Ds or Fs. The principal turned to the department chair, who had been teaching more than 30 years in the school district, and asked, "How long has this trend persisted?" "For my career," the department chair answered. When asked why this pattern had existed for so long, the following causes were identified, each by a different teacher: (1) Students don't do their homework, (2) students are inadequately prepared for algebra, (3) the counselors do not appropriately place students in courses, (4) students do not have an adequate grasp of fractions, and (5) the Algebra I curriculum is far too broad to allow for any reteaching for students who do not grasp concepts the first time they are introduced.

Additionally, as Lewin (1947) suggested more than 60 years ago, people do not resist change so much as they resist being changed. Others are more likely to change when they have been involved in decision-making and problem-solving processes (McGregor, 1960, 2006; Weisbord, 2004).

Leaders who perceive a gap between desired educational outcomes and current practices have reached an important realization. Their first challenge is to help others see the same gap. Transforming stakeholders into coalition members with a purpose can provide substantial momentum to a change effort. Consequently, collaboration must take place at the very beginning—as the instructional problem to be addressed is being articulated.

Consider the scenario from our experience presented in the sidebar. With at least five different beliefs about the causes of poor performance in Algebra I, this mathematics department is not likely to agree to one solution. They must agree on the underlying nature of the problem before they can move forward with a strategy to address it. Osterman and Kottkamp (2004) promote the idea that collaborative problem diagnosis begins with data and discussion. Looking more closely at the alternative definitions of the problem suggests different possible solutions. (*A caution:* We do not advocate solution identification without more systematic identification of causes at this point in the process, but we use hypothetical solutions for the purpose of illustration.) If the teachers agreed that the most important cause was lack of homework completion, then providing a supervised after-school setting for students to work on homework might be a good idea. If, however, they agreed that the cause was an inadequate grasp of fractions, then the mathematics curriculum or course offerings might need to change to address the problem. To come to agreement on the nature of the problem, the math department must examine root causes, a topic we take up briefly below and in depth in Chapter 6.

The exact problem-solving and planning process we endorse in this book is slightly different from the typical process outlined above, reflecting our observations about faults with the way school improvement planning is often enacted. We accentuate opportunities to enhance planning through the deliberate use of research (see Figure 1.1). The four-stage process is consistent with Osterman and Kottkamp's (2004) "cycle of experiential learning," thus connecting the school improvement process to what is known about effective techniques to promote reflective practice. Descriptions of these four stages follow.

Figure 1.1   Continuous Improvement Process

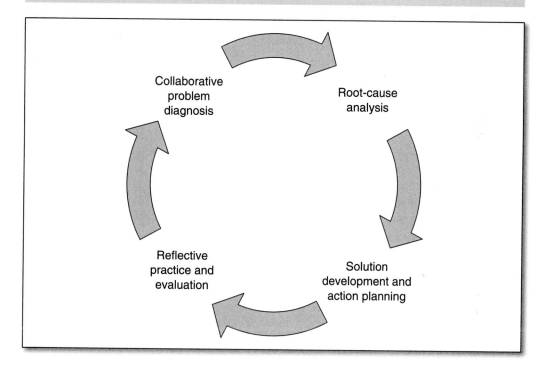

Collaborative Problem Diagnosis

For a variety of reasons, people would often rather keep doing what they are doing—even if it is not working—than change. Changing routines involves a certain amount of risk, because the outcomes are unknown. Lewin (1947) describes people in organizations as being frozen in their behaviors and beliefs. For individuals to change and for the organization to move forward, they must first become unfrozen. That may be an easy concept to grasp, but it is a difficult task to accomplish because teachers and administrators, similar to others, resist being changed. Unfreezing is most likely to come from an internal motivation to see the current situation differently, and it must be supported. Once a sufficient number of people are unfrozen, it becomes possible to move the organization toward change before it becomes frozen into a new pattern of action.

The pattern of unfreezing, moving, and refreezing is a simple way of approaching change but doesn't necessarily tell the whole story. Weisbord (2004) elaborates potential individual perspectives into four categories: (1) contentment, (2) denial, (3) confusion, and (4) renewal. Most relevant to those who aspire to lead school improvement, Weisbord argues that individuals in the stages of contentment and denial are likely to ignore external exhortations to change. Those satisfied with the status quo or oblivious to persistent problems will not be motivated to move to new ways of engaging in teaching and learning. A large proportion of teachers stuck in contentment and/or denial may be the most common problem with which prospective leaders are likely to wrestle as they strive to formulate and implement a school improvement project. Undoubtedly, someone will spout the old saw, "If it ain't broke, don't fix it."

A Common Pothole

A critical factor in unfreezing and motivating people to leave their states of contentment or denial is changing individuals' perspectives. We find that common practice in schools and school districts is to present faculty and administration with a mandate to implement a preconceived solution to an often unclear problem. This type of scenario usually takes place in a climate of urgency. "We are not making AYP with students in poverty. Therefore, we will implement an after-school tutoring program twice a week." From the teacher's perspective, this may be a ridiculous proposition. An elementary school student in poverty will have difficulty getting home an hour after school ends if there is no transportation provided. The after-school curriculum is unlikely to be substantially different from what happens in classrooms such that it compensates for the child's learning struggles. Who will ensure that the after-school curriculum is appropriately aligned with classroom teaching and students' specific needs? Preconceived solutions have a low probability of unfreezing anyone but those who happen to agree that they are good ideas.

Evidence of a Problem, Challenge, or Gap

Here and throughout this book, we use the term *data* more broadly than many educators. We have in mind both the standard definition that includes test scores and the degree to which groups of students test at various proficiency levels on state standards. We also mean qualitative data that help explain not only what exists but how and why (Maxwell, 2005). Today, quantitative data are easy to get—a positive outcome of the standards and accountability movements. Qualitative data requires more effort because it comes from talking to people, observing classrooms, and examining documents. Quantitative and qualitative data are evidence that something is happening. There are many types of evidence, including assessment data, craft knowledge, and published research.

We stress the importance of putting together a team of interested educators to collect and analyze evidence to figure out where the instructional challenges lie and the reasons behind their existence. Collaborative problem diagnosis helps build a common perspective among those who are interested in making a difference. The mathematics department described above might have come to agreement on the most important cause of difficulty in Algebra I had they engaged in data collection and analysis as a group.

Root-Cause Analysis

At the beginning of our research class, when we challenge our students to explain an instructional problem in their schools, most respond with some variation of "Test scores are low in [blank] among [a specific group of] students." We frown at this type of formulation—test scores are an *indicator* of a problem, but defining the "problem" in terms of a single indicator cuts off necessary probing about the nature of what's going on. Instead, we favor a formulation that focuses on student learning, such as "Students in poverty do not achieve in math at the same level as the majority population." Next, our students often suggest a solution. Thinking about the Algebra I scenario, teachers feared that the principal's emphasis on the rate of Ds and Fs would lead to pressure to give all students at least a C. While this might (seem to) treat the "problem" (i.e., students would not be getting Ds and Fs anymore), clearly that kind of solution would not address the instructional needs underlying the symptom of low grades.

Evidence such as test scores is better understood as revealing symptoms of an underlying problem—understanding the *reasons behind* indicators of student learning such as grades or low test scores requires root-cause analysis (Preuss, 2007). The concept is straightforward (see Figure 1.2). We notice the symptoms that reading test scores are lower than we expected for primary-grade students and that third-grade students are not making AYP in reading. Why is reading performance lower than expected (a root-cause question)? One

Figure 1.2   Why Causes Are So Important

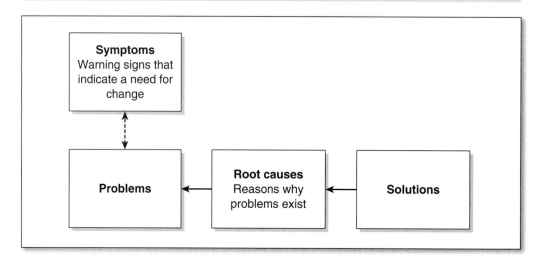

place to begin answering such a question is building an understanding of the local context. For example, if we know that teachers in the primary grades have committed themselves to implementing a specific reading program, it would make sense to observe (collect qualitative data) how they are implementing the program. If we find that implementation generally appears to be consistent with what the program intends, then we would look elsewhere in our root-cause analysis to find reasons behind disappointing performance. It may be that the program itself, though it made sense at first, turns out to be ineffective for the population of students most in need in our school. As we consider various causes of the problem of poor reading performance, specific solutions will begin to make sense as means to addressing the causes. To alleviate the problem, solutions must lessen or eliminate one or more important causes.

Without root-cause analysis, it is possible to get trapped in a shotgun approach to solving school problems. Suppose we adopted the "students don't do their homework" perspective from the Algebra I scenario prior to engaging in root-cause analysis. An after-school homework supervision idea might be put into place based on departmental folklore about the reasons for incomplete homework. Suppose, however, that the underlying cause is that students are weak in basic operations, especially with fractions. Thus, those who diligently stay after school are incapable of completing their homework because of concepts they have not yet learned. The supervising teacher ends up trying to teach basic operations piecemeal as students come to her with problems they cannot complete. All are likely to become frustrated as students wait for help and the teacher repeats instruction these students "should have gotten long ago." Alternatively, when root causes of problems are identified and addressed, problems are more likely to be solved.

Solutions and Action Planning

If a poor grasp of basic operations is one of the root causes of low achievement in Algebra I, then a more reasonable approach may be the one the high school in the scenario tried. They implemented an Algebra Skills class to be taken as a second math class for students who were not fully prepared for Algebra I. Students in the Algebra Skills class received the reteaching in basic operations that they needed and also received reinforcement for new concepts learned in Algebra I. This was not a perfect solution, but it helped move many of the Ds and Fs to Cs and better.

What happened in the example mathematics department is that they came to understand the causes of the achievement problem as rooted in basic skills. With that agreement, they moved forward with a plan of action to implement the Algebra Skills course, which is still in place more than 10 years later. But at its inception, the course encountered roadblocks that had to be cleared out of the way, and students and families had to be sold on the idea of students taking a second math course. Action planning involves anticipating how the school as an organization will respond to a specific change effort and laying out a course of action for implementation. Once this general context is understood, then numerous details must be worked out to ensure that implementation proceeds smoothly. From agreement on a solution, a detailed action plan is developed to guide implementation and allow leaders to anticipate possible roadblocks that might emerge along the way.

Reflective Practice and Evaluation

If the greatest weakness in school improvement efforts is failure to address root causes, then the next may be failure to evaluate attempts to address the problem. Our experience suggests that school improvement efforts are rarely evaluated carefully for two major reasons: (a) Time and resources are scarce and almost never applied to evaluation activities, and (b) once a new program has been implemented, stakeholders devoted to it will not easily give it up or make changes—they have become frozen into a new pattern.

If a school improvement effort begins from a reflective practice perspective that asks, "How well aligned are our actions with what we intend?" then it may be possible to sustain reflection that leads to formative evaluation over a longer period of time. Osterman and Kottkamp (2004) describe a never-ending cycle of data collection, collaborative analysis of gathered data, piloting solutions, collecting more data, more analysis, and refinement of solutions. The end result is a strong inquiry stance within a school that emphasizes learning among teachers and administrators in addition to students. We subscribe to this view of how to engage in school improvement.

At some point, however, summative evaluation must occur. Resources are always scarce, compelling us to ask the question, "Is this program more effective than some alternative way of organizing time and spending money?" A persuasive answer is based in reexamination of the data that originally described the gap between goals and outcomes. If we have narrowed that gap substantially, then perhaps the program should be sustained. Whatever the outcome, evaluation is the wellspring of organizational learning; tracking implementation through formative assessment is critical to making adjustments to action plans as they unfold, and summative assessment of progress toward objectives is vital to making judgments about how the school can promote continuous improvement in student learning.

CONCLUSION

In this chapter, we have begun to lay out a specific logic of action for fostering school improvement. To improve schools, leaders need first to understand what is not working. Quantitative and qualitative data, combined with other evidence, can help them identify gaps in performance and the nature of the root causes of particular problems. Published research, a topic we will discuss in depth in Chapters 7 and 8, combined with craft knowledge will help in the search for solutions that address root causes and therefore resolve long-standing problems. Yet there is no one magic answer necessitating evaluation and reworking of implemented solutions.

We acknowledged in the first portion of this chapter that expectations for school leadership have been shifting from manager to instructional leader. This is not an easy change to make. Prospective leaders may not have good role models for instructional leadership, and practicing leaders may not know how to make the change. Recognizing these challenges, the next chapter provides an in-depth analysis of the relationships among research, leadership, and efforts to improve student achievement.

REVIEW QUESTIONS

1. Which kinds of data are currently used in your school to assess student and school performance?

2. How would you describe the school improvement planning process in your school? In what ways is it similar to or different from the typical action planning process described in this chapter?

3. What kinds of opportunities currently exist in your school to engage in collaborative problem diagnosis and/or ongoing reflective practice?

4. In what ways might teachers or administrators in your school be "frozen" or unwilling to change regarding a long-standing program or practice that some may see as problematic or ineffective?

CHAPTER 2

RESEARCH, LEADERS, AND IMPROVING STUDENT PERFORMANCE

LEARNING OUTCOMES

Readers who grasp the most important ideas from this chapter will be able to

- appreciate the value of research to instructional leaders;
- differentiate between looking at individual behavior only and viewing schools and districts as organizations;
- analyze past school improvement efforts through four different analytic perspectives or frames; and
- begin to apply major organizational theory concepts.

The term *research* conveys digging into books and articles in a musty space, searching sterile databases on a computer, or experimenting on animals whose lives will ultimately be sacrificed in the name of science. Certainly libraries, the Internet, and laboratories are worthy places to conduct research. But those places also connote a degree of remoteness from the energy and promise students infuse in schools. We believe that research must take place in schools and classrooms because that is where the evidence that is most important to education leaders—teachers, principals, superintendents, and others—is located. This evidence forms the foundational knowledge for decisions about how best to improve schools so that all children have the opportunity to reach their potential.

A focus on research at the classroom and/or school levels reveals our organizational bias—schools are the units of change within school districts. The federal government, state legislatures, school boards, and superintendents can make all the decrees they wish. Little is really changed unless and until the will to change is manifest within schools (Cuban, 1993; Tyack & Cuban, 1995). Lasting change occurs only when teachers change their behavior and the behavior of their students within classrooms. The challenge is making change that actually improves student achievement and, by extension, school performance. An important part of making change worthwhile is basing it on what is currently known about how to educate children (i.e., grounding what we do in research).

Yet learning about research may seem like a very tall mountain to climb. Written analyses, tables, and charts can seem confusing at first, and applying them to specific situations can be even more difficult. Persistence is vital, however, because uninformed change is random and likely to fail. If education leaders understand how to read published research, how to carry out manageable research projects in their schools, and how to engage in action planning, implementation, and evaluation based on both published and action research, then children will be the fortunate beneficiaries. Accepting the premise that schooling opens lifetime doors for students, putting research to work to make education more effective for more students cannot come soon enough.

Fullan (2001) uses the phrase *knowledge creation* as descriptive of an important leadership behavior. Knowledge creation derives from collecting and interpreting evidence, at least in part. But knowledge must be put to work through action; otherwise, it provides only a small benefit. We explicitly and deliberately combine knowledge creation with an action orientation. Action, in turn, helps create new knowledge and modified actions intended to enhance student performance.

A CONCEPTUAL FRAMEWORK FOR INSTRUCTIONAL LEADERSHIP

Learning how to be a research-informed leader requires a sort of compass course we refer to as a conceptual framework. You can think of the conceptual framework we present as a road map that moves you from knowledge acquisition through action to outcomes. We perceive school leaders as operating within organizational structures and environments. We employ a logic of action that suggests decision making is better informed when it begins with an organizational perspective, combines what is known at the school site (action research) with what is known more broadly (published research), and involves others in collaborative process. Each of the concepts presented in the framework is discussed in more detail in this and subsequent chapters. A graphic representation of our conceptual framework appears in Figure 2.1.

Figure 2.1   Conceptual Framework for Leading School Improvement

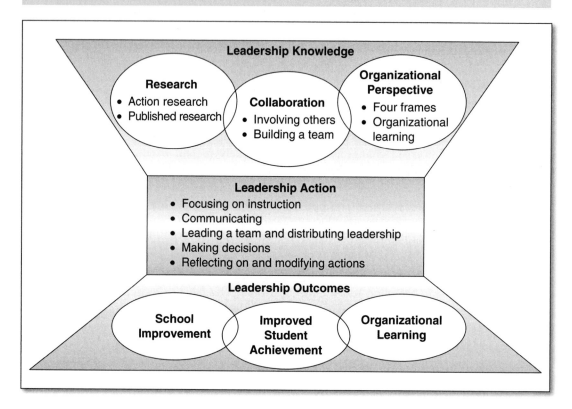

Who Are the Leaders, and What Do They Do?

We use the term *leader* broadly. Leadership can be formalized in roles, as with superintendents, principals, assistant principals, department chairs, grade-level leaders, and so on. Additionally, leaders may be in positions that have no authority but potentially a great deal of influence, such as teacher coaches, technology specialists, counselors, and librarians. Leaders can also be teachers who simply take the initiative to make change focused on instruction. Formal role, specific position, and teacher status do not automatically confer leadership status on anyone. Leaders are people who are willing to collaborate with others, make decisions, take action, and evaluate the results of what they have done. Worksheet 2.1 at the end of this chapter is designed to help you think about who plays leadership roles in your school, in what context they may be leaders, and how effective they are as leaders.

Different Kinds of Decisions

Education historian Larry Cuban (1988) has examined leadership in schools over a period of more than a century of U.S. education and concludes that teachers, principals, and superintendents lead in similar ways but in different realms. Cuban views leadership as occurring when there is a combination of autonomy and opportunity for choice. In other words, leadership happens when it is possible for those inclined to lead to make decisions. There is an important additional dimension to the decision making that makes up the grist of leadership, however. Decisions can be focused in one of three areas— management, politics, or instruction. Although not mutually exclusive, these categories of decision making help focus our thinking about the kind of leadership that is required to improve student and school performance.

Managerial decisions are the choices made about how the support structure of school works. Such decisions range from how to arrange student desks in the classroom (a choice typically made by the teacher) to formulating the master schedule (a school site administrative prerogative) to determining student rights and responsibilities (the decision of the school board and central office under the umbrella of the state education code). Good managerial decisions are undoubtedly critical to running a school and school district effectively. They will not, however, in and of themselves have a meaningful and long-lasting effect on student achievement. To be sure, students must feel safe in the schoolhouse to be able to learn. But the fact of their safety does not guarantee that learning will occur.

Cuban (1988) takes a somewhat unusual view of politics. Rather than emphasizing power relationships (see discussion in the "Using the Framing Tool" subsection below), he explains that political decisions are driven by values, as is political conflict. The principal who bends the rules for the child of wealthy and powerful parents does so in the belief that she is maintaining a degree of loyalty from an important constituency. Yet another principal may decide that equity and fairness are values that override the expediency of not ruffling powerful feathers. The consequences of each kind of choice are significant and different. Similar to managerial decisions, political decisions affect the quality of students' educational experiences, but they do not by themselves ensure quality teaching and learning.

We emphasize instructional decision making throughout this book and in our teaching because we believe that student achievement will improve most substantially when teaching and learning improve in meaningful ways. We are consistent with Cuban when we define instructional decisions as directly impacting classroom beliefs, attitudes, and behaviors—for teachers, students, and parents. The school improvement planning we endorse is focused on instruction with appropriate managerial and political decisions in support of the improvement effort. School leaders are the stewards of high-quality teaching and learning experiences.

Instructional Leadership and Decision Making

Although we may be focused first and foremost on instruction, managerial and political decision making should not be ignored. A common experience for our students is that they are passionate about the instructional improvement effort they have designed, only to be thwarted by a lack of practicality or school politics they had been unaware of in the relative simplicity of their classrooms. This is why we emphasize the importance of understanding schools and districts as organizations and why we recommend a specific set of tools for analyzing and understanding those organizations. To think more deeply about how managerial, political, and instructional decisions are mutually reinforcing, engage with Activity 2.1.

ACTIVITY 2.1   Management, Politics, and Instruction

Managerial, political, and instructional decision making intersect in various ways, depending on the focus of educational change and the tendencies of the person leading that change. Consider the three scenarios (all of which use pseudonyms) below and discuss with one or more critical friends the questions that follow.

Scenario 1

Nate chose to focus his school improvement project on creation and implementation of an online system for tracking alternative education students' achievement of state-mandated competencies. Nate put together a committee that consisted of teachers to provide expertise on classroom issues and user implementation, technical experts to design the software, and students to assist with design and implementation of the software. The connection to instruction was clear—if teachers were more aware of the competencies achieved by each student, they would be less likely to overlap other teachers' instruction or leave gaps in content. Some teachers were hesitant to implement, but the state was interested in adopting the software in all school districts and provided a grant to help fund the initiative.

Scenario 2

Anna resuscitated a moribund Positive Behavior System (PBS) policy in her elementary school. She discovered that record keeping about students who had recurring behavioral problems was poor, so she made improved record keeping an important first step in her school improvement project. Working with a committee she put together, Anna helped design an intervention for the most difficult students that involved having them check in and check out with a teacher on a daily basis. The purpose of checking in and out is for the student to have regular contact with an adult who cares about him or her and for the teacher to keep up to date on the student's behavioral and academic progress. Anna's overall goal for PBS was for students to acquire the ability to self-monitor their behavior so that they could avoid being in trouble with teachers and focus on their schoolwork. Anna faced some initial resistance from her school administration, but she convinced them to attend a training session on PBS, after which the principal joined her committee and helped with the training sessions for the faculty. Anna found that her collaborative team was so committed to the project that she was not sure whether she had actually led the effort.

Scenario 3

Sally was teaching sixth-grade science when she developed a project to use student work portfolios as a means for students to learn their academic strengths and weaknesses. Her larger goal was for students to understand their learning strengths and weaknesses so that they could take better advantage of classroom instruction. Similar to Anna, Sally pursued student self-monitoring as a device for improving academic behavior, but she approached it from a different perspective. During design and initial implementation, Sally worked with an enthusiastic team of sixth-grade teachers responsible for 120 students. All teachers fully implemented the portfolios in all subject areas. The following year, Sally voluntarily moved to a seventh-grade team. No one on the team was interested in using portfolios in their classes, the science department head did not want to promote portfolios in science classrooms, and the principal believed that focus on standardized test scores was more important. Sally was the only person using portfolios in the classroom in the seventh grade, but her old sixth-grade team continued to implement the project.

For one or more of the scenarios described above, discuss the following:

- What is the logic of action at work in the instructional decision? What leads to what?
- What managerial decisions supported or undermined the key instructional decision(s)?
- What political decisions supported or undermined the key instructional decision(s)?
- What decisions were left out that might have supported the instructional decision(s) more effectively?

Would you have chosen to focus on the instructional decision in each scenario? Why or why not? Decision making is the central behavior of leadership. Informing decisions with facts that come from data, knowledge that emerges from data analysis, and craft knowledge is imperative to good leadership. Leading change without a well-informed perspective is a risky enterprise, because parents and the public fear that change will make education worse. The stakes are high, because a child is in third grade only once. As a result, it is incumbent on education leaders not only to use research to make wise decisions but to educate those whom the leader presumes to lead about the utility of research as applied to instructional challenges.

There is a rich literature on the impact of leadership on student achievement. Although we are unable to go deeply into that literature here, we commend to your attention the work of Ken Leithwood and his colleagues in the Learning From Leadership Project (e.g., Leithwood, Seashore-Louis, Anderson, & Wahlstrom, 2004; Wahlstrom, Seashore-Louis, Leithwood, & Anderson, 2010) and a meta-analysis of research on the effects of transformational and instructional leadership on student learning. Robinson, Lloyd, and Rowe (2008) conclude that although transformational leadership has some effect on how well students achieve, instructional leadership is a more important factor. This major study reinforces our belief that properly supported instructional decisions are at the heart of the most important work school leaders should be doing.

SCHOOLS AS ORGANIZATIONS

As much as we wish to focus your attention on leadership, such a discussion is less meaningful without considering the context in which leadership occurs. We take the approach that schools are organizations and, as such, display certain characteristics that are common to organizations of different types, including hospitals, businesses, and government. That "school" is a type of organization may seem obvious to many, but we often find the idea of schools as organizations is a hurdle our students need to get over before they can come to a deeper understanding of leadership generally and instructional leadership specifically.

Most of the students who enter the education leadership program in which we teach are full-time classroom teachers. Their perspective tends to include the classroom, their relationships to their students, and teachers' individual and small-group relationships to one another. To put it another way, we find that teachers who aspire to work in administration most often explain what happens in schools through a human resources frame. Like most of us, teachers probably are not conscious of how they interpret the world in which they work, but Bolman and Deal's (2008) analytical framing tool is a useful way to look at what teachers and administrators do in their organizations. We recommend reading Bolman and Deal's *Reframing Organizations: Artistry, Choice, and Leadership* to gain a much more detailed and nuanced understanding of schools as organizations than we can provide in this chapter. This section presents a taste of what the authors have to offer and applies their kind of thinking to the challenge of school improvement.

Using the Framing Tool

Judging from certain phenomena in the world of education leadership, it is apparent that teachers are not the only educators who tend to focus their analysis of school events through the human resources frame. Firing superintendents when test scores appear inadequate, hiring "turnaround" principals to "fix" schools with persistent management and instruction problems, and requiring teachers to engage in generic professional development in hopes of improving their performance all suggest a human resources perspective. The idea is that individuals and their relationships to others have a substantial impact on organizational performance. Therefore, if a school board is unhappy with the overall performance of the school district, it makes sense to them to remove the current superintendent and bring in a new one who can motivate principals and teachers to perform better through improved relationships. In the current era of accountability and high-stakes testing, that motivation often seems to come in the form of demanding better performance from everyone and tightening bureaucratic monitoring. But it could just as easily come in the form of an emphasis on collaboration at multiple levels throughout the system or capacity building through professional development in target curriculum areas. The human resources frame emphasizes individual and collective motivation, the quality of working relationships, and group dynamics.

As one would expect, there is more than one way of looking at organizations. The first of three additional frames that Bolman and Deal (2008) provide is the structural frame. As the name suggests, this perspective looks at how the organization is put together and emphasizes rationality. (We should note that human interrelationships are rational as well, but the logic of action in the structural frame is different from that in the human resources frame.) It is common for education leaders to adjust organization structure among their earliest acts in a leadership position. They set goals, rearrange positions, and repair neglected or broken monitoring systems. In 2007, when Michelle Rhee took over as chancellor of the District of Columbia Public Schools, one of her first acts was to address the thousands of fire code violations in the district's school buildings. She went on to trim positions from the central office and fire poorly performing principals. As of this writing, she is involved in negotiating a new contract with teachers that would allow for a two-track salary system. All these changes are directly related to elements of organization structure, including rules (fire code violations and the teachers' contract), organization size (trimming the central office), and performance evaluation (firing principals). Structural changes are often the most accessible to leaders, which is why they come early in any new administration.

The mention of certain kinds of changes, particularly the example above about deviating from the standard teachers' salary schedule, brings to most readers' minds the notion that change is difficult because people resist. Resistance is strengthened when individuals coalesce into nonschool organizations, such as teachers unions, to make their voices heard through collective bargaining. The political frame (Bolman & Deal, 2008) helps explain this kind of behavior. In contrast to examining structure or motivation, the political frame focuses on interests and power. Access to resources, bureaucratic position, relationships to others with power, and coalition membership are all potential sources of power. How that power might be exercised to meet our individual or collective interests is a matter of leader judgment. Of all Bolman and Deal's four frames, this is the one that educators seem to enjoy the least because they perceive themselves as helping children in an apolitical manner. Nevertheless, schools and school districts would be unique among organizations if they did not exhibit political behaviors.

The central idea of organizational politics is that individuals (and groups) have somewhat divergent interests or goals. Since resources needed to fulfill these interests are inherently limited, we have a dilemma: How do we ensure that our interests are met? Further, individuals (and groups) have inherently limited power to influence others. To expand our influence, we form alliances with others that take the form of coalitions of people (or groups) with complementary interests. In other words, we coalesce to exert power to meet our needs. Unions are a classic example, but so too are grade-level teams or departments through which people work together to influence budget allocations or a modification in the master schedule. Note that there is nothing inherently dastardly or unsavory about striving to meet our interests or needs; indeed, the great majority of political action that goes on in the day-to-day world of school is about enhancing student welfare, safety, and learning.

The most challenging perspective for our students tends to be the symbolic frame. Based in anthropology, the symbolic frame emphasizes organization culture. Evidence for specific cultural characteristics comes from rituals, stories, and symbols. Educators commonly remark about the culture of schools they work in or visit. Teachers and others talk about the "feel" of a school as they enter the main hallway or the way children and adults seem to interact. All schools, as organizations, have a culture of their own—often described as the taken-for-granted "way we do things around here."

An example of symbolically laden action comes from the Fairfax County (Virginia) Public Schools. Aspiring administrators participating in a district-run professional development program make formal presentations of school improvement initiatives they have designed. They spend time in discussion with the superintendent to learn his reactions and receive his feedback. Undoubtedly, there is practical benefit from this exercise. Its symbolic importance may be much greater, however. This annual ritual symbolizes to those present and others across the district that the superintendent cares deeply about instruction and that he is personable enough to spend quality time with a handful of aspiring administrators who might otherwise be unknown to him in a vast school district serving 166,000 students. (Note that observing that an action has symbolic value does not suggest that it is more or less important but, rather, that its value extends beyond its functional benefit.)

A Multiple-Frame Perspective

Each of the four frames brings out different kinds of information about the nature of a school or district as an organization. The savvy leader is able to combine the frames analytically to gain a more complete picture of what is really happening in a particular setting. We believe that as leaders engage in the instructional improvement process—from conducting library research through action planning, implementation, and evaluation—they will be more adept in the change process if they have a multifaceted perspective similar to that provided by the human resources, structural, political, and symbolic frames. Organizational framing is an exceptionally useful tool for understanding root causes of instructional challenges, evaluating freezing problems and roadblocks to change, and assessing implementation results. Activity 2.2 provides one way of putting the frames to work. Because of their relative simplicity and their analytical power, we return to the frames in later chapters.

ACTIVITY 2.2   Back to the Future Through Bolman and Deal's Four Frames

This activity asks you to think about school improvement efforts you have experienced in the very recent past. You may have done something similar to this kind of reflection before, but we offer a twist—using the four frames to understand your experience a bit more deeply. Answer the prompts below with absolute candor.

- Last year, we tried to (insert your goal for improving student achievement)...
- by (insert your objective, or what you actually did)...
- because (insert the reason you thought this would help you reach your goal).
- What actually happened was (discuss the outcome in terms of your indicators of success)...
- because (say a little something about what you learned).

Now run your responses from above through the analysis provided by four-frames thinking by answering the questions in each of the boxes below.

(Continued)

(Continued)

Structural:	Human Resource:
• Did rules, roles, and relationships support the change you implemented? • Did the change support the stated mission and/or strategic objectives of the school? • Did the change require changes in the school day? Were these changes resisted?	• Were participants involved in decision making? • Were participants' needs met? • Were people motivated? How? • Did they have the skill and the will to support the change? • Who gained prestige, and who lost prestige?
Political:	Symbolic:
• Were participants involved in decision making? • Who were the significant interest groups affected by the change? (What did they want? What power did they have to impact the outcome? Where does this power come from?) • Were significant stakeholders who were affected by the change consulted? • Whose authority was needed? • Who were the "winners" and who were the "losers," and how did they react?	• Was the change consistent with "the way we do things around here"? • What were the "sacred cows" you challenged? • Was time provided for people to "unfreeze"? • What stories were told regarding the change? Were they positive or negative?

Thinking about your responses to the questions in the boxes above, which frame or combination of frames do you find most helpful for understanding the results of your previous school improvement effort? Why?

Why Persuasion Matters

More than 30 years ago, Karl Weick (1976) pointed out that schools and school districts resemble what he called loosely coupled systems. This widely accepted, yet rarely challenged, assertion is grounded in two general premises: (a) that what constitutes effective teaching is poorly understood and (b) that monitoring of teaching and learning processes is difficult. As a result, Weick says, what happens in one part of a school or school district does not necessarily have a direct effect on another part. Think about the wide variety of reactions to principal mandates in your own school.

If we accept the notion that in many ways, particularly in the realm of instruction, commands and actions are not always tightly linked, the power of persuasion becomes vital to leadership effectiveness. As an example, consider Scenario 3 introduced in Activity 2.1: One of our students implemented the use of student portfolios with her entire sixth-grade team. All team members were enthusiastic, and student learning results appeared to be positive. Nevertheless, no other sixth-grade team adopted the innovation, and when this teacher moved to a seventh-grade team, they showed no interest in adopting the apparently successful use of portfolios. Everett Rogers explains this seemingly peculiar result through his research on adoption of innovations (e.g., Rogers, 1995). A basic conclusion of his work is that adoption of innovations is not entirely rational. People adopt innovations when they have a high degree of regard for someone else who has adopted. This may be why the sixth-grade team who knew and respected our student readily adopted portfolios but other teams who knew her differently did not. She may have been unable or unwilling to persuade the seventh-grade team that portfolios were worth the time and effort required to implement them.

We believe that innovators can become more compelling advocates for their innovation ideas and therefore achieve more widespread adoption when they put diligent library research, insightful observation of the local situation, and strong personal and professional relationships together. In other words, one primary reason to learn to use research is to build a more persuasive case for adoption of change strategies that will lead to improved student learning.

Organizational Learning

Consistent with educators' tendencies to view educational problems in terms of individual students or teachers and relationships among them, many people think about student learning as separate from what the school as a whole learns. Our belief is different. We agree with Argyris (1999) that organizations learn. They do not always learn what we might intend, but they learn nevertheless. A school that does not learn as an organization seems destined to have difficulty helping students learn more effectively. Organizational learning is an important leadership challenge that ought to be embraced to improve the prospects for implementing meaningful change in the classroom.

Organizational learning begins with an examination of the alignment between what we as a school say we intend and what we actually do. Argyris (1999) refers to these two ideas as espoused theories (our stated intentions or aspirations) and theories in use (our actions). Imagine that you work in an elementary school that has at the core of its vision statement the idea that all children can learn. This is a commonly espoused theory. Many teachers in this hypothetical school work hard to differentiate instruction and use evaluation of student work to guide future instructional strategies. Such teachers' theories in use would be well aligned with the school's espoused theory. Other teachers, however, may use time-out a great deal in an effort to control unruly student behavior, or they may try to refer challenging students for special education testing before exhausting tried-and-true interventions. This other group of teachers' actions would not be well aligned with the school's vision.

Finding and examining gaps between espoused theories and theories in use is central to organizational learning within schools and, ultimately, vital to school improvement. You will see in Chapter 4 that we ask you to begin the school improvement planning process by identifying an important gap between what is espoused and what is practiced at your school. Osterman and Kottkamp (2004) provide helpful guidelines for pursuing discussions that explore differences between espoused theories and theories in use.

Argyris (1999) analyzes why discussions about gaps between aspirations and performance can be difficult or impossible. He coined the term *undiscussables* to describe those issues that are simply not talked about. A common undiscussable in schools is the poor performance of an administrator. Teachers and parents may be reticent to criticize someone in that role for fear of some sort of retribution. Furthermore, Argyris argues, members of the organization refrain from talking about the fact that certain undiscussables are not discussed. Therefore, undiscussables are self-sealing (i.e., they cannot be opened up because we do not even acknowledge that they exist; Argyris, 1999).

The whole point of identifying performance gaps and opening up undiscussables is to be able to make change. A final concept from Argyris (1999) answers the question "Change what?" Argyris refers to the forces that sustain the status quo as governing variables. These are the values that, unless they are modified in some way, prevent real change from occurring. In the example above of teachers who would refer their students to special education before engaging in extensive intervention efforts, the governing variable at work might be something such as "Difficult students must be referred to specialists so that all other students can learn." It is entirely possible that such a governing variable, being out of step with current beliefs about how to work with students, is inaccessible behind a wall of self-sealed undiscussables. The governing variable will need to be named if it is ever to be changed. That process requires opening up undiscussables that may include the fact that some teachers in the school just do not understand how to differentiate instruction.

When our students engage in action research, they find gaps between espoused theories and theories in use. In the process, they run head-on into undiscussables that protect governing variables. This kind of activity inevitably leads to some degree of conflict and discomfort. Nevertheless, the gaps between what we say we do and what we actually do, our unwillingness to discuss specific issues, and entrenched governing variables stand in the way of improved student achievement. If leaders are unwilling or unable to open up undiscussables, the school cannot learn and improve.

Summary

Schools and districts are more than masses of individuals doing their work and forming a handful of relationships. As organizations, they work in ways that are often predicted by organization theory. The few theories we have been able to present here should guide you as you engage in analysis of what is happening at your school and how you and your collaborative team should address a specific challenge. We hope that you will refer back to this section, if necessary, as we use these organization theory concepts in later chapters.

RESEARCH THAT INFORMS LEADERSHIP PRACTICE

In our careers before we entered academia (one as an education consultant and the other as a high school principal), we encountered countless teachers and administrators who dismissed research as "too theoretical," too much embedded in the "ivory tower," or irrelevant to their local situations. These attitudes may stem from a perspective that assumes that what one reads in an article or a book will be directly applicable to a particular situation. If not, it is worthless. We hold a different view. We envision education leaders understanding research and figuring out how specific aspects of the research they have read can inform the decisions they need to make about instruction. Instead of adopting without question a recommendation made at the end of a scholarly article, the research-informed leader asks, "How do this author's conclusions relate to what our teachers and students are doing?" In the process, teachers and principals examine information they already have about their students to determine where the similarities and differences are between their school and the research sites contained in the source(s) they have read. This is not a process of adopting or not adopting. It is a synthesis of what is known about one's school and what others have found who have studied similar and different educational circumstances. We challenge leaders to engage in this type of synthesis and to take action to improve instruction.

ACTIVITY 2.3   The Intersection Between Leadership and Research in Your School

Discuss with classmates or interested colleagues your school's current perspective on the relationship between leadership and research. The prompts below may help stimulate conversation.

- Who are the research "stars" in your school, the people who seem to be well read and who are able to reference research in their discussions of student achievement?

- Who in your school understands and can use the district's data warehouse system? Are these people able to analyze student achievement data in a manner that is helpful for school improvement planning?

- How focused is your principal on instructional issues? Does this focus include interest in and knowledge of the school's student achievement data and/or some relevant literature on learning challenges?

- How interested in and aware of contemporary published research are teachers in your school?

- What steps could you take to begin to put your school on a path toward using research for school improvement?

Using research to lead school improvement is not a simple task. Research can be confusing and intimidating. Combining leading with research is, consequently, a substantial challenge. This section describes our conception of the intersection of theory, research, and practice so that prospective and practicing leaders can grasp the larger, practical meaning behind working with published literature, thus preparing the reader to go into greater depth in subsequent chapters.

Theory, Research, and Practice

Many of the instructional challenges schools face are complicated and difficult to understand without help. Published literature is a great source of assistance when approached in the right way. Unfortunately, some of the least useful literature is often what is most attractive to practitioners because it is easily digested. Although opinions and perspectives from respected scholars and persuasive speakers can be informative, they do not usually untangle specific problems or provide effective means of working out solutions. Engaging with actual research requires a greater investment of time and intellectual energy, but the payoff is much more substantial. The good news is that reading research is like practicing a skill; the more one does it, the easier it gets.

Theory

Theory is often dismissed as not being part of the "real" world and appears intimidating when we think in terms of Einstein's theory of relativity or Darwin's theory of evolution. These are grand theories that inform different areas of science, and they are still being tested. We have something much more modest in mind when we think of theory that is part of education research. A theory is merely speculation about the relationships among people and phenomena (Weick, 1989). Theories help organize our thinking about what is going on in a particular situation. The underlying theory of this book is that prospective and practicing leaders who understand how to apply research to their local school instructional challenges will experience greater success in their efforts to improve student performance. The most elegant theories are simple and easily understood.

Theory helps researchers think about the research questions they are pursuing. For this reason, a theoretical perspective or conceptual framework is a section commonly found in research journal articles. Researchers often explain their data in terms of how it supports or contradicts a theory or set of theoretical principles. Yet it is possible that an article will be entirely theoretical—its sole purpose is to explain a framework that could be used in subsequent analyses. This kind of article has the potential to provide an enlightening new way for an instructional leader to think about a learning problem in her or his school.

Activity 2.4 is designed to help the reader develop a simple theory and understand the connections between theory, research, and practice. Our hope is that it will also build confidence that anyone can understand theory that is well presented.

ACTIVITY 2.4   Connecting Theory, Research, and Practice

As school leaders, you have spent a considerable amount of time pondering the question *"What makes an effective leader effective?"* Focus for a moment on the question of *how teacher leaders impact school improvement.* To frame your conception of teacher leadership, you are going to conduct some case studies of yourselves.

1. In your tenure as an educator, *how have you witnessed teacher leaders impacting student performance and achievement?* Pick a single event or occurrence and jot down some notes:
   - What characterized the situation?
   - Who was involved?

(Continued)

(Continued)

- How did leader(s) motivate others or enlist their support?
- What was accomplished (and how did you know it)?

2. Use these data to frame your theory of leadership for school change. To begin to frame your theory, complete the following steps:
   - List the factors that you think contribute to a leader's "effectiveness." Create a list of constructs. A construct is an abstraction that cannot be directly observed, a concept invented to explain behavior (e.g., intelligence, stress).
   - How do these factors relate to one another? Create a model that displays the *relationships among these constructs.* (Draw a concept map.)
   - What's the underlying logic? Describe your model in plain language—how do these things work to promote student effectiveness?

3. Now, extend the research:
   - How would you study the efficacy of your theory?
   - How would you test your model?
   - How would you measure the factors involved, from whom would you collect information, and what techniques might you use to see if relationships exist?

4. Now, extend the research to practice:
   - How would your theory and research be useful and to whom?
   - Who would you seek to influence and in what ways?
   - What is the practical value of your theory and research?

Questions for Discussion:

1. In what way is what you just did theorizing?

2. In what ways would your conceptual framework define or influence your research?

3. How does this framework connect to subsequent questions, relating to how you would use the framework in your study?

Research

Up to this point, we have made many explicit and implicit references to data as part of research, but we have not yet named research that is grounded in data. This is generally referred to as empirical research. An empirical article is one in which the authors collected and analyzed specific kinds of data as they set out to answer a set of research questions. Their theoretical framework likely provided categories in which their data could be fit. Results might validate, contradict, or extend the theoretical constructs the authors applied.

A common misconception our students hold is that data will reveal answers to the instructional challenges that they face. Answers are not found in data, but they may be found in *interpretations* of data—this is true for both data embedded in published research and data available at the school site. Human beings need to interact with data to understand messages that may be embedded there and to create responses to local problems. Theory and the conceptual frameworks it helps build are tools that assist researchers in understanding what the data they find means. Published empirical research is important because it presents interpretations of data (both quantitative and qualitative) that both improve the knowledge base within a particular subject area and enhance the theoretical foundations for understanding new situations.

Practice

By now, many readers are probably wondering, "How could published research possibly have anything to do with what teachers and administrators face in schools every day?" The answer is that the best education research applies theory and empiricism to practical problems that occur in schools and school districts. Classrooms, schools, and other educational settings are these researchers' hunting grounds for meaningful data. Thus, many are striving to bridge research to practice in a manner that helps teachers and administrators work with students more effectively. The consumers of this research—instructional leaders—thus have an avenue to broaden their understanding beyond their individual experience bases.

A reminder at this point is important. We made the argument in Chapter 1 that education leaders should *use* research as a means of informing their thinking, not necessarily *implement* research conclusions without question. Our position is that educators interested in research should always begin with a clear understanding of their local context and the craft knowledge they have acquired over an entire career. Figure 2.2 is intended to demonstrate how you might put theory and empirical research to work. It is very deliberate that your big idea about what is happening is at the apex of the pyramid, because it is the most important construct through which theory and research ought to be considered. What individuals learn from reading theory and empirical research informs their big ideas about how to address instructional challenges.

Being well informed through reading research is a critically important part of moving down a path toward school improvement, but knowing about research relevant to a particular achievement gap is worthless without concerted action. Making research practical is the responsibility of the instructional leader. This involves taking what is known about the local situation, considering that in light

Figure 2.2   How Research Ought to Be Used

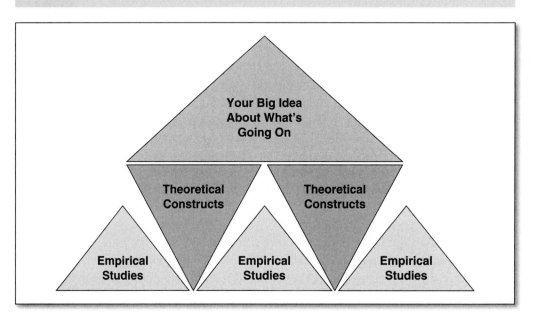

of published research, and formulating decisions for action based on this knowledge. In other words, leaders put research to use in their practice.

Collaboration to Improve Student Achievement

Up to this point in the book, discussion of collaboration has been sporadic. We focus specifically on collaboration in the next chapter, but we wish to emphasize here that effective leaders work collaboratively with a variety of stakeholders from the original conception of their ideas for making change through action planning, implementation, and evaluation. We subscribe to the view of Osterman and Kottkamp (2004) that collaboration is critical from the moment problem identification begins and that it is reinforced through data-informed reflection as solutions are tried and evaluated.

Understanding that others should be involved in decision making and implementation is an easy concept to grasp. In practice, this can be one of the most frustrating aspects of creating change. Too often, members of a group prove themselves incompetent in some key way or drop responsibilities that were handed to them. This common behavior causes those with passion for an issue to take all the work on themselves and to keep more of the critical decisions away from the group because they cannot be trusted anyway. The result may be that the leader becomes isolated and finds himself or herself in the position of issuing mandates when the original intent was the opposite. Commitment within the group is weak, and the school beyond the group has little understanding or interest in the leader's initiative. For these reasons, we have devoted Chapter 3 to the topics of involving others and teamwork.

CONCLUSION

Most of this chapter has focused on the top portion of Figure 2.1. Our belief is that leaders understand their schools and districts from at least four different perspectives characterized by Bolman and Deal's (2008) four frames. Instructional leaders, as the name suggests, focus their leadership efforts on instruction but not exclusively. They are able to provide managerial (e.g., efficient structures) and political supports (e.g., connections to core values, power sources in the community and at the central office, access to resources) that enhance the likelihood that improvements in teaching and learning will get implemented and be sustained over time. To gain a deeper understanding of school challenges and to identify potential solutions, instructional leaders conduct action research and consult relevant literature. Key colleagues collaborate with the leader to inform decision making throughout the process and to build a sense of commitment to both the problem at hand and its ultimate solutions. We assert that leaders who are reflected in the description just given will find that their schools engage in organizational learning as student achievement and overall school performance are enhanced.

Becoming a reflective, insightful leader who makes data-informed decisions is obviously more complex than we can convey in one chapter. Nevertheless, we have laid down conceptual markers to which we will return numerous times in later chapters. Instead of engaging in a longer discourse about what we intend for all the characteristics of a change-adept leader, we would rather show you how they work as you encounter each phase of school improvement planning.

REVIEW QUESTIONS

1. Under what conditions is instructional leadership more feasible?

2. What kinds of insights come from looking at schools and districts as organizations?

3. Which important factors make implementation of good ideas challenging?

4. What benefits are instructional leaders likely to gain from engaging with published research?

WORKSHEET 2.1   Who Are the Leaders in Your School?

The table below is intended to help you make explicit who the leaders are in your school—and who they are not. It is also intended to help you think about what you are already doing in the realm of leadership. Finally, the table will help you see where your leadership and leadership in your school generally is currently focused. You may want to save your work in a file so that you can return to it when you get to the action planning phase of your school improvement project. It will help you identify potential supports for and roadblocks to your school improvement planning efforts.

In thinking about these questions, you may want to consider your observations and experiences with your school's improvement efforts over the past year. Since leaders emerge within specific leadership contexts, this may help ground your thinking and help you understand who in your school may best lead different kinds of challenges.

Tasks

1. First, list all the people in your school who hold official leadership positions.

   - Put a plus (+) next to the names of those who you believe lead effectively.
   - Put a minus (−) next to the names of those who you believe are not effective leaders.

2. Do the same for the next two rows (though it seems likely that the "Leaders by Action" category will not have ineffective leaders in it). Names may appear in more than one row.

3. In the last row, give brief descriptions of circumstances in which you have exercised effective leadership.

4. Consider the nature of each leader's activities *as a leader*. Going back through your list, indicate each person's *dominant* focus—instructional, managerial, or political.

Leaders by Position (Those who hold official leadership positions, such as principal)	
Leaders by Reputation (Those who may or may not hold official positions but who are thought of by others as leaders)	

Leaders by Action (Those who you have seen lead, however you may define that)	
My Leadership Accomplishments (What have you done?)	

Questions

1. How robust is your school's leadership? Are there enough leaders? Are they working cooperatively enough so that one could say they are all pulling in the same direction?

2. How might your own leadership complement the strengths and/or mitigate the weaknesses of one or more leaders in your school?

CHAPTER 3

INVOLVING OTHERS, FORMING A TEAM

The final ingredient of effective team performance—and one of the most critical—is team leadership. Our research strongly indicates that the right person in a leadership role can add tremendous value to any collective effort, even to the point of sparking the outcome with an intangible kind of magic.

—Larson and LaFasto (1989, p. 118)

LEARNING OUTCOMES

Readers who grasp the most important ideas from this chapter will be able to

- understand the value of involving others informally and formally in school improvement planning and implementation;
- discern who belongs on a team and who can assist the reader's project from a greater distance;
- differentiate among different kinds of team members; and
- identify team members whose skills, knowledge, and dispositions complement one another.

At this point, students in leadership preparation programs may be thinking, "How can I possibly lead a meaningful school improvement and still meet the obligations of my full-time job?" A similar dilemma faces in-service school leaders with already-full agendas. The short answer is that you can't—at least, not alone and not in a brief period of time. This is one of the core reasons why involving others is so important. The burden is heavy, and it must be carried by several individuals working together. The other reality, of course, is that complex problems demand the best thinking of many; the collective knowledge, experience, and judgment of a team are often critical to success of any school improvement effort. Despite this basic truth, deliberately and systematically involving others and ultimately creating and maintaining a well-functioning team is a major test of leadership ability.

This chapter helps you see collaboration through a more analytical perspective than you might otherwise. The result is that you will learn how to make best use of the skills, abilities, and perspectives of a variety of people in your school community and avoid some common pitfalls—all in the name of creating, implementing, and evaluating a successful project that will positively impact student achievement. To accomplish all this requires that you develop habits of mind that lead you to be strategic about whom you involve in your project and how and ways in which you distribute leadership opportunities to others.

The "work" that you need to do as a result of thinking carefully about collaboration will become clear as you progress through the various stages of the process that unfolds in the remainder of this book. As we suggest later, in the early stages of problem identification and root-cause analysis, as you are building your understanding of the instructional challenge you want to work on, you will be involving others informally. As you identify your action plan and contemplate implementation, you will solidify your team. As such, it is worthwhile to think of your reading of this chapter as setting the stage for your deliberations about team building—work that will continue as you move toward taking action.

THE VALUE OF COLLABORATION

Working with colleagues is vital for problem articulation, effective research, action planning, implementation, and evaluation for the following reasons: (a) Knowledge from data collection and analysis should be socially constructed (i.e., multiple perspectives help create a deep understanding); (b) bringing multiple perspectives to bear when figuring out the nature of a challenge, potential solutions, implementation, and evaluation broadens the set of possible choices and forms a stronger footing for decision making; and (c) collaboration helps build common perspectives based on the interaction of various points of view. The last point is particularly important because school improvement efforts fail when taken on by the Lone Ranger. In contrast, the process of developing a common understanding among a substantial portion of teachers and administrators helps create a coalition of support for a particular project. When this coalition becomes enthusiastic about addressing the problem in a specific way, the motivation to implement will spread more widely through the school as friends and colleagues talk to one another.

Engaging partners who can help with the legwork of collecting data seems an obvious advantage, but why involve others to help make sense of the data? On the surface, it appears simpler to have one person retreat with the fruits of data collection and figure out what is going on without a lot of "noise" from other people who are less informed. But the problem with the do-it-alone approach is that one person looks at the data with blinders and biases that prevent her or him from seeing all of it. For example, a teacher who does not have a deep understanding of appropriate interventions for students with special needs may look at low math achievement for special education students and teacher comments and conclude that the problem is that these students simply don't pay attention and take notes during class. A special education teacher may discover in the data, however, that teachers are not appropriately structuring class activities to make them accessible to students who have difficulty processing numbers. These two teachers engaging in analysis and discussion together are likely to articulate the math achievement problem differently from either teacher working alone. Working together, they may think and talk about the intersection between teacher choices and student responses. What we have described here is the process of transforming data into knowledge (Fullan, 2001). Knowledge develops more completely when generated collaboratively.

A more subtle problem with the do-it-alone approach to data collection and analysis is the limitation of our own cognition. March and Simon (1993) elaborated the concept of limited or bounded rationality more than 50 years ago, and Simon spent a good portion of his academic career experimenting with and refining the idea (Simon, 1993). In a nutshell, bounded rationality means that one person's ability to comprehend his or her world and what is happening in it has limitations. When the limits to our rationality or understanding are not recognized, then we miss important evidence in our environment. Those limits or boundaries can be expanded when we collaborate with others. In short, two heads are better than one.

Despite the value of collaboration, merely bringing people together will not reliably create a positive outcome. Human beings are complex. They have multiple and conflicting motivations and goals. Creating a group or team increases the intricacy of work exponentially. Despite the challenges of working with a group of people, the complexity of instructional challenges we face in today's schools necessitates teamwork (Larson & LaFasto, 1989). Taking what might otherwise be an unruly collection of individuals and forging them into a reliable, high-functioning team makes collaboration far more effective.

ACTIVITY 3.1   Roundtable Discussion: A Team That Worked

Consider a time when you had a positive experience working with a team to accomplish something important, either professionally or in another kind of social setting. Reflect on each of the following:

- What problem or challenge characterized the situation? What was the team trying to accomplish?
- How did the team come into being? Who convened the team?
- Who served on the team, and how were they selected?
- What motivated members to participate?
- What common values or beliefs guided the team's work?
- What did the team accomplish?
- What specific factors most contributed to the team's success?

Share your reflections about this "team that worked" with one or more critical friends. As you think about the experiences described, can you generalize the necessary attributes of an effective team? What kinds of things seem most important across team contexts? What role does leadership play?

Different Degrees of Collaboration

This chapter explains two essential kinds of involvement or collaboration. The first is looser and more episodic; think of working with people in brief spurts for very specific reasons. The second is tighter and more consistent and is demonstrated through working with an explicit team. Both kinds of involvement are key ingredients of successful project planning and implementation. Knowing which individuals should participate in various ways involves leadership judgment.

Figure 3.1 is a schematic drawing of what we generally have in mind for working with others. The cloud represents the somewhat amorphous thinking and communicating that needs to occur more broadly in your school, and possibly your district, as you think about how to define the problem, challenge, or gap you wish to address and as you consider potential team members. The early stages of thinking about your project are likely to involve more informal discussions. Later, you will be seeking more formal commitments. The collaborative team is the engine that does the specific work of bringing your school improvement project to life.

Figure 3.1   Collaborative Project Development

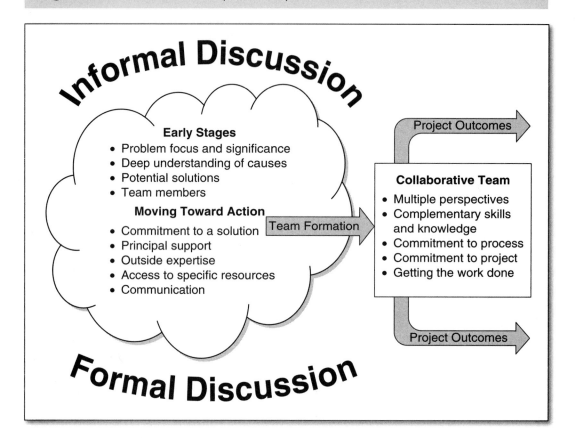

INVOLVING OTHERS

Despite substantial efforts to the contrary, the practice of teaching still tends to be solitary. We notice among our students that the work-alone ethic remains strong through much of their coursework in our leadership preparation program because, as we discussed above, working with others is complicated and can be annoying and slow. Instead of adopting this common view, however, we recommend that you look at the challenge of school improvement through multiple frames (Bolman & Deal, 2008) to see how other members of your school community can help you develop and achieve your project goals. Not all the people discussed below will end up on your collaborative team, nor should they. Nevertheless, they can be involved to greater or lesser degrees, and all have the potential to help you at various stages through design and implementation of your project.

The Principal

If you are currently serving as a principal, then you have substantial authority in your school site, depending on how much autonomy the superintendent allows. Most others in the school have little to no authority over anyone except students. From a structural perspective, this means that most people reading this book will rely primarily on their own *influence* within the school community to accomplish work, rather than exercising authority (i.e., a final say). How much influence you have depends largely on what you know and your relationships with others, particularly with your principal.

Enlisting the principal in your improvement effort is vital because he or she is held responsible for everything that happens in the school. If you can bring to your principal a viable approach to a persistent problem, you will win valuable support. Yet your principal must understand and agree with your articulation of the instructional challenge and believe that the solution you ultimately propose is both effective and practical before he or she commits to providing the symbolic and practical assistance you will need. In other words, you will need to be persuasive, a topic we explore in Chapter 5.

Building a strong professional working relationship with your principal is necessary groundwork. She or he must trust you and believe that you act with integrity. This is the human resources aspect of your involvement of the principal. Politically, you need the principal's backing to acquire necessary resources and to help get other people in the school community to pay attention to you. In other words, you need some of the principal's authority to flow through you and into your project. You can strengthen your human resources and political ties to the principal through regular communication and, ultimately, by bringing in an attractive solution.

Beyond talking with you and privately supporting your efforts, your principal can help you by using the great symbolic strength of the position. When the principal speaks at faculty meetings, to parent groups, and to the central office about the promising project you are leading, people pay attention, primarily because the principal is the person in charge. Your principal describing your project sends the strong symbolic message that what you are doing is important and worthwhile. Teachers, especially, will pay little attention to you if they believe that the principal is either not interested in or against what you are doing. With the principal acting as your cheerleader, you gain a substantial amount of credibility and influence.

Teachers

Although they may not share your perspective yet, there are likely to be many teachers in your school who have experienced the problem, challenge, or gap on which you choose to focus. This means that they can provide you with insights that either support, refute, or augment your own. Talking with teachers familiar with the problem you are addressing not only enhances your understanding of the problem, it also helps you identify the motivations, frustrations, and beliefs of teachers who will ultimately implement whatever solution set you and your collaborative team devise.

Every teacher in your school has some measure of subject-matter expertise that is enhanced by insights into instructional techniques that are derived from multiple years of experience in the classroom. Tapping into this expertise helps you learn the nature of current successes and difficulties and how those vary from teacher to teacher. Perhaps more important, by discovering the expertise of more teachers in your school, you learn your colleagues' strengths and limitations and begin to learn the challenges you will face both in obtaining agreement that your problem should be addressed and in fostering the will to implement your solution.

Teachers represent another important resource to you—relationships with other teachers. As we noted in Chapter 2, adoption of innovation depends largely on who the early adopters are and whether or not they are respected and valued by peers (Rogers, 1995). By engaging in discussions with teachers, learning from them, and sharing your perspectives, you could be laying the groundwork for early adopters who are enthusiastic about your efforts. The human resources frame suggests that people are motivated by work they find gratifying. To the extent that your improvement project fosters enhanced learning, teachers will want to support it as they seek professional fulfillment. Later adopters will tend to trust and emulate early adopters whom they respect.

As the primary implementers of your action plan, teachers can teach you a great deal about the nature of the problem, the potential for your solution's success, and potential roadblocks you will encounter along the way. It pays to listen carefully to them. At the same time, you should see yourself in the role of persuading those people who are crucial to implementation that your team's analysis of the problem and proposed solution(s) make sense.

Central Office Personnel

Depending on the size and wealth of your school district, there may be subject-matter experts who work from the central office. If so, it would be a good investment of your time to find out who in your area of interest might be able to work with you, your team, and your school. In addition to their capability in a curricular area, they often have access to small amounts of money, supplies, books, professional development time, and personnel. If they take interest in your project, they may lend important practical assistance. Furthermore, by virtue of their residing at the central office, such individuals have high potential to have access to upper-echelon district leadership and are imbued with power symbols. In the face of principal reluctance or lack of interest, having friends at the central office can be a big help in winning support for your project.

In small districts that do not have large central office staffs, it is a good idea to cultivate a working relationship with the superintendent and/or members of the cabinet. You need to be careful not to go behind the back of your principal (pay attention to local norms), but central office administrators often have a great deal of respect for and interest in classroom teachers. Sharing what you are doing in your project helps keep them informed about what is happening in the schools. Serious interest on their part has the potential to bring additional resources into your project and signal that what you are doing is important.

Parents and Students

Although it is practically a cliché to state that parents need to be involved in their children's education for students to be successful, it remains unusual for us to involve parents in the process of planning instructional improvement. Even more outlandish is the notion of asking students how they might respond to an effort to improve their performance. We suggest that you rethink these old habits.

A mechanism for involving parents is to recruit one or two for your collaborative team (described in detail below). Obviously, you want to involve parents who both have an interest in your focus problem and population and have some expertise to offer. Many parents who work in professional jobs combine both of these with the flexibility to devote some volunteer time to the task. As with others you involve, parents can also become strong allies who promote your program in the larger community.

How strange we are in education not to ask students what they think about why they have difficulty succeeding in certain areas and what ought to be done about it. Yet it is uncommon for us to involve students in these ways. In Chapter 4, we recommend conducting student surveys and interviews to learn more about the problem you identify in your school, which would be a fine start for involving students. Depending on the age of the students in your school and your focus area, you may want to go further by consulting with small groups about potential solutions you and your team consider. This kind of strategy of asking the "customer" what she or he thinks has been advocated in business for more than a generation (Collins, 2001; Peters, & Waterman, 1982). It informs change and helps build widespread support in the community. At the high school level, it may even prove desirable to recruit one or two students to the collaborative team, being careful not to reveal individual confidential student data.

Maintaining Relationships

If you are successful in involving people from the groups discussed in this section, you will be well on your way to developing a coalition of individuals who are interested in and possibly devoted to the success of your project. By involving others, you are harnessing their power and influence to your project and giving it a greater probability of success. This is likely a new role for you, one that involves moving in a much wider circle than a classroom teacher or administrator typically does. Much of this work involves talking with and writing to others on a regular basis.

Communication is critical to involving others, both on your team and apart from it. Communication does not need to be sophisticated or lengthy, but it does need to be regular. If you can write periodic pieces for your in-school newsletter, speak for a few minutes during faculty meetings, and talk informally with colleagues, they are more likely to understand and support what you and your team are trying to accomplish. More active involvement of individuals from multiple constituencies pays even greater dividends in terms of building enthusiasm and support for your project.

Some of the people you involve in your project in the manner described above may end up on your collaborative team, though most probably will not. Different people will have different roles to play at various stages of planning and implementation. For example, you may want to involve your school's data expert in the initial stages of problem finding but not necessarily during the action planning phase, when more curricular expertise is needed. Not everyone needs to serve on the collaborative team to be involved in a meaningful way. Use Worksheet 3.1 periodically as you move through various stages of planning and implementation to identify specific people who can most help you be successful in your school improvement efforts.

ACTIVITY 3.2   Leading a Team

In an effort to present working with teams in a logical fashion, we offer a series of steps to help you think about how to do it. We understand, however, that none of this work is simple. We believe that having a discussion that is both retrospective and prospective about working on a team and/or as a team leader will help you and your peers think about what to anticipate in your work with teams.

With one or more critical friends, consider each of the following questions in relation to your role as team leader. If you are in a graduate class, then this discussion might be enhanced by the presence of a school leader who is particularly adept at leading teamwork.

Discussion Questions

1. What will you need to lead your collaborative team effectively? What resources or factors in your school will support your efforts to build an effective team?

2. What roadblocks do you anticipate that might make your creation of and work with a team more difficult?
   - In what ways is authority an issue (if you are not the principal of the school)?
   - To what degree is your school district centrally controlled such that the discretion of the principal is circumscribed? What are the implications for your team?

3. What do you fear most about leading a team in a school improvement project?
   - What additional learning do you need to help you lead a team more effectively?
   - Is there anyone at your school site who might be able to mentor you in the area of team leadership?

4. In summary, describe your vision for how your team focused on instructional improvement will carry out the project. What would an "ideal" team look like?

BUILDING THE TEAM

Many people will have their fingerprints on your project in a variety of ways, but particularly as you move toward implementation of your project, you need a consistent group that is devoted to the success of your project and is as much or more on the job than you are. This group is your collaborative team. Your working relationships with some of the people you involved in the processes described above may suggest they would fit well with your team. First, there are several considerations to make.

What Is a Team?

Committees are a standard feature of most schools and school districts. They conduct important work that helps maintain critical functions and lends an aura of participation, if not outright democracy, to the enterprise of schooling. Committees are often referred to as teams—as in the term *leadership team*—but they rarely function as such. A complicating factor is that committees also spawn the activity that many educators love to hate—meetings. The main difficulty of both the concept of committees as teams and meetings is that they frequently have no central, clearly articulated, understood goal. Consequently, committee membership and meeting time can easily seem purposeless.

In contrast to the typical committees on which most of us have served, a team has a clear purpose for its existence as articulated in its central goal and/or objectives (Hackman & Walton, 1986; Larson & LaFasto, 1989). With more of a goal orientation, as opposed to a process orientation, a well-functioning team will exist for as long as it takes to achieve its goal, and then it will disband. This kind of structure is ideal for school improvement projects because once fully implemented, if they are indeed effective, they should no longer require meeting time in and of themselves. As the project becomes an integral part of how school happens, it no longer requires special support. Thus, once teachers know how to teach in the manner your project suggests, the reason for your team's existence will disappear, as should the team (Hackman & Walton, 1986; Katzenbach & Smith, 2003).

Who Should Be on the Team?

In his popular book about leadership and organizational success, *Good to Great*, Collins (2001) recommends "getting the right people on the bus" (p. 55) to move the organization forward. This advice is problematic in schools, where we rarely get to choose teachers and administrators uniquely suited to help resolve a particular school's central instructional problem. The beginning of a school improvement effort, however, is a rare opportunity to put at least some of the "right" people on your bus. Figuring out who belongs there can be difficult, especially if you do not already have a great deal of influence in your school and/or you are not very familiar with many other members of your faculty. In the next three sections, we describe ways in which leaders commonly pick teams and the weaknesses of these tactics. Each method has its own logic of action that seems rational on its face, but each is fraught with different kinds of problems. We follow these sections with a discussion of more effective ways of thinking about who should be on your team.

Picking My Friends

It is common and sensible to enlist the help of those whom we trust when putting together a team for a specific purpose. Our friends make us feel good because they generally agree with our own perspectives and we enjoy their company. Motivation is strengthened when working toward a common goal with people we like. The problem is that by thinking as I do, my friends may not bring a fresh enough perspective that truly expands the boundaries of my own rationality. Furthermore, my friends may not represent the necessary knowledge and skill sets for the goal that I have in mind. If my primary recruitment criterion is working with people I like, then my team could be limited by my own personal strengths and weaknesses.

There is a more substantial problem with picking one's friends to be on a team. Doing so projects a clubby attitude: "If you're part of my crowd, then you are one of the chosen ones to participate." In schools, this is felt most keenly when the principal appears to consult with only a small subset of the faculty with whom he or she has particularly close relationships. This kind of inner circle tends to isolate the principal from the knowledge and expertise of others, and teachers often resent not being invited into the decision-making group. It can also result in groupthink (Janis, 1971). Envisioning yourself as an instructional leader, enhance the likelihood of widespread implementation of your project by reaching out to those beyond your circle of friends.

Volunteers

In an effort to be fair and open, it is tempting to put out a call for volunteers to serve on a team engaged in school improvement. Such an inclusive approach has the advantage of conveying the desire to welcome widespread participation in the project. But there are serious disadvantages, because it becomes difficult to control team membership—a critical factor in creating high-functioning teams (Katzenbach & Smith, 2003; Larson & LaFasto, 1989). There are three kinds of problems with the all-volunteer approach:

1. People volunteer for the wrong reasons. For example, the principal may have conveyed that everyone in the school must serve on at least one committee. Unable to find acceptance anywhere else, a particularly

unmotivated teacher chooses to serve on your team because it appears to be the least-bad choice.

2. Teachers who tend to volunteer for everything sign up for your team because improving student achievement is an engaging issue for them. Although they bring a great deal of energy and ideas to their work, such individuals tend to be spread too thin across many projects and may not be reliable enough to make meaningful contributions to your team.

3. Controlling the mix of expertise is impossible if the team is open for anyone to join. The team is then vulnerable to having overlapping expertise in some areas and gaps in others. Consider volunteers, of course, but you also need to engage in some active recruiting.

One of Each Flavor

In an effort to strike a balance among team members and mitigate the kinds of problems identified with the other two strategies of team recruitment, many leaders decide to include team members who collectively represent multiple interests or constituencies. But what people represent in terms of curricular area or years of experience in a particular role is less important than what they are willing and able to do. Although role can be a key factor, it is not sufficient for determining potential contribution to a team. You must also assess both the expertise and the willingness to engage in the work required by your project when considering potential team members. Teachers who have strong reputations among colleagues, students, and parents may be the strongest candidates. Administrators and teachers who can subordinate personal goals to the goal(s) of the team and wish to join your team are more likely to have the motivation to move your project forward than others who have ulterior motives (Larson & LaFasto, 1989).

Getting the Right Mix

Enlisting the right members for your team requires considering three key characteristics of potential team members: (a) Their expertise—are they *capable* of engaging in this work? (b) Their motivation—do they *want* to engage in this work? (c) Their habits of mind—how will they *approach* the work? We elaborate these characteristics in the next section and discuss practical steps for getting a mix of personalities on your team that have high potential to be productive.

Understanding Expertise, Motivation, and Habits of Mind

The three basic elements that potential team members bring with them to your school improvement effort are easy to understand but may be difficult to determine in the pressure of day-to-day work. Additionally, making team selections based on these criteria will require considerable fortitude, because it may mean that friends and others will suffer bruised egos if they are not chosen because of weaknesses in expertise, motivation, and/or habits of mind or simply because they are not part of the right mix for the team. Remember that your team is not a social club designed to help its members feel good. It is a small organization that is tightly focused on its primary goal. Being distracted by egos and/or conflict will seriously compromise the effectiveness of your team.

Expertise

The knowledge and ability to succeed in a particular effort constitutes expertise. It is much more than one's role. For example, if your project addresses limited-English-proficient (LEP) students' needs across the curriculum, then you may want to choose at least one teacher from each of the core content areas. But you must also consider who is able to teach the LEP population most effectively. That person could be a math teacher or a specialist who assists students whose first language is not English, or both kinds of experts may be available in your school. A lack of expertise could and should exclude a person from serving on your team despite the apparent centrality of that person's role to the problem you wish to address. Furthermore, multiple kinds of expertise are necessary. For example, making instructional change is very likely to involve changing the structure of the school day for some students, at least to some extent. This suggests that you will need administrative expertise in addition to classroom proficiency.

Motivation

Having exceptional expertise on a team does not necessarily guarantee success. If, for example, the assistant principal identified as having the necessary administrative expertise is not particularly interested in addressing the unique challenges of improving achievement for LEP students, then her or his expertise is not likely to be put to good use on the team. If this assistant principal were to join the team, you might observe behaviors such as missing meetings, putting up roadblocks to change, or nay-saying other people's ideas, all in an effort to avoid the time-consuming nuisance of making change. Similarly, teachers may have expertise that is not aimed in the right direction. There is a high probability that your improvement project will require some measure of professional development. Therefore, you will need team members who not only are good teachers but who also understand and enjoy working with adults as they learn.

Motivation is a powerful engine for action but is not always easy to understand. McGregor (1960, 2006) explains that people working in contemporary organizations have their basic physical and emotional needs met and are therefore seeking a higher level of gratification from their work. Frankl (1984) named this kind of search for deeper meaning *self-transcendence*. Both McGregor and Frankl present views that are optimistic for school improvement efforts because they suggest substantial, largely untapped energy available from educators who would like to make a greater impact on student achievement. Although we believe this to be true to some extent, we also know that several factors can seriously inhibit motivation. Not everyone is equally excited by the same kinds of instructional challenges. Personal histories that include past efforts at improvement may contain negative experiences that make teachers and others cynical in the present situation. Perhaps most important, individual motivation to engage in a change effort may be heavily influenced by what respected peers think and do (Rogers, 1995). A leader seeking positive group dynamics in a focused, well-functioning team must understand the motivation of potential team members before making choices. Expertise without motivation may generate a great deal of heat in terms of conflict and debate but inspire little action.

Habits of Mind

The ways in which we think and act are evidence of our habits of mind. In his study of master chess players, Simon (1993) found that they maintained approximately 100 chess game patterns in their heads. The typical habit of mind for a master chess player was to analyze an opponent's move, then choose the appropriate counter-move based on his or her beliefs about the pattern that was emerging. This habit of mind represents the application of standard operating procedures that can be adjusted as the game progresses. In the area of fostering school improvement, we are seeking analytical and reflective habits of mind—the desire to know more about a particular learning problem, challenge, or gap and a willingness to engage with others about what data mean and how to take action that will improve current outcomes. These habits of mind may be more difficult to find than expertise and motivation, suggesting that it will be the leader's responsibility to cultivate them. (See Osterman & Kottkamp, 2004, for a full discussion of reflective practice habits of mind focused on instructional challenges.)

Different Types of Collaborators

Our experience suggests that educators fall into four broad categories in terms of expertise, motivation, and habits of mind. This simplifying scheme may help you think more quickly about promising team members, but it also requires learning about and understanding the personal characteristics of potential team members more thoroughly. We offer the caution that not everyone fits neatly into boxes and that it would not be wise to stereotype potential team members. Figure 3.2 presents general categories of potential participants. Expertise, motivation, and habits of mind should be considered in terms of their relationship to your school improvement project.

Figure 3.2   Four Types of Potential Team Members

Novice	*Experienced, Successful, Not Active*
Low expertise	High expertise
High motivation	Low motivation
Developing habits of mind	Reluctant habits of mind
Experienced, Not Successful	*Experienced, Successful, Active*
Low expertise	High expertise
Low motivation	High motivation
Poor habits of mind	Analytical, reflective habits of mind

Novice

Novices are teachers or administrators new to their positions. In both cases, they may have high levels of energy—partly because of their newness to their jobs and partly because they are in a phase of their careers in which they are eager to please others. People new in their jobs often bring new ideas and are not bound by old habits prevalent in the school. Such individuals could be highly motivated by your improvement effort because they came into their positions intent on helping students and your project looks like an opportunity to them. This motivation is worth a great deal on your team, but it is tempered by a lack of experience and potential gaps in expertise. There is much that they will not know (about the nature of your project's problem, about how things function in your school, etc.). This lack of knowledge can lead to critical errors in judgment and operational mistakes. Individual novice team members have high potential to learn and contribute to the team and may be excellent workers, but they will need support from others with higher levels of expertise. Too many novices on one team may lead to poor choices and weak influence schoolwide.

Experienced, Not Successful

Administrators and teachers in this category have been working in their jobs for a number of years, but they have never been particularly successful. Their lack of success could be due to poor aptitude in their jobs, organizational lack of acceptance for their ideas and goals, or some combination of the two. The result after several years of this kind of experience may be poor habits of mind that have stunted their expertise development. A pattern of negative feedback or being ignored may have eroded such individuals' motivation to the point where they just try to get through the day, week, or month. Obviously, it would be unwise to put a large number of this kind of person on your team, but the involvement of one or two on your team also represents an opportunity for professional refreshment and rejuvenation that could help bring them out of their low-performing status. It is your role as leader to give people who fit this category work to do that can help them expand their expertise and enhance their motivation.

Experienced, Successful, Not Active

Many teachers are highly successful in their classrooms but choose to refrain from taking part in collaboration opportunities. Likewise, an administrator may have carved out a comfortable niche for herself or himself (such as building the master schedule or managing counseling services) that narrowly defines responsibilities. Teachers and administrators in this category have a great deal to offer others who may be less expert, but they choose not to do so. This may be a general predisposition, but many teachers attempted to be more collaborative and more involved in the lives of their schools at an earlier point in their careers and got burned in the process. An improvement effort on which they may have worked very hard could have been scuttled by the principal or the central office, or they might have taken a risk that stirred up controversy they prefer to avoid in the future.

Whatever the case, such individuals are potentially high-performing team members, but it is up to the leader to help improve their motivation and bring them out of their reluctance. Building trust is a critical part of improving motivation and fostering collaboration (Bryk & Scheider, 2002; Larson & LaFasto, 1989; McGregor, 1960, 2006). Trust with this type of participant must be developed over time through clear communication, treating the individuals as adults by giving them meaningful responsibilities, and supporting them through difficult times. Nevertheless, as the team leader, you must be on the lookout for negative habits of mind from these veterans that are expressed in phrases such as "We tried that 10 years ago and it didn't work then."

Experienced, Successful, Active

This kind of individual clearly requires the least amount of coaching and nurturing from the team leader. Ready, willing, and able to participate in teamwork to improve student achievement, such persons will help the team greatly. Nevertheless, difficulties may arise in terms of group dynamics. Team members who can operate at this level often become impatient with and discouraged by others on the team who appear to be slowing them down or not pulling their weight. Conversely, other team members may see these individuals' impatience with the pace of group process as arrogant, pushy, or worse. It is the responsibility of the leader to manage group dynamics productively and keep everyone's ego in check and intact. Although team members who are consistently successful and active are probably capable of intimidating everyone, the leader must coach them as needed about working with others in a manner that maintains harmony and productivity on the team.

It is probably a good idea for you to assess where you best fit in Figure 3.2. What is your personal history within your school? How are you perceived by others? Your project is an opportunity to overcome any weaknesses you may have displayed and take advantage of your strengths, but as the team leader, you may need to address others' perceptions of your expertise, motivation, and/or habits of mind. Figure 3.2 gives you the opportunity to identify the kind of collaborative participant you aspire to be.

Two More Considerations

As the leader of your school improvement project, it is your responsibility to recruit the most capable team you can. We suggest that you begin by having a conversation with your principal, who should be kept well informed about the progress of your project from initial conception through implementation. Competent principals know their faculty very well and can give you insights with respect to expertise, motivation, and habits of mind of potential team members. The principal is also likely to give you clues about important internal politics and organization culture issues that could affect your team's functioning.

Political and Symbolic Team Members

Our discussion of general involvement and specific team membership up to this point has relied heavily on structural and human resources frame analysis (Bolman & Deal, 2008). We have been focused on who fits where in the school and the district, what roles they play, and how you as a leader might interact with various individuals and groups. As we suggested in Chapter 2, it is best to use multiple frames when trying to figure out what is happening in the organization we call school. The political and symbolic frames may be harder to understand, but they are well worth considering.

Remembering that politics focuses on access to resources, power, and coalitions, thinking about the characteristics of potential team members in these terms may help you recruit a team that can improve the probability that your project will be implemented well. One or more teachers who interact in the principal's inner circle are essentially part of a powerful coalition that can lend strength to your team. If they are not already too busy with projects, they represent promising team members. In many settings, the teachers' association is the most powerful coalition that has the power to block or facilitate changes at the school site. A building representative or association officer with the right kind of expertise and a modest amount of motivation might bring with him or her resources and influence that will enhance the success of your project. Membership from among the ranks of teachers and administrators who will be directly involved in implementing your project is both a structural and a political issue; building a consensus with this group may be critical to planning, implementation, and evaluation of your work.

Every school has its classroom heroes—the teachers who are able to reach the most challenging students and build positive relationships with them, those who help develop the skills and knowledge of their fellow faculty, and the ones who create classroom magic. Their presence would carry a great deal of symbolic weight that could help your team. Your school community knows many stories about these individuals and their successes in the school setting. When they serve on your team, they can be influential ambassadors to the rest of the community. When they help create the improvement project, others will take notice and trust the work of your team because of their belief in the capability of the classroom heroes working with you. Whether or not others choose to adopt the innovation you ultimately design depends in large measure on their perception of the individuals who are recommending the innovation and those who adopted before them (Rogers, 1995). Classroom heroes who are early adopters may enhance the implementation of your project.

Time to Decide, Time to Lead

It is obvious by now that building your team requires thinking along multiple dimensions. The most important message of this chapter is that you as a leader must be strategic about how you involve others in your school improvement project. Yet the task of selecting your team is made just a bit more challenging by the fact that you do not have full discretion over who serves on it. Ideal candidates may not be willing. It is possible to end up with too many people who are eager to help but do not yet have the skills and knowledge to do a great job. You may feel compelled by your school administration or other influences to select someone with low expertise and low motivation. As a leader, you must play the hand you are dealt the best way you know how. If you use the factors identified in this chapter to make choices where you can, then you will have a stronger team than if you used, for example, the one-of-each-flavor strategy.

Thinking about all your team members in terms of expertise, motivation, habits of mind, organizational politics, and symbolism helps you gain a better understanding of strengths and weaknesses of individuals and the team as a whole. This knowledge, in turn, helps you decide how you (and others you involve) might develop the skills and knowledge of individuals as you work through the school improvement planning and implementation processes. If you can select a team in which the members complement one another's personal characteristics, you will have chosen well. Worksheet 3.2 is designed to help you figure out the various characteristics of potential team members so that you can be strategic in your recruitment efforts. (Again, you might use this worksheet multiple times at various stages of planning as you move from more informal involvement to establishment of the collaborative team that will help lead your school improvement project.)

Our emphasis on developing a well-functioning team is consistent with the collaboration theme that runs throughout the book. As the team leader, you have an important role to play in determining the nature of the collaboration you expect from team members. As a result of their study of numerous high-performing teams, Larson and LaFasto (1989) identified the following six leadership principles to guide you in your work as team leader.

As a team leader, I will

1. avoid compromising the team's objective with political issues,

2. exhibit personal commitment to our team's goal,

3. not dilute the team's effort with too many priorities,

4. be fair and impartial toward all team members,

5. be willing to confront and resolve issues associated with inadequate performance by team members, and

6. be open to new ideas and information from team members. (p. 123)

Team members will assess whether or not you act on these principles, and they will look to you to make team processes work well. In other words, they will look to you to lead the team.

PUTTING THE TEAM TO WORK

We have devoted considerable space to explaining how to think about who should be on your team, emphasizing the importance of the team's composition. How you work with that team once they are assembled is even more important. Motivation will build and habits of mind will be sharpened when team members believe they are involved in important work and their time is well spent.

When your team is engaged in learning about the instructional problem, challenge, or gap that you have identified and finally creating action plans, there will be many decisions all of you will need to make along the way. The decisions drive the direction that your school improvement effort ultimately takes, so how you make them becomes very important. As team leader, the most important decisions you will make are centered on how the group will decide. We explain what we mean by this in the next section.

Collaborative Team Decision Making

Rather than being an all-or-nothing proposition, collaboration can be categorized according to the kinds of decisions being considered. McGregor (1960, 2006), Vroom and Yetton (1973), Vroom and Jago (1978), and other situational leadership theorists inform our description of these different kinds of collaborative decision making. In Table 3.1, a summary of decision types follows our discussion.

A common mistake of many leaders who wish to be collaborative is that they fail to see the relative value of different types of collaboration for different types of decisions. Thinking about your team, much time could be wasted on thorough discussions of managerial issues such as where and when the team will meet. Feedback on these kinds of logistics is certainly important, but your team will appreciate your leadership if you make the managerial decisions expeditiously and allow for much more time and participation on decisions affecting the planning and operation of the improvement project itself.

Time-dependent managerial decisions lend themselves to being made by the leader alone. We refer to this kind of decision as Type 1. Nevertheless, a small degree of collaboration is warranted. In Type 1, you as decision maker explain the rationale behind your decision to team members so that they can understand why the decision was made and so that they are able to implement the decision as you intend. This may seem simple, but we have all witnessed leaders who made decisions that few people understood because the leader did not bother to explain them. By coupling explanation with decision, you treat team members as adults and help them do a good job following you as their leader. Scheduling provides a clear example. Arranging a common time for your team to meet will be challenging. If you consider each person's needs and set the least-objectionable day and time to meet, then you will have made the best decision possible. Explaining your rationale to the group will help them understand the choice you made and will reduce bickering over the schedule.

Type 2 decisions are somewhat more involved. In what is probably a managerial decision that may not be as clear as the day and time to meet, you could present an idea about how to handle the reading of a set of articles relevant to your focus improvement area. You might propose that each person volunteer to read a different article and make a brief written and oral presentation to the group to facilitate group learning. As you present this idea, you would need to enlist considerable cooperation from the group, so getting their feedback on the strategy seems prudent. To build trust, you must be sincere in your solicitation of feedback for a decision not yet fully made. Considering the feedback, you would make a decision and then explain how the feedback was used and why some feedback was rejected as you explain the final decision. Feedback brings team members into the decision-making process, while clear communication demonstrates their role in the final outcome.

Our focus on instructional improvement and the decision making that goes along with it strongly implies a more sophisticated kind of decision making for the key elements of school improvement projects. Type 3 decision making is the most collaborative between leaders and constituents, and it requires the highest degree of trust—trust that may be enhanced by well-executed Type 1 and Type 2 decision making. In Type 3, you position yourself to work as a peer with the team, neither dominating nor removing yourself from discussion and debate. Instead of saying some variation of "I make this decision," you are communicating, "Let's decide together."

The Vicissitudes of Collaboration

Anyone who has participated in group process around an important issue knows that discussion is often contentious and making a final decision can be very difficult. Despite your best efforts to maintain an inquiry stance within your team, competition is likely to creep in at more high-stakes moments in the school improvement planning process. This leads many to conclude that collaboration doesn't work and/or that meetings are a terrible waste of time. To the contrary, we see the arguments that might ensue as an important part of honest reflection on issues such as reasons for students' poor performance. The process of discussing what has previously been undiscussable and identifying governing variables that need to change (see the discussion of organizational learning in Chapter 2) may not be cordial, but it is crucial to making meaningful change in schools that benefits students. The leader's job is to manage the collaborative process so that it is as productive as possible.

Making decisions together requires working to achieve consensus. If your group is contentious, you may be tempted to resort to voting, but before you do, remember that voting creates winners and losers. Bitter losers on your team are likely to erode its effectiveness. Consensus is probably equal parts agreement and a willingness not to stand in the way of the will of others (see box). For more about forging consensus over contentious issues, we recommend *Getting to Yes: Negotiating Agreement Without Giving In* by Fisher, Ury, and Patton (1991) and *Getting Past No: Negotiating in Difficult Situations* by Ury (1993).

DEFINING CONSENSUS

Consensus is widely misconstrued as majority rule. Democracy is great, but any important political fight yields winners and losers, and the losers often seek revenge. Consider the battle over health care reform being waged as we write this book. An important question for you as an educational leader is whether the cost of creating losers is worth the benefit of voting. We think not in most cases of important school change.

Our definition of consensus is that a whole group can agree to *live with* a particular decision, path, or outcome. There may be variations in agreement (i.e., some may love the solution, others may be willing to try it but are skeptical).

Consensus is neither automatic nor instantaneous. When people on your team disagree on a course of action, you may find the following discussion points helpful:

1. Figuring out which interests are met by being in favor of an action and which interests are met by being opposed to it

2. Discovering unanswered questions that people have regarding the decision

3. Getting more facts or data that clarify the situation so that the course of action makes more sense

4. Modifying the course of action so that additional interests can be met without losing the original rationale for the action

When seeking consensus, be sure that all participants have been heard. Give your team time to reach consensus. Be open to persuasion so that you set a good example as a reflective leader.

A different type of collaborative decision making is delegation, which we label as Type 4. If you wish to delegate a decision or set of decisions to a subgroup from the team, your role will be prominent before and after key decisions are made. In the beginning, you and those to whom you are delegating a decision will determine the goal or desired outcomes and the standards by which the outcomes will be measured. You will also set boundaries around the decision. For example, you might delegate to a subgroup of your team the task of comparing your school's data with that of other schools at the same level throughout the district. You would want to be sure that this subgroup does not duplicate the work of others on the team and that no one else encroaches on its assigned task. You would also be certain to set a clear deadline for the subgroup's completion of its task so that the work of the entire team would not be delayed. As the subgroup engages in its work, you should stay out of the way, only checking on progress to make sure the group is on track. When the subgroup has completed its task, your responsibility is to provide feedback based on the goals and standards agreed on when they began. We find Covey's (1992) *Principle-Centered Leadership* to be an excellent source on the process of delegation.

As you take on the responsibility of deciding how collaborative decisions should be made, Table 3.1 can be a handy reference to help you think about the various decisions you face and the best way to handle them with your team. Depending on your personality, style, and level of trust with your group, you may

Table 3.1   Gradations of Collaborative Decision Making

Type of Decision	Degree of Collaboration	Application
Type 1	Leader decides and explains decision rationale so that followers understand and know what to do	Simple managerial decisions, such as bureaucratic procedures
Type 2	Leader decides after receiving feedback; leader explains how feedback was used	Managerial decisions that affect the work life of followers, such as how data will be collected, who will perform which tasks, and sharing information
Type 3	Leader and collaborative team decide together as equal partners; leader determines decision boundaries and plays a part in forming consensus	Complex instructional and political decisions in which multiple sources of expertise are required, such as pedagogy taught as professional development
Type 4	Leader delegates decision to collaborative team, helping set goals, standards for evaluation, and boundaries for decision	Decisions for which specialized knowledge is required and ideal team members are available

tend to choose one type over another, but two cautions are appropriate: (1) Be clear and explicit with your collaborative team about which type of decision making you are entering into and why, and (2) be sure not to overload your process with too many Type 3 decisions, because they tend to take a great deal of time. Activity 3.3 is designed to help you figure out which type of decision making might work best for different kinds of decisions your collaborative team will face.

ACTIVITY 3.3   Deciding How to Decide

With one or more critical friends, brainstorm a list of 5 to 10 decisions you and your collaborative team need to make to create and implement a school improvement project. Be inclusive—no decision is too small or too great to consider. Use the table below to help you figure out which type of decision making you need to use with your collaborative team for each decision and why. When the answers to the questions are predominantly yes, then you are in the appropriate quadrant for the type of decision making that will probably work best for a specific decision.

At the time you read this chapter, much of your thinking about decisions will be hypothetical. That's okay—think of this activity as practice for the time when you are actually working with your team on problem articulation, root-cause analysis, and action planning. One approach might be to consider a school improvement project you participated in implementing in the recent past and consider the decisions your team had to make en route to implementation. Another might be to consider a project your school is already contemplating and analyze the decision making involved in this project.

Type 1	*Type 3*
1. Is the decision primarily managerial? 2. Is my timeline short? 3. Is the decision minor? 4. Am I responsible for the decision outcomes?	1. Is this decision instructionally and/or politically focused? 2. Do I trust this collaborative team to make good decisions? 3. Do we have the time necessary to engage in this level of collaboration? 4. Can I live with whatever decision occurs, given the boundaries I have set? 5. Will the collaborative team and I be willing to be collectively responsible for the decision outcomes?
Type 2	*Type 4*
1. Is the decision primarily managerial but affects the work life of many? 2. Do I have time to consider feedback carefully? 3. Is the decision important enough to take the time to consider feedback? 4. Am I in a unique position to make this decision? 5. Am I responsible for the decision outcomes?	1. Is this decision instructionally and/or politically focused? 2. Do I trust the members of the collaborative team sufficiently to delegate this decision to them? 3. Can I set clear boundaries, goals, and standards for this decision? 4. Will I be able to step aside and let the team do its work without hovering or interfering? 5. Can I live with any decision made within the boundaries, goals, and standards that we have set?

CONCLUSION

Engaging productively with a group of dedicated professionals functioning as an authentic team greatly enhances the probability of success for your school improvement project. Building a coalition of capable, dedicated individuals who work well with one another and collectively wield influence within the school helps integrate your school improvement project into the mainstream of your school community's thinking and actions. Thus, choosing your team wisely and nurturing its development over time ultimately benefits the students who are the focus of your improvement effort.

We advocate that you seek collaboration in all stages of the planning process, starting in the next part of this book with problem identification. But as we have said, the involvement you seek as you begin the planning process is likely to be informal in nature; until you fully understand the nature of the instructional challenge you identify, it is hard to know who really needs to be involved, whose expertise is most needed, and so on.

The value of a high-performing team becomes even clearer in the final two chapters of this book. You will see how critical your team is to effective action planning (Chapter 9) and implementation and evaluation (Chapter 10), because it would be impossible for a full-time teacher or administrator acting alone to execute all the necessary tasks embedded in the numerous activities and phases of putting a plan into action and understanding its educational outcomes. Furthermore, even the most superhuman educator acting alone would never understand well enough the complexity of the learning challenge you have chosen to improve student achievement.

REVIEW QUESTIONS

1. What are the important ways in which collaboration helps make you productive as a leader?

2. In what ways does collaboration make the leadership process more difficult?

3. How can you tell the difference between someone who belongs on your collaborative team and someone who should be involved but on a less consistent basis?

4. How many members and what sort of mix would you seek for a collaborative team?

WORKSHEET 3.1   Who Can Help Me?

As you move from problem identification to implementation, your notion of who might help you most in your work may change. Periodically, brainstorm on your own to identify specific people who could assist you as you engage in various stages of your work. Put their names and positions in the cells in the leftmost column. Place Xs in the other cells according to why you want each individual to be involved. For example, the school principal may be a symbol of the importance of your project, the mathematics department head may have access to resources, and the central office school social worker might be an expert on poverty issues and also have access to resources. Compare your table with others' in an effort to broaden your thinking about who might be involved in your school improvement project.

Level	Role	Expert	Symbol	Access to Resources
School				
District				
Other				

WORKSHEET 3.2   Assessing Potential Team Members

This worksheet is intended to help you assess the expertise, motivation, and habits of mind of potential team members. It can be expanded and duplicated to accommodate additional individuals and to give you a sense of the kind of balance you might achieve on your team. Obviously, given the nature of the information contained in this worksheet, it would be best to keep its contents strictly confidential. It is for your use alone as you decide whom to recruit to your project. It is important to be honest with yourself about your own beliefs. Be sure to ask yourself what specific evidence you have that supports (or contradicts) your perceptions and the perceptions of others.

The second part of the worksheet asks a series of questions intended to help you think about how well individuals will fit together on your team. You may find it helpful to have a conversation with yourself about potential team members so that you can enter into team leadership with your eyes wide open.

Questions About Fit

Answer the questions below as honestly and thoroughly as you can. If you are lacking information, you should seek it from others in an objective and confidential manner. Your principal may be the person who can best help you answer these questions.

1. Is there anyone who has a history of personal and/or professional conflict with anyone else?
   - If so, is the conflict manageable and largely in the past for those involved, or would it seriously damage team function?

2. Who in your pool of potential team members is among the most powerful and influential people in your school community?
   - Are there any individuals who are particularly well connected politically?
   - Are there any classroom heroes?
   - Which potential political agendas and/or super-developed egos will I need to monitor?

3. Which individual(s) will be required by the general circumstances of your school to participate on this team regardless of expertise, motivation, or habits of mind?
   - Are there potential team members who can counteract any negative characteristics this person might bring to the team?
   - What is my relationship to this person? Do I have influence? If not, then who does?

Type 1: Novice	***Type 2: Experienced, Not Successful***
Name: _____	Name: _____
Position: _____Years: _____	Position: _____Years: _____
Expertise for your project: _____	Expertise for your project: _____
Evidence:	Evidence:
Motivated for your project? ___Yes ___No	Motivated for your project? ___Yes ___No
Evidence:	Evidence:
Political and symbolic considerations:	Political and symbolic considerations:
Type 3: Experienced, Successful, Not Active	***Type 4: Ideal Team Member***
Name: _____	Name: _____
Position: _____Years: _____	Position: _____Years: _____
Expertise for your project: _____	Expertise for your project: _____
Evidence:	Evidence:
Motivated for your project? ___Yes ___No	Motivated for your project? ___Yes ___No
Evidence:	Evidence:
Political and symbolic considerations:	Political and symbolic considerations:

(Continued)

(Continued)

4. Do possible members of this team have the potential to learn from one another?
   - Is there mutual respect within the group of potential team members?
   - Do I respect potential team members, and am I willing to learn from them?
   - Which potential team members have the greatest respect for me?

5. Is it possible to select a team from among potential members that would enjoy spending extended periods of time together?
   - Is membership on the team likely to enhance individuals' motivation?
   - Looking at my selection, will I enjoy working with this team?

6. Having made my team selection, will the principal and the school community at large respect and trust the expertise represented on the team?

7. What kind of coaching and nurturing will the team need from me to sustain high performance?
   - Who will need more regular, sustained contact with me?
   - Who will require being shown what to do and how to do it?
   - Who needs more autonomy to sustain motivation? How comfortable am I with that?
   - Whose personality requires guidance to avoid negative group dynamics?

PART II

PROBLEM ARTICULATION

Using Evidence to Find Improvement Needs

In the next two chapters, we focus on clearly articulating the nature of the instructional problem, challenge, or gap you wish to address in your school. As we discuss in Chapters 4 and 5, a deep understanding of an achievement gap is a vital part of the foundation for finding viable solutions to puzzles that have existed for a long time. Chapter 4 focuses the reader on finding evidence of an instructional problem in his or her own school. There is a great deal of data that is easily gleaned from school, district, and state websites that reveals substantial information about which students are succeeding, which are not, and in which subject areas they appear to have the greatest difficulties. Likewise, schools and school systems amass a variety of data that are available to stakeholders, including such things as formative assessment data and summaries of school climate surveys.

BIG IDEAS: USING EVIDENCE TO FIND IMPROVEMENT NEEDS

1. Student learning takes place in a specific context—your school
   - What are your school's stated aspirations for student achievement?
   - How well are your students doing, collectively and in subgroups? What is the level of achievement?
   - What gaps exist between aspirations and achievement?

(Continued)

(Continued)

- What are the student demographics?
- How well prepared is your faculty to teach this student population?
- What are some of the important characteristics of the community your school serves?

2. Finding evidence of a specific instructional need
   - Define the instructional problem, challenge, or gap you wish to address
   - Think in terms of an identifiable group of students
   - Communicate with data; build a persuasive case
   - Triangulation → Trustworthiness

Finding school site information is an important first step that will likely teach the seeker more than he or she expected. Communicating what is learned is critical at this point and along the way in the school improvement process. To facilitate helping others see the school's instructional challenges from your perspective, Chapter 5 provides step-by-step application of the principles explained in Chapter 4. The final product is an Improvement Target Proposal that brings a specific instructional problem, challenge, or gap into sharp focus so that all in the school community are able to understand the need to address the issue you identified. The fundamental purpose of the Improvement Target Proposal is to create knowledge from data. Doing so requires finding evidence of a specific gap, collecting relevant data, presenting the data in an easily digested format, and interpreting the meaning of the data so that others can understand the problem. The Improvement Target Proposal establishes a baseline for the school's performance in a specific area, compares that baseline to what the school says it intends for students—either explicitly or implicitly—and clearly articulates an argument for addressing the problem, challenge, or gap that has been identified.

The figure shown here will help you see the path toward producing a persuasive Improvement Target Proposal and the major school improvement documents that follow.

The first two products that we explain in the chapters that follow provide the basic reasoning and structure that go into the School Improvement Project Proposal. The Research Brief is the focus of Part III, and the School Improvement Project Proposal is the focus of Part IV. But it all starts with a clear and persuasive articulation of the school improvement area—the Improvement Target Proposal.

Improvement Target Proposal

- Identify the school's published data (school, district, and state websites, printed materials)
- Find the school's performance objectives (vision/mission, improvement plan, other)
- How well is your school doing?
  - Assessment data—at least two years' worth
  - Multiple sources of quantitative and qualitative data—"triangulate" data
  - "Craft knowledge"—what teachers know from experience
- Figure out the highest-priority need areas—where achievement gaps are most compelling
- Prepare an Improvement Target Proposal that clearly articulates the problem, challenge, or gap that you wish to address (no solutions discussed or proposed yet)

Research Brief

School Improvement Project Proposal

To help illustrate the scope of this performance and to facilitate its use in an academic context, a full description of the task as we use it in class and a grading rubric are presented below. Note that the Educational Leadership Constituent Council (ELCC) standards are embedded in the rubric for easy cross-referencing between aspects of the assignment and specific standards. The assignment description and assessment rubric are intended to be used in tandem. It will be necessary for professors to discuss in class a preferred structure for the paper. The rubric is quite detailed in order to give professors and students a clear sense of how the work is to be assessed. Student work rarely fits the descriptions perfectly, however, so professor discretion in grading is always necessary.

Improvement Target Proposal
Description and Rubric

Overview

Data are tools—they represent a primary source of knowledge building for school improvement. As leaders in your school, one of your primary tasks is to understand available data relating to your school's performance in meeting its goals and objectives. Additionally, you need to learn how to communicate about these data to various stakeholder groups. In this assignment, you are asked to assemble some of these data and prepare a short summary suitable for presentation to a school leadership team.

Tasks

1. Identify the variety of published data relating to your school's demographic characteristics (e.g., enrollment, attendance, composition of the student body, staffing), measures of student learning, and any perceptual data that might exist relating to such things as school climate. These data may be available on your school or school system's website, on related websites (e.g., state education department), or in published material.

2. Determine your school's primary performance objectives: What is the school expected to achieve? Dig deeper than routine accountability requirements; examine the school's current improvement plan, for instance, to identify current improvement priorities.

3. Examine relevant assessment data for *at least a 2-year period.* To do this, you will need to **triangulate the data** available to you—look across various sources to answer the question "**How well are we doing?**" As a leader in your school, you will add value to your analysis by using your craft knowledge to interpret what these data mean. You may limit your focus to one or more areas identified as priorities for your school (i.e., you do not need to present data on each and every curricular objective, but you should provide a reasonable synopsis of "how well we're doing").

4. Identify any areas that reflect priorities—for instance, areas in which students are achieving at a level below your school's goals and objectives. Be careful to identify performance indicators that clearly relate to the school performance objective(s) you've identified. The goal here is NOT to "solve" an identified problem but to highlight areas that are in continued need of attention in your school's improvement plan.

5. Prepare an Improvement Target Proposal that includes a synopsis of the school's demographic characteristics, improvement goals, current levels of performance, and challenge area(s). Use the attached rubric as a guide to structure your paper.

This is an exercise in *leadership communication.* Be selective—you cannot provide an overview of all the data that might be available. Craft your examination to focus on important areas of concern. *Note: The tone of the paper is persuasive.* You are providing your expert judgment based on your analysis of school performance data, and in the end, you are lobbying the team to adopt the focus you identified as important.

Direct the paper to your school's leadership team as the audience—the team may include new members, such as one or more parents or community members. Avoid jargon, and be aware of the clarity of your presentation—if you confuse your audience or present a lot of disparate data that don't connect to your school's objectives, you've failed to add value to the discussion. *Use tables or graphs* sensibly to briefly summarize the discussion and direct the reader's attention.

This is a short paper (around 7 pages) and should be written in a fashion that is suitable for the audience described above.

(Continued)

(Continued)

Improvement Target Proposal Assessment Rubric

	Exceeds Expectations	Meets Expectations	Approaching Expectations	Falls Below Expectations
Introduction and Thesis Weight: 10%	Paper starts with an introduction that provides a clear road map for the reader, foreshadowing what the executive summary is intended to provide in the way of information. The thesis appears as the last sentence of the introductory paragraph.	Paper starts with a brief introduction that alludes to the purpose of the paper and provides a general foreshadowing of what is to be included in the document. The thesis may not be entirely clear or appropriate.	The introduction provides only the barest hint about the purpose of the paper and the information to be shared. The thesis is either confusing or missing.	The paper lacks an introduction entirely, or the introduction fails to provide useful information that is linked to the intended purpose of the document.
Characteristics of the school and diversity of the school community (ELCC 4.2) Weight: 20%	Paper includes a thorough and concise overview of the demographic characteristics of the school, school staffing, and school community. The school's current improvement objectives are highlighted, and (if available) data related to characteristics of the school climate are described.	Paper includes a general overview of the demographic characteristics of the school, school staffing, and school community; the school's current improvement objectives; and measures of school climate. Some important demographic data are not evident.	Paper includes a limited review of demographic and staffing data, the school's current improvement objectives, and measures of school climate. Important data are omitted or inaccurately presented.	The presentation of demographic data is missing or wholly inadequate.

74

	Exceeds Expectations	**Meets Expectations**	**Approaching Expectations**	**Falls Below Expectations**
Use of data to analyze school performance related to the school's vision and objectives (ELCC 1.2) Weight: 25%	Paper includes a clear and concise summary of the school's performance based on an assessment of important educational outcomes reflecting the school's vision and objectives over at least a 2-year period.	Paper includes a summary of the school's performance over a 2-year period, using general measures of important educational outcomes.	Paper includes a summary of the school's current performance in general terms. Specific indicators or educational outcomes are unclear or missing.	The assessment of school performance is missing or wholly inadequate.
Identification of improvement area (ELCC 2.2) Weight: 25%	Paper concludes with a recommendation of one or more focal areas to improve instruction. The identified area(s) are well supported by the analysis of school data and are clearly connected to the school's improvement objectives and the emerging needs of the school community.	Paper concludes with a recommendation of one or more focal areas to improve instruction. The identified area(s) are generally supported by the analysis of school data and are at least loosely connected to the school's vision and improvement objectives.	Paper concludes with a general recommendation of one or more focal areas to improve instruction. The identified area(s) are not clearly supported by the analysis of school data.	The recommendation is missing or wholly inadequate.

(Continued)

(Continued)

	Exceeds Expectations	Meets Expectations	Approaching Expectations	Falls Below Expectations
Use of tables and graphs to summarize data Weight: 10%	Tables and/or graphs are powerfully used to present demographic and/or school performance data. Tables and/or graphs are clearly labeled and discussed.	Tables and/or graphs are used to present demographic and/or school performance data but in some cases are mislabeled or otherwise difficult to interpret accurately.	Tables and/or graphs are used too sparingly to be effective or are largely distracting, mislabeled, or otherwise confusing.	Tables and/or graphs are not evident.
Mechanics Weight: 10%	Paper is nearly error free, which reflects clear understanding and thorough proofreading.	Paper includes occasional grammatical errors and questionable word choice.	Paper includes errors in grammar and punctuation, but spelling has been proofread.	Paper includes frequent errors in spelling, grammar, and punctuation.

CHAPTER 4

ASSESSING THE LOCAL SITUATION

LEARNING OUTCOMES

Readers who grasp the most important ideas from this chapter will be able to

- find the differences between aspirations and results at their schools;
- identify various sources of evidence for gaps between aspirations and results;
- understand and apply the concept of triangulation to create a more trustworthy rendering of evidence-based conclusions; and
- think more broadly about how to identify a learning problem, challenge, or gap.

Too often, we hear common laments in schools and school districts about decision making that follows a ready-fire-aim pattern or school improvement planning efforts that become highly ritualized. Both outcomes are based more on needing to meet arbitrary deadlines than on careful inquiry. Efforts to improve student performance take place in an atmosphere driven by local politics and a sense of urgency that borders on panic. After many years of ready-fire-aim in which waves of fads crash on the school district's shores with each new superintendent, teachers become demoralized and cynical (Schlechty, 2001). These unhappy results stem from a strong tendency to recommend and implement solutions to problems before the problems are fully understood. Consider the Algebra I problem discussed in Chapter 1. Commonly imposed solutions are to spread Algebra I over four semesters instead of two, offer variations of pre-algebra, or some combination of the two.

We challenge you to collect the data in any high school. You will likely discover a high rate of Ds and Fs no matter what the course sequence. Instructional problems cannot be solved until they are fully understood within the local context.

In this chapter, we focus on the challenge, learning gap, or instructional problem as the place to begin school improvement efforts. This is the moment in which you become a researcher, focused on collecting data in your own school site. It is not just about you, however. As a leader, you will need to help others understand the problem in similar ways. In many respects, this is the most challenging part of the school improvement process. The desire to impose and implement preconceived solutions is so strong among administrators, teachers, and parents that you are likely to find yourself under extreme pressure to skip the problem diagnosis portion of the school improvement process and jump to implementing a new program. But sustaining a systematic inquiry process is vital; when the problem is thoroughly understood, promising solutions will be much more evident and will have a higher probability of success. Further, you will clearly understand *why* the proposed solution is likely to have the impact you desire and how to sustain the effort over time.

A cautionary note before digging into the content of the chapter: Although we tend to believe that problems are seeking solutions, one of countless insights from James G. March (1994) is that it is often the case that solutions float around searching for problems. March and others developed an entire model about how this happens (Cohen, March, & Olsen, 1972), but think about it intuitively. How often have you or someone you know walked into a meeting thinking, "I already know how to solve this problem. I just need to think about how to sell my idea to others." Chances are good that you have been searching for a problem to link with this pet solution for some time. There are many preconceived solutions out there just waiting for problems to come along that they can solve. We implore you to resist this model by understanding that preconceived solutions are not likely to make the impact you desire. Unless or until the problem is well understood and agreed on by you and your collaborators, it would be pure coincidence that an "off-the-shelf" answer could begin to remedy the situation.

The end result of this chapter is a thorough understanding of how to identify a worthwhile instructional problem, challenge, or gap to address in an effort to engender school improvement. The next chapter helps you apply the concepts and strategies described in this one. Activity 4.1 is intended as a warm-up to thinking about the process of problem articulation by creating a retrospective on your school's most recent improvement effort.

ACTIVITY 4.1   How Did We Do Last Year?

Change is a leader's friend, but it has a split personality: Its nonlinear messiness gets us into trouble. But the experience of this messiness is necessary in order to discover the hidden benefits—creative ideas and novel solutions are often generated when the status quo is disrupted.

—Fullan (2001, p. 107)

To understand today's problems more deeply, it is worthwhile to take stock of your school's improvement history. Take some time to reflect on your school's efforts to improve last year. Answer the following questions to stimulate your thinking:

- What were your improvement objectives last year?
- How well did your school do in meeting its objectives? How do you know? What evidence are you using to assess the impact of your school's improvement activities?
- What were the (un)expected problems or barriers that cropped up?
- What were some lessons you learned? Knowing what you know now, what would you do differently?

An alternative means for reflection involves returning to Activity 2.2 and reconsidering your answers to the following questions:

- Last year, we tried to (insert your goal for improving student achievement) . . .
- by (insert your objective, or what you actually did) . . .
- because (insert the reason you thought this would help you reach your goal).
- What actually happened was (discuss the outcome in terms of your indicators of success) . . .
- because (say a little something about what you learned).

THE DIFFERENCE BETWEEN ASPIRATIONS AND RESULTS

In Chapter 2, we briefly discussed the concepts of espoused theories (aspirations) and theories in use (actions). In this chapter, we explore ways to discover some of the espoused theories and theories in use active in any given school. The former concept is embodied in state standards that clearly, explicitly, and specifically lay out what all students should know and be able to do in the various content areas over the range of grade levels. Presumably, you are well acquainted with your state's standards appropriate for your level of teaching and/or your subject area. We advocate exploring aspirations that are derived more locally, too. We also introduced some elements of change theory, which highlights the notion that the need for change is defined as a gap between the real and the ideal—where you are and where you want to be. Your job, initially, is to explore where such gaps exist and determine where you believe your school should invest its energy and resources to work to reduce this gap.

Schools and districts articulate local aspirations with one eye toward state standards and the other eye focused on local needs and interests. These more local espoused theories appear in part in statements of a school's vision or mission and core values. Related theories in use are more difficult to determine by looking at documents, but results or outcomes of teaching and learning efforts provide some evidence for the degree of alignment between theories in use and espoused theories. In the next two sections, we lead you through discovery of the differences between aspirations and results.

Aspirations for Our Students

Consider the following mission statement excerpted from an elementary school website identified somewhat randomly and disguised by a pseudonym:

The Rolling Hills community is united in fostering a safe and nurturing environment that challenges students to reach their highest academic and personal potential. Staff, students, parents, and volunteers work together to promote and model intellectual curiosity, creative expression, acceptance, and respect for all people and cultures as we continue our growth as lifelong learners.

Statements such as this one are suffused with aspirations and values. Although the two seem to overlap, statements that appear to be primarily aspirations are highlighted in light gray. These are the characteristics the school community members have determined they wish to foster in the organization and within the students they serve. In summary, the school aspires to be a safe place for all children, where they develop academically and personally into successful human beings. The values of unity, collaboration, growth, and lifelong learning are highlighted in dark gray. Additional values of academic excellence, interpersonal tolerance and respect, and personal responsibility are strongly implied in the aspirations.

The Rolling Hills Elementary School mission statement establishes a benchmark by which results can be assessed. This could take place on many different levels—individual student, classroom, grade level, or schoolwide. Data can be collected that indicates whether or not the school is achieving the benchmarks it has established. We will say more about that in the "Data as Evidence of Results" subsection below.

ACTIVITY 4.2   Roundtable Discussion: Comparing the Ideal With the Real

Osterman and Kottkamp (2004) remind us that all potential changes have a *real* and an *ideal*. The reason a real situation requires attention is that there is a gap between your real and ideal. The larger this gap, the greater the need for change. One way to begin to get a feel for your school's change priorities is to reflect:

1. Start by exploring the real—imagine that you were asked by a long-lost friend to explain what a day is like in your school. What would you say?
   - Describe the school climate or environment—how would you describe the general mood of the school?
   - Describe the kinds of activities that might typically be going on in classrooms—what are students doing?
   - Describe how the adults in the building go about their work—is there a lot of collaboration going on, for example?

2. Next, explore "where you want to be," or your preferred future.
   - How would you like to see any of the above change to support a more powerful or effective school?
   - What are some important goals you would like to see your school pursue?

Share your thoughts with one or more critical friends. Consider the answer to this question as a way of communicating about your thinking: If you could change something about the teaching and learning process in your school that would significantly improve student learning, what would that be?

School improvement plans, the kind mandated by most U.S. school districts, are another valuable source of information regarding a school's aspirations. The plans are much more detailed and specific because school and administrator performance are often assessed against them. The plans tend to weave together the aspirations embedded in state standards and the school's mission or vision. The following excerpt from Franklin Middle School's (a pseudonym) school improvement plan is an example of how the two sets of aspirations work together. This information appeared under the category "Evidences of Need":

90% of all students passed the state reading test.

47% of LEP [limited-English-proficient] students passed the state reading test.

67% of economically disadvantaged students passed the state reading test.

60% of Special Education students passed the state reading test.

96% of white students passed the state reading test.

90% of Black students passed the state reading test.

71% of Hispanic students passed the state reading test.

86% of Asian students passed the state reading test.

Four important implications about aspirations are presented in this listing of state testing results: (a) Students are generally succeeding at a high level in reading, (b) an achievement gap between some student groups and the majority population exists, (c) there is still a good distance to travel to achieve the goal of all students succeeding at grade level, and (d) the school is committed to meeting state standards with the implication that all children can in fact meet them. We infer that the school aspires to improve at least some students' achievement in reading, because this list appeared under the heading of needs. Also noteworthy in the list is its shift from aspirations to results. The aspirations are implied, but the results are quite specific.

Discussion of school aspirations probably needs to go deeper than just remembering state standards and thinking about a vision or mission statement. It is important to know how those aspirations were developed, the degree to which they are widely known, and the extent to which faculty, students, and/or parents are committed to acting on them. In short, we need to know the degree to which aspirations are shared in the school's community. Thus, an important element of assessing the local situation is informal discussion about individual and collective aspirations with respect to student achievement.

The goals embedded in state standards and school missions are descriptions of what students are supposed to learn and how schools are intended to be. The gap between these ideals and what students actually learn and how schools really function defines the need to make change. Argyris (1999) points out that for change to occur, the ways in which organizations learn must change, because organizations are inherently defensive of the status quo. Questioning "how things are done around here," as we advocate throughout this book, is your first step in changing how your school and community learn, and it is an important part of moving the school improvement process out of the realm of pro forma activity or knee-jerk response to emergencies. Exploring the gap between the ideal and the real begins with data.

Data as Evidence of Results

As much as educators might chafe under accountability rules and expectations embedded in federal regulations and state testing regimes, reforms and innovations of the past 10 years have caused a great deal of student achievement data to be readily available. Furthermore, much of these data are easily accessed from school and district websites. As a point of optimism, the current emphasis on accountability and contemporary technology greatly eases the challenge of discovering state and local aspirations and results. It required fewer than 5 minutes for us to retrieve, copy, and paste references to overall goals and state testing data from two schools in different school districts for use in this chapter. Easily retrieved data found in school improvement plans is a productive place to begin.

In the example above, white and Black students have a high level of reading achievement based on statewide test results. The lowest-performing group is clearly the LEP students, followed by special education and economically disadvantaged students. The immediate question for any leader intending to focus on improving student achievement is "Which group(s) requires near-term intervention?"

ACTIVITY 4.3 Roundtable Discussion: Sources of Data

We make the distinction in this chapter between evidence and data, noting that data may be considered a subset of the kinds of information you might consult to understand the performance of your school. Take a few moments to discuss the following with one or more critical friends: What are the sources of data in your school that might inform your understanding of how well the school is meeting its learning objectives?

A caution about the ways in which we label students is appropriate here. Under the federal guidelines spelled out in No Child Left Behind (NCLB), categories of students (often referred to as "subgroups") provide a focus for school improvement because of the need to achieve adequate yearly progress (AYP) for all groups and to report student data using these categories. An emphasis on data, however, can lead to treating students as data points rather than as children. For example, one common practice is to try to improve the performance of those students whose scores were not far below passing on state-mandated tests. They quickly get labeled "bubble kids" because their scores are "on the bubble"—that achievement region in which the differences between passing and not passing are small. A focus on students who are nearly passing is a pragmatic approach to coping with scarce time and resources as the school strives to achieve AYP. The problem with this kind of thinking, however, is that it ignores the fact that students far from passing state tests are those who really need the most help and whose life chances are at the greatest risk. It seems unethical to provide less to the neediest within a group simply because they have the lowest probability of helping improve the school's testing profile.

Understanding that not all students can be assisted to the same degree at the same time, we encourage manageable projects that address the needs of an entire sub-group. Moving beyond the numbers and school profile, it is easy to determine that if the program for LEP students at Franklin Middle School doesn't change, then the majority of such students are at risk for failure and dropping out in high school. Looking a bit further into the school's website, we discover that LEP students number 46 and make up approximately 5% of the school population. The small proportion of students who are not yet proficient in English may help explain their low achievement—their needs may be invisible to the school as a whole. Leaders find themselves in a difficult dilemma: be socially just by addressing the needs of a (potentially) marginalized minority or allocate resources to serve the greatest number of students? Special education and economically disadvantaged students are also struggling with reading but not in proportions as high as in the LEP group. Yet special education and economically disadvantaged students represent larger proportions of the student body—11% and 16%, respectively. Should we assist the group that has the lowest achievement level or the group(s) with the largest number? This is the kind of decision that cries out for collaborative discussion and decision making. The school community must make a deliberate decision about where to allocate resources, weighing the myriad criteria that create the complexity of this decision.

A Closer Look at Data

We have already been looking at two types of data—achievement test scores and demographics. In the latter case, we started to think about issues of importance (i.e., Is the LEP population large enough to be addressed through a school improvement project, or are there other factors such as improving the chances for later success that are more important than sheer size of the student subgroup?). Importance (note that we are avoiding the term *significance* because it has a specific statistical meaning we will discuss later in Chapter 8) is also a relevant concept for the test data. Is the 47% passing rate in reading for LEP students truly different from the 60% passing rate for special education students? There is a statistical process for answering this type of question, but consider the numbers themselves. There are only 46 LEP students in the school, so a 47% pass rate means that about 22 LEP students ($0.47 \times 46 = 21.62$) passed the reading test. If the LEP students achieved the same passing rate as the special education students (60%), only about six more students would need to pass the test ($0.60 \times 46 = 27.60 - 21.62 = 5.98$). This basic arithmetic may suggest that the LEP group passing rate does not yield a substantially different outcome compared with the special education group. In a scenario such as this, local knowledge might indicate that some students are counted in both groups. It might be best for a school improvement project to take in both LEP and special education because their passing rate profiles are more similar than they appeared to be at first and some students are double-counted.

Whether or not designing a project to work with LEP and special education students together seems to be a good idea depends on the nature of the learning difficulties suggested by the test data and the reasons behind relatively low pass rates for the reading test. A deeper understanding of the nuances of why students are not meeting standards requires root-cause analysis—getting to the bottom of the problem. Until we know more about root causes (the subject of Chapter 6), it is impossible to think productively about a *strategy, action,* or *solution* to improve student achievement, because it is only when at least some of the root causes are removed that improvement will happen. At this point, the focus is on identifying areas most in need of improvement; the ultimate decision about whether to work with a larger number of students in an effort to use resources more efficiently may come later, as you develop a deeper understanding of the nature of the problem.

Worksheet 4.1 helps the emerging leader/researcher get started picking up data from today's most available sources, some of which may be in print form (e.g., common assessments within a grade level or subject area) and many of which are electronic. The reader will also benefit from thinking about different and complementary types of data that create a fuller picture of what is happening in a particular school. The most easily accessed data includes state testing results, district-required benchmark test results, student grades, and student demographics. A good strategy might be to look at and think about those data sources to begin to get an idea about the patterns of results related to the important aspirations of the school.

Other Assessments

Moving beyond the easily accessible test data—the "low-hanging fruit" of student achievement information—in the Franklin Middle School example, we ought to know how teachers view the performance of students who have not passed the standardized reading test. Presumably, language arts teachers and specialist teachers for both English as a second language and special education regularly test students' reading abilities with assessments they have created themselves and/or districtwide benchmark tests. For each of the students who did not pass the state reading test, we would want to know if their profile is mirrored in teacher-made and/or districtwide tests. If the answer is yes, then we may conclude that curriculum and assessments are aligned. If the answer is no, then we would want to dig deeper into why students' achievement profiles differ depending on how they are tested. Both LEP students and special education students are likely to be taught and tested on material that contains different content compared with the majority student population because of the very nature of the learning challenges these students face. They are caught in a testing dilemma rooted in policy: Students may not be developmentally ready for tests at their grade level because of circumstances beyond their control (e.g., not having grown up speaking English; having a specific, measurable learning disability), yet they are required to be tested at their grade level anyway. Leaders must figure out ethical means to compromise around such dilemmas for the sake of their students.

Locally created assessments tell us more than just the degree of alignment with the state testing regime. Their more frequent occurrence and greater specificity allow for more detailed measurement of a learning problem, challenge, or gap. In organizational learning terms, classroom assessments provide finer-grain evidence for the difference between espoused theories and theories in use. As a result, they can be more useful tools for achieving the results to which the school aspires than state assessments alone.

Before leaving the topic, we wish to make our position on assessments clear and explicit. As we explained in Chapter 1, assessments are not the learning problem, though we often hear learning problems expressed in terms of whether or not a student passed a particular test. In much the same way that a cough or a sniffle isn't the flu, test results are only *symptoms* of a problem—these may be indicators of an underlying illness, but they are not the illness itself. A test score is an indicator of a potential problem. A problem may be lodged in the classroom, the school as a whole, the district, the student's attitude and belief system, the student's home situation, or some complicated combination of two or more of these. An effort to improve test scores without understanding the underlying causes of test failure will lead to ineffective and possibly unethical strategies to boost test scores. We believe that understanding the root causes of unsatisfactory test results is a prerequisite for creative and effective solutions. More than just assessment data is required in this effort.

Affective Data

Anyone who has ever taught and/or raised a child understands that motivation is an important factor affecting cognitive performance. There are many influences on student motivation. Our experience suggests that one of the most important contributors to low motivation as students age is frustration with schoolwork. Many others are possible, such as hunger, instability at home, the need to work after school to support the family, or taking care of younger siblings while both parents work multiple jobs. On the positive side, relationships between teachers and students appear to have great potential to inspire students to do their best work. Assessment data will not tell us about student background factors and classroom rapport that impact the best instructional efforts and therefore cannot shed light on students' motivation.

Mandated school improvement processes often require school climate surveys, and schools often develop and implement other, more specific kinds of surveys (e.g., surveys dealing with parental satisfaction, school safety, or service learning activities). Depending on how the surveys are written, they may provide a window into the level of student engagement, parental involvement, teacher attitudes and beliefs, and broader community perceptions. The surveys themselves are likely to have been negotiated into not offending anyone, so the data they provide may paint only a broad-brush picture of whether or not students, parents, and the community are pleased with school outcomes. That is helpful information, but as with assessment data, alone it doesn't tell us enough about student motivation.

Thankfully, teachers have contact with students every day and know a great deal about how they appear in classrooms. Teachers will not necessarily know all the specific causes behind any particular student's level of motivation, but they might know some. They will certainly have a sense of personal factors affecting specific categories of students. For example, working evening and graveyard shifts is common for high school–age LEP students because, as immigrants, they often come from economically disadvantaged families that depend on them for income. Motivation may be low if LEP students are tired during the school day and cannot see the benefits from applying themselves in school. Special education students, on the other hand, have often experienced many years of academic disappointment by the time they reach high school, despite teachers' and counselors' best efforts to help them adapt their learning strategies to cope with their specific disabilities. Why would we expect such students to be highly motivated in the school setting that has been a largely negative experience for them? We do not intend to stereotype, and we recognize that not all LEP or special education students share the dampers on motivation described here. Yet what we describe is the experience of many and is worth noting and exploring.

The kind of evidence we have discussed in this section is generally referred to as qualitative data. As the term suggests, it helps illuminate qualities as opposed to quantities; it helps explain why and how things happen, not just what happens. Qualitative data is often overlooked by novice researchers, but we encourage you to see quantitative and qualitative information as complementary in your quest to discover what is happening in your school.

Piecing the Puzzle Together

The multisource, somewhat complex process we describe for collecting data about the differences between aspirations and results provides the information that helps you identify the problem, challenge, or gap where you want to focus your school improvement efforts. That is the limited goal we have for this chapter—limited, but central to your efforts and the essential place to begin.

Why pursue so many data sources? There are two answers to this question. The first answer is that multiple data sources are critical to obtaining a clear picture about a school's current situation. Medical analogies come easily to mind. At the time of this writing, nations around the world are concerned about a strain of flu that appears to be spreading rapidly and may have serious medical implications for those who become sick. The fundamental question for any individual is "Will this flu kill me?" Medical researchers are not able to provide a definitive yes or no answer because it depends on multiple factors such as the individual's age, access to health care, other medical complications, and health and hygiene history. Likewise, with school improvement, the answer to a question such as "Should our school be focused on reading?" will depend on our interpretation of the data. Different data may support the same conclusion, or they may not.

Collecting information from different sources (e.g., state testing results, teacher-made tests, district benchmarks) and of different types (e.g., testing, student perceptions, teachers' classroom impressions) helps the researcher/leader understand trends with greater certainty. We call the process of using data from multiple sources triangulation (Maxwell, 2005). We can feel much more confident that reading is an important issue for LEP and special education students if the state testing data, teacher impressions of student performance, and student survey responses about their reading behaviors are pointing in a similar direction. Triangulation improves the trustworthiness of our ultimate conclusions and our confidence that what we think we are seeing is real.

This point is worth emphasizing; indeed, it is a theme of this book. It is incumbent on the leader to *triangulate* data to fully establish a *trustworthy* argument about the instructional problem. Any one data point might raise an eyebrow or get the attention of school leaders, but to have confidence in the notion that a problem truly exists and merits consideration, it is important to examine related data to gain confidence in this conclusion. Any one source of data has inherent limits, both in form and in terms of implementation. Thus, the leader as researcher might look at a number of standardized tests and/or teacher-made tests, look at data over time, or both. Discussions with groups of teachers that reveal their craft knowledge and understanding of student needs based on daily interactions with them are important sources for triangulation. Triangulation produces a sense of trustworthiness, or confidence in this case, in the proposition that an instructional problem needs attention.

An important implication of our discussion of data collection and analysis is that data-informed decisions require substantial amounts of time before they can be made. The time required to gain a more complete understanding of the chosen learning challenge is a wise investment that will pay dividends in the action planning and implementation processes. Worksheet 4.2 provides a tool to help you determine the profile of data you need to collect and examine to analyze your school's performance.

IDENTIFYING A CHALLENGE, PROBLEM, OR GAP

After identifying some ways in which your school's results are out of alignment with stated aspirations, you will need to narrow your thinking down to a manageable school improvement area. It seems best to follow the advice we give to our doctoral students: Start with your passion. The project is something you will be working with for a long time. There will be moments of glory and periods of frustration. It is important that you have a deep commitment to the area you select so that your vision and goals will sustain you through some inevitably difficult times. But also consider what is important in the context of school and district priorities. As a practical matter, we urge our students to talk first with their principals about which areas they believe are most in need of attention. In the sections that follow, we present some areas worth considering, which may help guide the discussion you have with your principal.

ACTIVITY 4.4   Developing a Critical Eye

As you access various sources of data about your school, it is important to reflect on the general utility of the data and the quality of the source. For each table, chart, or graphic you amass, think about each of the following questions—or better still, discuss these with members of your collaborative team or a classmate.

1. What are these data? What are the data supposed to inform you about?

2. Based on an examination of these data (alone), what are you willing to say about student learning (or school climate or staff opinions)? What can you conclude? What questions do you have?

(Continued)

(Continued)

3. How good are these data? Do you trust the source?

4. How useful are the data and for what?

5. Considering the presentation of data (e.g., chart, table, narrative), is this data communicated well? Why? What is accentuated, and what is hidden?

And one more—extremely important—question:

6. What more do you want to know? What other data—or other presentations of the same data—would you like to see?

Low Achievement That Persists Over Time

Many of the achievement problems schools face are not new. There are many suggested strategies for various challenging student populations, but results are often disappointing. NCLB has caused our attention to turn immediately to groups such as students with learning disabilities, second-language learners, and students from poverty. There is great value in studying the learning challenges of these student categories, of course, but they are not the only ways in which we might focus on students who have learning difficulties. Sometimes it is more important to explore a particular aspect of curriculum (as with the Algebra I example from Chapter 1), a particular grade level, or a grouping of students such as a "house" within a middle school.

It is not entirely clear why some learning challenges are so widespread and intractable. We suspect that deeply rooted achievement problems become part of the woodwork, part of how things happen under "normal" circumstances. Learning gaps such as poor reading comprehension or an inability to perform basic math operations do not have simple solutions once students reach high school, so schools and students cope as best they can. Many schools experience difficulty year after year with special education students who are unable to pass tests in reading and/or mathematics and second-language learners who progress through an English as a second language curriculum only to flounder when they have a schedule of all college preparatory classes.

Persistent problems that have not yielded easy or effective solutions in recent years provide fertile ground for a meaningful school improvement project. At the same time, working on them will not be easy, because they are deeply embedded in the status quo. Choosing to focus on a problem, challenge, or gap that has persisted over time means that teachers and their administrative teams will need to examine teaching practices and how students progress through school to understand learning problems thoroughly. The investigation process may feel invasive of sacred ground.

Blind Spots

One of the frustrations we face in teaching our research class is when a student approaches us with something similar to the following statement: "My school is making AYP, and 90% of our students are passing the state-mandated tests. I can't find a learning gap in my school." Our reaction: You're not looking hard enough. We have already made the case that there is more evidence regarding student achievement than state-mandated tests. Furthermore, we have yet to find a school in which all students are successful. In contrast to the fictional quotation above is the story of a student who worked in perhaps the highest-performing middle school in a very large system. He and his colleagues found that student achievement in mathematics dipped as students moved from sixth grade to seventh grade. This was not an issue of AYP or even state test failure. The challenge was to keep students on a high achievement pathway so that they would be maximally prepared for high school.

One of the most effective ways to see what others miss is to adopt a bias for inquiry, which can start with the question, "How can we do better?" Not only better in terms of obvious performance measures but also in terms of the journey that students travel in school. When the school experience has negative aspects, even some of the most capable students perform poorly. The importance of affective learning seems to be lost in the race for higher test scores, but it may be every bit as meaningful as our emphasis on cognitive development.

Importance

Finding an interesting gap to address is a good start, but working in this area may not seem important to others. Leaders using research effectively must be able to answer the "So what?" question. Why is it important to address the achievement problem for students whose families are in poverty? Some might argue that if the numbers of students in a particular subgroup are small enough, then it is not worth allocating scarce resources to their needs because it won't "make a difference" in terms of the school's overall achievement profile. We find such a position unethical on its face, yet we recognize budget constraints and the fact that choices must be made.

Demonstrating importance often requires making the case that addressing a specific issue will improve a particular group of students' life chances. U.S. education is generally predicated on a fundamental human capital argument: The more students learn, the more valuable they become in the labor market, thereby increasing their earning potential. This theory has been difficult to validate in specific, but it is generally true that high school dropouts earn less and have a harder time being employed than high school graduates, who in turn earn less than people who have earned a bachelor's degree. The implications for K–12 education are that we have a duty to help students increase their future earning potential by educating them well enough at one level so that they can progress to the next level. At the same time, the human capital argument states that a well-educated society supports a thriving economy that benefits everyone. If a school's improvement efforts help more children achieve proficiency in key academic subjects, then the prospects for the students as individuals and for society as a whole improve.

There are certainly many more bases for the importance of a particular focus than the human capital argument alone. Our point is that demonstrating importance, and therefore enhancing the persuasiveness of your arguments in support of a particular challenge or learning gap, requires a combination of suggesting a clear need (e.g., "If students who fail reading tests are not helped, then their probability of succeeding in higher levels of school is greatly diminished") and reaching a critical mass that will make a clear impact on school performance. This is a balancing act, because an improvement proposal that promises too much in terms of outcomes and reaches to a number of students beyond what available resources can support is doomed to failure and may engender substantial cynicism within the school. Remember, we are at the stage of identifying a gap to address. The scope of the ultimate project remains to be determined later.

CONCLUSION

Assessing your school's current situation is probably best approached as a mini research project to answer the questions "How well are we doing as a school?" and "How do we know?" What seems obvious in the beginning becomes more subtle and complex as you search for ways to explain how and why your school may not be living up to its aspirations in a particular area. Comparing locally available data to state standards and the school's mission is the first step to surfacing an aspect in which your school could and should improve. Examining additional quantitative and qualitative data begins the process of finding the root causes of a gap you have identified, something that you will return to often in the school improvement process.

Sometimes it is not clear that an issue we may have identified is really a problem, challenge, or gap worth pursuing. The box below helps you think about whether or not the focus area you have identified is worth pursuing.

DID I IDENTIFY A MEANINGFUL PROBLEM?

Three aspects to any issue will help you figure out whether or not you have identified a problem, challenge, or gap that merits your creation of a school improvement project:

1. *Progress:* Are the students on whom you have focused making academic progress? Are they progressing at a rate commensurate with peers in an appropriate comparison group? What does the trend look like over time? For example, a literacy program designed to help students who enter high school two or more grade levels behind in reading should be expected to help students progress at a rate faster than peers. If not, these students will not make it to the 10th-grade reading level required for the graduation exam in time to graduate with their class. If students cannot meet that goal, then the literacy program may be inadequate and in need of replacement.

2. *Perspective:* How are similar schools performing with respect to the instructional need and the focus group of students you have identified? If students in similar schools are performing better, then there is a case to be made that your school could be approaching this particular challenge more productively.

3. *Proficiency:* How does student performance compare with standards established at the district, state, and/or national levels? Scores may be getting better over time and your school may be outperforming similar schools on some measures, but if students are not meeting standards, then the consequences for their future education and career opportunities remain.

Answers to the questions posed by the three Ps above help you build a case for the existence of an instructional problem, challenge, or gap and its significance in specific terms based on criteria that are important to educators, students, and parents. These kinds of questions also serve as a guide to the kinds of evidence you may need to amass to be confident that the issue you identify is an important one.

Throughout this chapter we have been writing about conducting action research to begin your understanding of a local academic problem, challenge, or gap. Given the knowledge you have acquired about your local situation, it is time to choose your focus. Worksheet 4.3 is designed to help you do exactly that. If you are unable to complete the worksheet satisfactorily, you probably need to go back and collect more data and/or engage in more discussion and thinking about ways in which your school is not meeting some of its aspirations.

In Chapter 5, we move to the process of persuading others that the instructional problem, challenge, or gap you have identified is a worthwhile place to focus attention, energy, and resources. Before moving on, however, consider the map of the school improvement planning process we provide in Figure 4.1. Thus far, we have addressed the left one-third of the figure. You are in the

Figure 4.1   A Map of School Improvement Planning

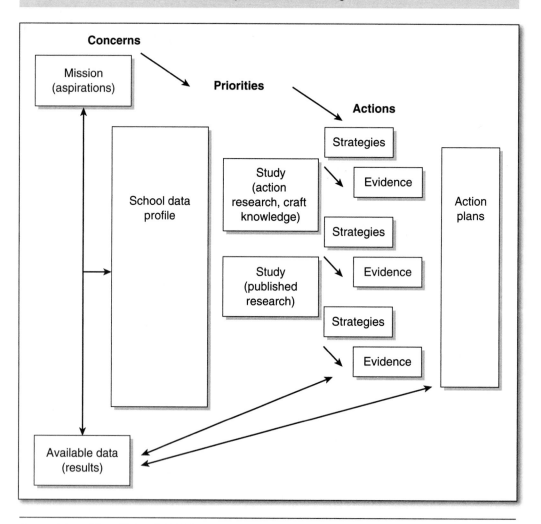

Source: Adapted from Holcomb (2004).

process of identifying concerns and figuring out which sources of evidence will help you make your case about a target improvement area.

In the next chapter, you will make your case by continuing the process of data collection started in Worksheets 4.1 and 4.2, engaging in some rudimentary data analysis (covered in much more detail in Chapters 7 and 8), creating data displays, and learning how to make persuasive arguments about the nature of the problem you wish to address. In short, Chapter 5 is the bridge between abstract thinking about problem articulation and the practice of communicating to the leadership team and others the nature of the problem you have found.

REVIEW QUESTIONS

1. What are important sources that will convey the aspirations and results in your school?

2. Name valuable sources of data other than state-mandated test results.

3. What is your improvement focus? How do you know it is important?

4. What are multiple data sources that would help you triangulate information regarding your problem, challenge, or gap?

WORKSHEET 4.1   Finding Data

As you begin your search for data that will help you identify an instructional problem, challenge, or gap in your school, it is a good idea to think about how to organize the data in your mind so you can develop a coherent picture. Begin with your school's aspirations. From your school's website (or a more appropriate source), read the vision or mission statement, and then record the following information:

1. What are your school's aspirations for all students?

2. What are the values expressed in the vision or mission that would be considered central to the school's purpose? (If there is a specific list of core values, use that.)

The above information may give you a helpful baseline for what your school intends to accomplish educationally with all students. Sometimes, however, vision or mission statements are not up to date and/or are so general that they are of limited help. Examine aspirations embodied in state curriculum standards and school district goals. What aspirations and values are embedded in those sources? Establishing a starting point is important work that should not be avoided.

Assuming you can articulate your school's espoused theory of learning, search school, district, and state websites; review printed sources; and engage in discussions with teachers for information related to these aspirations that can begin to answer the question "How are we doing right now?" Use the diagram to assist your thinking.

Questions to consider:

1. What is your school's performance at present?

2. How has your school evolved over time?

3. Did you find conflicting or contradictory data?

4. How do different school factors interact to create a particular outcome?

Demographics

Student number, gender, ethnicity, learning needs, income

School location, history, relationship to community, staffing

School community location, history, ethnic makeup, size, housing, crime

District history, student demographics, organizational structure, tax base

Perceptions

School climate
Classroom climate
Program quality
Faculty skills and aspirations
Leadership quality
Student ability
Parental involvement
Trust
History

Student Learning

Achievement tests
Norm-referenced tests

Criterion-reference tests
Authentic assessments

Teacher-made tests
Teacher-assigned grades

Performance assessments
Standards-based assessments

Motivation for learning

School Processes

Case descriptions, flowcharts and/or analyses of how programs and practices are implemented
Measures of characteristics of instructional and learning programs (e.g., instructional strategies, grouping, student/teacher ratios, time on task, organization of learning, team teaching, cooperative learning)

Source: Adapted from Bernhardt (1998).

WORKSHEET 4.2   Your School's Data Profile

What do you need, and where can you find it? Use this worksheet to create a data-mining plan that will help you develop a clearer and more persuasive picture of your school's current situation.

Data Type	Data Source/Location/Collection Strategy
Standardized test scores	Where will I find this data? Who will help me access this data if help is required? Who is stronger than I with data analysis? Can I enlist this person's help?
District assessments	Is this data reported back to school sites? Who has it, and who can help me get it? Is the data reported in a manner parallel to the state testing regime? If not, how is it reported? How accessible is disaggregated data that reports the progress of subgroups?
Teacher-made tests	Can I persuade teachers to share students' scores on these, at least in some areas? Would it be sensible to start with teacher-made test data from members of my collaborative team?

Data Type	Data Source/Location/Collection Strategy
	Is there a scheme I can use to create student profiles using different test results?
	Do teachers use common assessments? Can I get access to the results?
Demographic and affective data	Can I get access to information about which students are in various subgroups? Who can/will help me with this?
	Has my school conducted a climate survey recently? Who carried it out, and who has the results?
	Can I find time to interview teachers about their perceptions of the students I have targeted for my improvement project?
	Is it possible for me to conduct classroom observations, even if only for brief periods of time?
	Is it possible for me to interview selected students to gather their perceptions of school?

WORKSHEET 4.3   Finding a Focus

Your explorations of data available from your school site, district, and state have likely stimulated your thinking about what is happening in your school site with respect to student achievement. We encourage you to put this information together with your own local knowledge about your school as you determine the appropriate place to focus your school improvement project. As best you can, follow these steps:

1. Write your district vision or mission statement here:

2. Write your school vision or mission statement here:

3. Add any core values, goals, or objectives you believe are important indicators of school aspirations for students:

4. Fill in the quadrants of the diagram below. As you look for trends in the information you have collected so far, see what matches your own passion for instructional improvement.

5. Write a brief statement that explains your focus for school improvement.

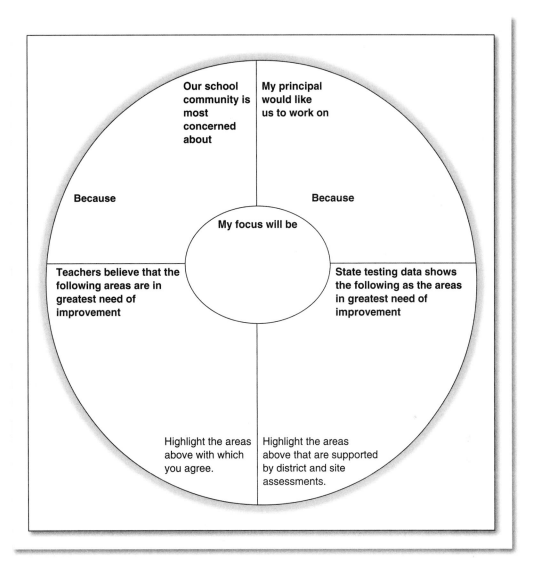

CHAPTER 5

COMMUNICATING A MESSAGE WITH DATA

LEARNING OUTCOMES

Readers who grasp the most important ideas from this chapter will be able to

- understand basic characteristics of well-structured writing;
- practice writing the major components of an Improvement Target Proposal;
- write a coherent, persuasive set of arguments in support of addressing the problem, challenge, or gap they have identified; and
- create tabular and graphic displays of evidence that complement written text.

Chapter 4 focused on the thought processes involved in understanding your local situation and identifying an instructional problem, challenge, or gap within that context. This chapter takes the next step by explaining how to communicate what you have learned about your school's context and the specific gap between aspirations and results that you wish to address. Creating knowledge about a particular instructional problem that interests you puts in place a critical piece of the foundation for making change that leads to improved student performance. As we emphasize throughout the book, however, you are not likely to succeed in this work by yourself. This chapter addresses the question of how to communicate what you have learned in a manner that accomplishes three goals: (1) *explains* to others "what is going on around here"; (2) *persuades* others that the problem, challenge, or gap you have identified is an important one that ought to be addressed sooner rather than later; and (3) *enlists* others in the cause that you have identified. On this last point, the most important persons to enlist in your cause are likely to be the principal and her or his leadership team, but the broader your support throughout the school, the better. Refer back to Chapter 3 regarding the others to whom we refer.

THIS CHAPTER'S DESTINATION

The Improvement Target Proposal, as discussed in the introduction to Part II, is a document that explains to administrators, teachers, and interested parents the situation your school is in at present. It provides both context and specifics about the gap you have identified. The Improvement Target Proposal has very limited goals. It only identifies a problem. It does not engage in root-cause analysis or proposing solutions, because at this point you are ready to conduct a local investigation but have not explored published research (see Chapter 7) that will inform your and others' understanding of the problem you have identified. Until this is accomplished, you are not ready to fix on an action or solution. This may appear to be excruciatingly slow progress, but moving forward carefully is an important aspect of collaboration. Furthermore, a central theme of helping your school become change adept (Schlechty, 2001) is developing among the administration and faculty habits of mind that inquire into the true nature of a problem before trying to solve it.

The Improvement Target Proposal establishes everyone's baseline for thinking about the problem you have identified. When all your potential collaborators can agree that you have discovered a legitimate instructional gap that warrants full attention, then it is much easier to examine the problem more deeply and ultimately discover promising solutions. Additionally, a clear statement of the problem and its importance becomes a useful tool for communicating to stakeholders in your school community and focusing their energy on the instructional improvement area you have identified.

There are five distinct components of the Improvement Target Proposal, each designed either to set up or to reinforce the others. It begins with (1) an introduction that brings the reader into the topic and continues with (2) a discussion of school, student, and faculty characteristics; (3) an analysis of the school's performance relative to its aspirations; (4) the identification of a specific area in need of improvement; and (5) a conclusion that reinforces the arguments made throughout the document. Charts, tables, graphs, or figures provide a sixth component that is incorporated into the body of the Improvement Target Proposal and helps convey data more clearly. The Improvement Target Proposal is based entirely on the quantitative and qualitative data you collect from school, district, and state sources to obtain a clearer picture of a specific instructional challenge at your school.

Helping Others Understand

One aspect of this chapter that may surprise you is our emphasis on the quality of your communication. As a leader, you are using this proposal to communicate the findings of your initial inquiry and to persuade others to follow your lead. Effective communication is vital to persuading others about a particular improvement effort. Communication occurs in three ways central to this chapter—in writing, graphically, and orally. We will discuss the first two in detail. Although oral communication is not, strictly speaking, a part of our discussion, we anticipate that you will have opportunities to present your ideas orally to people who have or have not read your document. Therefore, we provide guidance on how to prepare and deliver an oral presentation in addition to focusing on preparation of the Improvement Target Proposal (see Activity 5.1). In all three communication avenues, making compelling arguments is the central theme.

ACTIVITY 5.1   Presenting Your Improvement Target Proposal

Putting your Improvement Target Proposal in writing is a large and crucial step in the process of school improvement planning and implementation. Though it strikes fear into the hearts of many, an oral presentation of your Improvement Target Proposal is an important leadership activity that educates both your collaborative team and your school administration. Remember, most of us have an enhanced understanding of complex material when we receive it in at least two modes.

Oral presentations have many pitfalls, the most egregious one being that they take too long. The steps below are designed to help you create an engaging oral presentation and meet the needs of your audience.

1. **Plan the length of your presentation.** Keep in mind that members of your audience have engaged with the written text to varying degrees, but you should assume that they have read it or at least looked at it. Therefore, your goal is to guide your audience's thinking to the most important points made in the text and allow enough time for questions and answers so that they can be actively engaged and come to a deeper understanding of what you have presented. Our recommendation is that your presentation take no longer than one-third of the time you have available on an agenda. If you are given 15 minutes, speak only for 5. If you have 30 minutes, keep your presentation to 10. The rest of the time is for Q & A.

2. **Create visual support for what you have to say.** Microsoft's PowerPoint presentation program is easy to learn and use. Beware of death by PowerPoint, however. The two most common mistakes that presenters make with PowerPoint are that they put too much text into each slide, and then they read the slides verbatim. Imagine how boring such a presentation would be for someone who had carefully read your Improvement Target Proposal! A much more effective strategy is to use your PowerPoint slides as prompts for your own thinking and for that of your audience. Plan no more than one slide per minute of presentation time. Each slide might contain one or two ideas in verbal and/or graphic form. Remembering that the purpose of your presentation is to hit the highlights of your Improvement Target Proposal, use your graphs, charts, or diagrams in your slides and talk about them conversationally as each one comes up. PowerPoint is not the only means to support your presentation. You can use any software you wish, or you may be most comfortable using hand-drawn displays. Whatever you choose, your oral presentation will be stronger with visual aides.

3. **Prepare for Q & A.** You will build more self-confidence if you spend some time thinking about the kinds of questions you are likely to get from your audience and how you would like to respond to them. If you can work closely with a colleague on the Improvement Target Proposal, then it would be a good idea for that person to generate questions and ask you to respond to them impromptu. This will test your own understanding of your Improvement Target Proposal and your clarity in conveying that understanding. Weaknesses will be exposed, and you can find ways to mitigate these before you present.

4. **Practice your presentation.** It may seem awkward, but practicing your presentation helps improve its quality. Even if you practice alone, hearing yourself say certain things will tell you whether they are clear or awkward. Naturally, it would be even more effective to practice in front of one or two trusted friends who will give you honest feedback. Most oral presentations are weak on a number of counts. Practicing ahead of time will help you be better than other presenters, because you will be more familiar with your material and you will make corrections before your actual presentation.

In Chapter 2, we mentioned Fullan's (2001) notion of knowledge creation—in this case, the interpretation of data as presented in the Improvement Target Proposal is your first attempt at knowledge creation that will become public. You will take the quantitative and qualitative data that is readily available in your school and make sense of it in a way that helps create common understanding. This is why communication is so important. The data alone mean nothing and everything. We may not know what to make of the fact that 46% of students with disabilities failed the fourth-grade reading test, or we may read into the data all kinds of interpretations—from the malfeasance of third-grade teachers to the notion that inclusion is not an effective teaching strategy for this type of student. As an instructional leader in your school, it is your responsibility to help others understand specific messages that can be discerned from the data—what Fullan calls coherence making. Your ethics, values, beliefs, and expertise guide how the data will be understood through the vehicle of the Improvement Target Proposal.

If you choose to follow the steps we recommend in this chapter, you will emerge with an Improvement Target Proposal that provides the basic rationale for addressing the instructional challenge you have identified. Your focus may shift somewhat, and your understanding of the problem is likely to evolve as you work with a collaborative team (Chapter 3), revisit your local situation and conduct root-cause analysis (Chapter 6), and engage with published literature (Chapter 7) to develop a deep understanding of the nature of the problem. This kind of evolution is normal and beneficial; in fact, it is evidence of quality learning. Despite the changes that will inevitably take place, the Improvement Target Proposal provides a great beginning for your project.

Writing the Improvement Target Proposal also addresses three specific national standards as articulated by the Educational Leadership Constituent Council (ELCC) of the National Policy Board for Educational Administration (as well as the Interstate School Leaders Licensure Consortium standards for in-service school leaders). Writing this document requires you to discuss the characteristics of the school and diversity of the school community (ELCC Standard 4.2), use data to analyze school performance related to the school's vision and objectives (ELCC Standard 1.2), and identify an area for improvement (ELCC Standard 2.2). Although our primary focus is on improving the performance of students in your school, you may find it helpful to know which national standards you are addressing as you do so. As we discuss the additional two major components of the school improvement planning process in subsequent chapters, we will refer to the ELCC standards being addressed along the way.

Portions of the Improvement Target Proposal will be embedded in your School Improvement Project Proposal, the culminating performance-based activity of this book. As a result, you will have a choice: Either share your Improvement Target Proposal with interested administrators and teachers early in your project planning as a way of soliciting their interest and support or wait until you have completed your School Improvement Project Proposal. If you have a trusting relationship with professional colleagues, we recommend the former path as part of an effort to build the interest and support of others and receive constructive feedback as you move forward. More important, the Improvement Target Proposal can be a tool for unfreezing key constituents in your school, because it provides a vivid picture of an achievement area in need of attention. Sharing your analysis may be critical in building trust with others whose involvement will be important to the success of your School Improvement Project Proposal. Choosing to wait until your School Improvement Project Proposal is complete has the advantage of presenting a more finished product, but it also contains the hazard of your investing a great deal of work into a final product that others may perceive to be off target. Thus, you are faced with the first leadership decision of your effort to improve student and school performance. It is up to you.

FIRST, SOME GENERAL NOTES ON WRITING

In our careers, we have found that administrators fear writing nearly as much as they fear public speaking. Many tend to have difficulty with specific mechanical aspects of writing—word choice, use of commas, and sentence and paragraph structure. Another part of their fear is that they find writing time-consuming. Overcoming roadblocks to writing is a vital aspect of leading schools and districts, because many times, the written word is the first encounter a stakeholder has with you, your school, and your ideas. The writing you do for public consumption makes an important first impression and is a key means of communicating ideas and building common perspectives. Most important, high-quality writing can be an effective persuasion tool.

Good writing can be difficult to describe. It is often a case of "I'll know it when I see it." The two of us and our editors sometimes disagree about how ideas should be expressed. Nevertheless, there are some helpful principles you may have learned in middle school that are worth repeating.

Start With a Helpful Structure

Imagine a reader uninformed about the ideas you wish to present, distracted by a busy schedule, and inclined to be skeptical about plans that did not originate with him or her. This may well describe those whose support or approval you need as they sit down to read your Improvement Target Proposal. All your writing should be structured in a way that provides easy access to your thinking for such a reader. In your first paragraph, it is best to bring the reader gradually into what you want to convey. Then, within the same paragraph, narrow down to the main idea—your thesis—for what you wish to present (in this case, the school improvement area you are advocating to adopt as your focus). This is the right-side-up funnel portion of Figure 5.1. If your thesis is very specific and explicit, then it structures the subsequent paragraphs of your document. Body paragraphs each

Figure 5.1   Structuring Writing

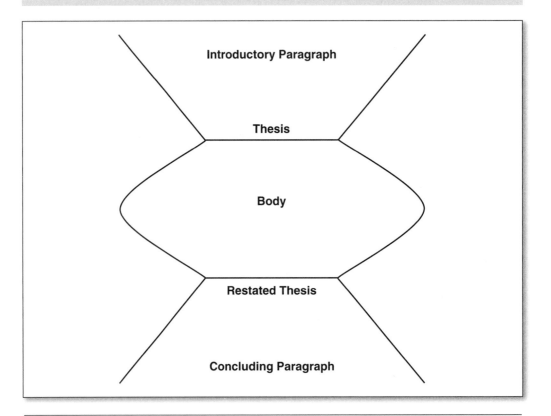

Introductory Paragraph

Thesis

Body

Restated Thesis

Concluding Paragraph

Source: Adapted from Baker (1977).

name a specific idea; elaborate or explain that idea with examples, logical arguments, and/or presentations of data; and explain their significance with respect to the thesis. The document ends with a conclusion that restates the thesis in new language that reflects what the reader has learned through the body, broadens to explain the meaning behind what has been presented, states logical arguments that will be important in the School Improvement Project Proposal, and/or explains next steps. This last portion is the upside-down funnel in Figure 5.1.

When the structure makes your writing accessible to others who are not familiar with your thinking, persuasion becomes much easier. Once again, the thesis is the place to start. The thesis contains your main idea—your firmly held belief—about something. In the case of the Improvement Target Proposal, the main idea is advocacy for addressing a specific instructional gap occurring in your school. There are probably at least three specific characteristics of the gap you have identified.

These ought to be listed in your thesis to plant them in the minds of your readers so that they look familiar when you elaborate on them in the body. In the process, you will present arguments about how the characteristics combine into an important challenge—arguments supported with data and/or logical reasoning. Your reasoning is reiterated in the restatement of your thesis in the conclusion. When you have written a persuasive document, the introduction and conclusion provide bookends for a tightly structured, persuasive set of arguments.

WRITING THE IMPROVEMENT TARGET PROPOSAL

Introducing the Reader to Your General Topic and Main Idea

Sometimes the most difficult part of writing any document is getting started. You may be more productive if you just start writing and ignore structure. Once your ideas are on screen or on paper, computers allow for easy reorganization. We assume that you engage in prewriting and free-writing exercises to get you started. We pick up the story in the organizing and refining stage.

The introduction to your Improvement Target Proposal orients the reader to your general topic and provides a road map for where this document is headed. This road map is central to the reader's understanding of your ideas. You are not writing a mystery. To maximize comprehension, you must preview for the reader the most important facts, interpretations, and arguments that are just ahead in the body of the paper.

SAMPLE INTRODUCTION: IMPROVEMENT TARGET PROPOSAL FOR GEORGE WASHINGTON MIDDLE SCHOOL

Read the opening paragraph and note how the two obligations of drawing the reader into the topic and providing a road map are met. The first portion, highlighted in light gray, is the broad part of the right-side-up funnel from Figure 5.1. This explains the general context of the school—performing well but with some danger signals. The dark gray portion explains the context a bit more and narrows down to the focus of the school's improvement plan. The thesis appears in light gray, underlined text. We might have preferred a more specific thesis that names the subject areas in which limited-English-proficient (LEP) students are struggling, but this thesis works quite well.

(Continued)

(Continued)

George Washington Middle School (GWMS) has had a long history of success. The school's motto is "Unveiling the Genius in Every Student," but recently, GWMS has begun to struggle with maintaining accreditation and making Adequate Yearly Progress (AYP). GWMS's school improvement plan targets priorities for regaining accreditation and meeting federal requirements for AYP, most notably in Math. In addition to these priorities, GWMS must address the needs of Limited English Proficient (LEP) students who are underachieving in multiple subject areas.

Source: Rob, "Improvement Target Proposal: LEP Achievement at GWMS." Used with permission.

This example is typical for our students, because most of them are working in school sites. It is, however, also possible to engage in improvement project planning from a central office position. The next example of an introductory paragraph for the Improvement Target Proposal takes that perspective and is somewhat more detailed than the previous one. The shading is done in a similar manner, showing that this student engaged in quite a bit more narrowing before she arrived at her thesis. In both cases, the road maps for the papers are clear and the theses explain these authors' areas of focus for their improvement projects. In the process, the authors have established a burden of proof for this particular document.

SAMPLE INTRODUCTION: IMPROVEMENT TARGET PROPOSAL FOR ROARING BROOK PUBLIC SCHOOLS

In today's data-driven educational world, schools strive to demonstrate that progress is being made by all students. In Virginia, Standards of Learning (SOL) tests are administered to measure proficiency in various subject areas. Data is collected and used to improve instruction throughout school districts to facilitate an increase in student achievement. Although these numbers appear to be extremely helpful to schools, all students may not be accurately represented. The Roaring Brook Public Schools strive "to provide free and equal education that meets the needs of all students." Although much information is available on many student subgroups, it appears that the free and equal education that is provided may not be meeting the needs of every child. One area of weakness that should be addressed is the instructional programs that are offered to Limited English Proficient students who are also identified as students with disabilities. Elementary Reading SOL scores suggest that the Roaring Brook Public Schools are not meeting the instructional needs of Limited English Proficient students who are also receiving Special Education services.

Source: Laura, "Investigating the English as a Second Language/Special Education Conundrum in Roaring Brook Public Schools." Used with permission. (The school district name has been disguised at the author's request.)

Worksheet 5.1 is designed to assist you in prewriting, writing, and editing your introductory paragraph. You may want to preview the worksheet now, but wait until you have collected and analyzed your local data before trying to write your introduction and thesis.

Establishing Context

Knowing the unique challenges and opportunities present in your school or work situation is important for being able to understand the specific characteristics of the gap you have identified. For example, minority student achievement in mathematics may be very different in one school where minority students are also the highest proportion of students in poverty compared with a school in which this is not the case. Yet many of our students are reluctant to write about context because we tell them that the audience for their Improvement Target Proposal should be their school administration and fellow faculty. Students assume that everyone in their school already understands the context quite well. Nevertheless, we insist on writing about the context, because doing so helps focus the reader and because people in schools can be remarkably isolated from general background information about students, faculty, and the community the school serves. Also, the Improvement Target Proposal may be very useful for communicating priorities to other, less informed stakeholders, such as parents who serve on improvement teams. There are three contextual factors that are the most critical: (a) demographics of the student body, the faculty, and the community the school serves; (b) characteristics of school climate; and (c) the school's current improvement objectives.

The Student Body

Rob was able to tell the story of student demographics at his school in one brief paragraph. This paragraph would be strengthened with a more comprehensive topic sentence such as "GWMS is a medium-sized middle school with a diverse student body." Nevertheless, we learn that Rob's school has a majority minority population and is challenged by a slight majority of students who are considered to be in poverty because of their eligibility for free and reduced-price meals. The pie chart on the following page helps us see the demographics more clearly, but used alone, it leaves out some equally important information. (We will say more about graphics later in the chapter.) Given that Rob's target population is LEP, it would be helpful to know if they are in overlapping subgroup categories.

GEORGE WASHINGTON MIDDLE SCHOOL DEMOGRAPHICS

According to the current GWMS School Improvement Plan, 946 students attend the school. The average class size is 20. The average daily attendance of the school is 98%. As with other schools in its district, GWMS is ethnically diverse. Figure 5.2 illustrates that over 60% of the student population are African-American or Latino. Free and reduced lunch is provided to 51% of the students. Additionally, 18% of the students are Special Education students and 18% are English-Language Learners and are receiving support services geared toward language acquisition as well as content knowledge.

Figure 5.2   George Washington Middle School Demographics

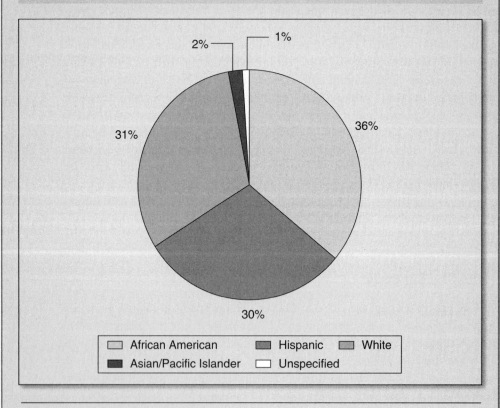

Source: Rob, "Improvement Target Proposal: LEP Achievement at GWMS." Used with permission.

Laura's interest was in how the Roaring Brook school district was serving (or not) students who were dually identified as eligible for English as a second language (ESL) and Special Education services. Consequently, when she wrote about the demographics of the faculty, this is where she focused her attention. It is possible to see in the following box that Laura is setting up the problem of appropriately educating dually identified students. If teachers lack the necessary background and certification to serve students who have both ESL and Special Education learning needs, then it seems logical that there would be a gap in such students' achievement. Understanding the inadequate preparation of teachers serving these students is an important background feature that helps build an argument for addressing the achievement gap that Laura found.

ROARING BROOK PUBLIC SCHOOLS FACULTY DEMOGRAPHICS

In the Roaring Brook Public Schools, there are 7 full-time-equivalent elementary ESL teachers and 52 full-time-equivalent elementary Special Education teachers. None of these teachers are dually certified in ESL and Special Education. Of the ESL teachers, five hold master's degrees and three hold bachelor's degrees. Five are only licensed to teach ESL, and three hold other endorsements. Only one ESL teacher has a provisional teaching license.

Source: Laura, "Investigating the English as a Second Language/Special Education Conundrum in Roaring Brook Public Schools." Used with permission.

Rob and Laura presented demographic facts they believed to be most relevant to their focus areas. This is a generally effective strategy because it prevents the Improvement Target Proposal from wandering off topic. Nevertheless, thinking about demographics more broadly, at least in the beginning, is a useful analytical device. General information that includes the size and structure of the school and how these characteristics compare with other schools in the district may be helpful for putting your focus area into perspective.

Moving from more general demographic indicators to more specific, the federally defined student subgroups provide convenient and consistent ways of categorizing students. Thus, it would be possible to discuss student demographics according to the numbers and percentage of various ethnic groups, economically disadvantaged students, students with disabilities, and students who speak a first language other than English. Equally important is thinking about these groups in relation to one another. What proportion of students is categorized as belonging to more than one group, and which groups do they overlap? Relevance remains key. For example, a project that focuses on the role of parents in academic success might add an explanation of how the parents of their students are employed, the rate of transience for families in the school attendance area, and the extent to which students attend neighborhood schools. The stability of families in the community tends to have substantial influence over parental involvement and support for school and district goals. Understanding the nature of the student body and the community from which they come helps the reader have a more detailed and nuanced sense of why the school may be facing specific instructional gaps.

School Climate Data

School climate can be a vague term that means different things to different people. Our working definition of school climate is the way the school feels to stakeholders. A school might feel like a caring community, a stimulating place, a dangerous building, or a competitive environment. Climate is influenced by numerous factors. Evidence of the nature of the school climate might be available from recent surveys of student, parent, and faculty attitudes and beliefs. States often require the collection of other data indicative of climate, including the rate and nature of student disciplinary incidents (easily found in school safety reports). It is difficult to provide all the desirable climate information in one brief paper, but considering the climate factors impinging on school improvement efforts is an important aspect of understanding the context within which one is attempting the arduous task of making change that improves student achievement.

Student Improvement Goals

Both of the students whose work is featured in this chapter used current school goals to good effect, but they did so in different ways. Rob showed in his Improvement Target Proposal that the school had focused its primary attention on mathematics achievement and was therefore not seeing the problem of ESL students underachieving across the curriculum (see the following box). As Rob concludes his discussion of current goals, he transitions into explaining his target population's challenges, the topic we discuss in the next subsection. By doing so, he demonstrates how the focus of his school improvement project complements the overall school improvement plan.

GEORGE WASHINGTON MIDDLE SCHOOL: PERFORMANCE GOALS

Since GWMS has been accredited with warning* in Math for the third consecutive year and did not make AYP for Math, the current School Improvement Plan focuses mostly on Math. The current School Improvement Plan goal indicates that students will meet or exceed state accreditation and AYP Math benchmarks. Three objectives are listed to meet this goal:

1. At least 70% of students will meet the accreditation math benchmarks.

2. Students will meet AYP benchmarks in mathematics.

3. Percentage of students receiving pass advanced on SOL tests will increase by 5%.

To help teachers meet these objectives, the School Improvement Plan outlines a continuous staff development plan. Staff development sessions are conducted by instructional coaches and are embedded during the school day through weekly grade-level department meetings, grade-level meetings, and monthly department meetings. The focus of staff development is AYP and SOL accreditation support and differentiation of instruction.

In addition to the need to make improvements in student achievement in Math, LEP student performance on high-stakes testing indicates that LEP students are underachieving in *all content areas*. As Tables 2–4 [not included here] indicate, LEP students in mainstream content areas are underperforming when compared to their grade-level peers on SOL tests.

Source: Rob, "Improvement Target Proposal: LEP Achievement at GWMS." Used with permission. Emphasis added.

*Accreditation in Virginia is contingent on a school meeting or exceeding its AYP targets.

Working from the central office, Laura takes a districtwide perspective on goal setting and school improvement planning, as one would expect. In the next box, she also adds the important contextual factor of categorical funding, her reference to the Consolidated Grant Proposal.[1]

---

[1]Most categorical funding is obtained by school districts through the submission to their states of a proposal or application that explains how federal money that passes through the states will be spent at the local level. State departments of education are expected to monitor local compliance with federal regulations through the mechanism of the consolidated application and occasional site visits.

> ## ROARING BROOK PUBLIC SCHOOLS:
> ## DISTRICTWIDE PERFORMANCE GOALS
>
> The federal No Child Left Behind (NCLB) act includes a goal that states that "all limited English proficient students will become proficient in English and reach high standards, at a minimum attaining proficiency or better in reading/language arts and mathematics." In accordance with NCLB, Roaring Brook Public Schools submitted its goals and objectives in a Consolidated Grant Proposal. The proposal outlines several goals that relate to LEP student achievement, including that we will have "high-quality learning environments and differentiated groups in appropriate class sizes for learning" and "a strong early literacy program" (Consolidated Grant Proposal, 2007). These objectives are designed to lead the county toward meeting the goal for LEP students in NCLB.
>
> *Source:* Laura, "Investigating the English as a Second Language/Special Education Conundrum in Roaring Brook Public Schools." Used with permission.

As we emphasized in Chapter 4, explaining current goals establishes aspirations or what we often prefer to call espoused theories. It is in the Improvement Target Proposal that espoused theories are compared with theories in use for the first time as students develop their school improvement projects. Remember, change theory establishes that a *problem* exists to the extent that there is a gap between the *real* and the *ideal*. Both Rob and Laura have laid the foundations for demonstrating that their school and district, respectively, have fallen short in meeting their explicitly stated aspirations for specific target populations. The actual demonstration of this gap comes in the next section, which explicitly compares aspirations with student performance.

Using Data to Assess the Gap
Between Espoused Theories and Theories in Use

At this point in writing the Improvement Target Proposal, you have staked a claim in your thesis that there is a particular instructional gap that merits attention. Now it is time to prove your point with data. This task is best accomplished if you combine verbal explanations with graphic representations of relevant data.

An excerpt from the mission statement of Chavez Middle School (a pseudonym) emphasizes standards-based academic excellence with the implication that all students are included in this aspiration: "An emphasis is placed on learning by staff, students, and families that promotes excellence on local, state, and national standards. The developmental needs of every child are purposefully addressed." In working through the Chavez example, we first present the school's most relevant student demographic data in Figures 5.3 and 5.4.

Figure 5.3   Sample NCLB Subgroup Distribution

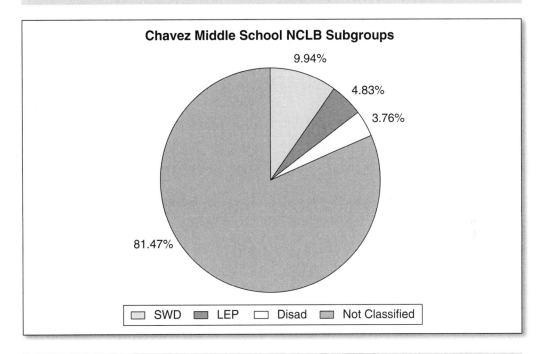

Chavez Middle School NCLB Subgroups

9.94%

4.83%

3.76%

81.47%

☐ SWD   ▨ LEP   ☐ Disad   ▨ Not Classified

Figure 5.4   Sample Student Ethnic Data

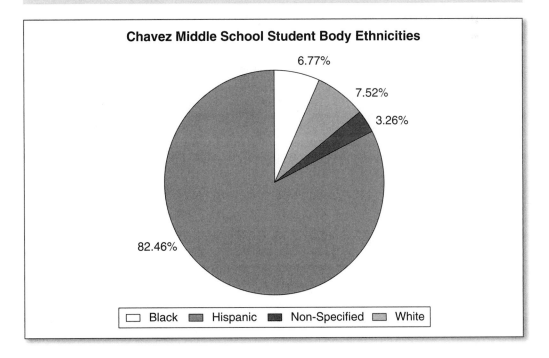

Chavez Middle School Student Body Ethnicities

6.77%

7.52%

3.26%

82.46%

☐ Black   ▨ Hispanic   ▨ Non-Specified   ▨ White

This school's state report card, available online from the state department of education website, provides multiple years of achievement data in mathematics, making it relatively easy to generate the bar chart in Figure 5.5 using Excel.[2] The dashed lines superimposed on the bar chart show this state's required passing rates in 2008–2009 and 2009–2010 (i.e., the dashed lines show future goals that must be met for this school to achieve AYP). The box titled "Making the Case for an Improvement Focus" provides verbal discussion of the data in Figures 5.3, 5.4, and 5.5 and begins to make the argument in favor of addressing a specific instructional gap.

Figure 5.5   Two-Year Data Sample

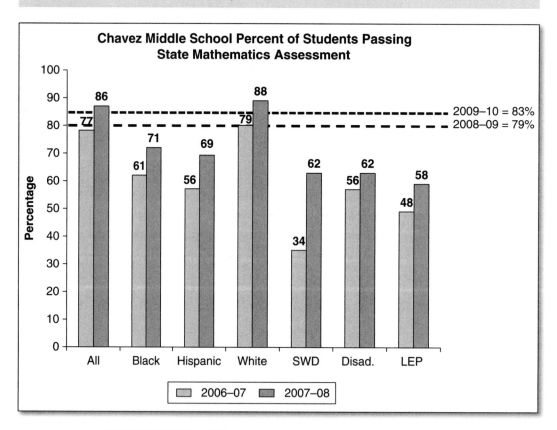

_____

[2]In this case, the report card data was available in an Excel spreadsheet that was easy to manipulate to create Figure 5.4. Bar charts can also be created in Word by hand-entering or copying and pasting data into a table, then creating the chart.

MAKING THE CASE FOR AN IMPROVEMENT FOCUS

Figure 5.5 indicates that ethnic minority students, students with disabilities, students who are economically disadvantaged, and LEP students are not performing as well in mathematics as their white counterparts. Although the trend improved somewhat between 2006–2007 and 2007–2008, white students pass the mathematics assessment by margins of 12 to 30 percentage points above students in other categories. All subgroups other than white are well below the passing benchmarks set by the state for 2008–2009 and 2009–2010 (dashed lines in Figure 5.5). If their learning needs in mathematics are not addressed very soon, then some number of students' academic opportunities will be curtailed and the school will be in danger of not making adequate yearly progress in mathematics. The question arises, however: How many students? Total student enrollment is approximately 1,000. Given the percentages presented in Figures 5.3 and 5.4, this means that there are between about 40 and 100 students in each of the categories where we have concerns. Approximately 30% to 40% of these students are not passing state mathematics assessments. Given the possibility that some students will overlap two categories or more, our focus should be on the following three groups: students with disabilities, disadvantaged students, and LEP students.

The statement from a hypothetical Improvement Target Proposal in the box above would go on to look at additional information available at the school site, including the number and percentage of students dually categorized as disadvantaged and students with disabilities or LEP, the extent to which those who fail are below the passing mark, and teachers' perceptions of these students' needs. The box and Figures 5.3, 5.4, and 5.5 taken together help the reader see that an instructional gap exists between specific subgroups and the majority of the student body. The verbal and graphic presentations of this problem support each other and are integrated in the Improvement Target Proposal.

Details Tell the Story

At this point, it seems helpful to note some of the details we have put into Figure 5.5, remembering that our goal is to communicate as clearly and persuasively as possible. The title for the chart is descriptive so that there can be no mistaking what data is included in the chart. The vertical axis is labeled as "percentage" so that the units are clearly understood. The scale of the vertical axis is manually set to 100 (the default in Excel was 90, because that was slightly above the highest value) so that if we were to compare additional charts with percentages, we would be working from a standard scale and data would not be distorted. In the original spreadsheet from which the chart was created, we were careful to label each row with the type of student (All, Black, Hispanic, etc.) and place the years as column headings. As a result, each set of bars is clearly labeled and the legend indicates which shade represents which year. Most important for purposes of persuasion, we have indicated in Figure 5.5 the moving goal posts required by state policy as the NCLB-determined deadline of 2014 approaches and all students are required to be achieving state standards. In this case, the Commonwealth of Virginia has determined that 79% of students are required to pass the mathematics assessment in the 2008–2009 school year and 83% are required to pass in 2009–2010. Having this last piece of information represented clearly on the chart is an important component in conveying the urgency of the mathematics achievement problem.

The combination of graphics and verbal explanation reveals what may have been hidden for some time at Chavez: Many students with disabilities, students in poverty, and LEP students in the 2007–2008 school year did not meet state requirements and were far away from passing rates required in the following 2 years. Measured against Chavez's aspirations for academic excellence (see mission statement on p. 116), current practices are not benefiting an identifiable portion of the student body up to an acceptable level. This kind of reasoning may help unfreeze administrators and faculty currently committed to the status quo.

An Alternative Display With More Data

The case for addressing the mathematics instruction of students in specific subgroups might be refined and strengthened by presenting additional data from the school report card website and/or using somewhat different graphics. Figure 5.6 presents a line graph for three years of data that may make a more vivid case that specific subgroups of students are in danger of not meeting state standards.

Additional information might include more comparisons among this school's performance, the performance of the district as a whole, and statewide performance; further breakdown of the data is possible—for instance, into the performance categories of advanced, proficient, pass, and fail. It would be wise to determine the absolute numbers of students failing the mathematics assessment in each subgroup and avoid double-counting students classified into more than one subgroup to have a clearer understanding of the magnitude of the problem. Discussions with teachers would provide more detail about the challenges that all the subgroups face as they work to succeed in mathematics.

Worksheet 5.2 is designed to help you articulate the difference between aspirations and results in your own school; using this worksheet can help you

Figure 5.6   Three-Year Data Sample: Line Graph

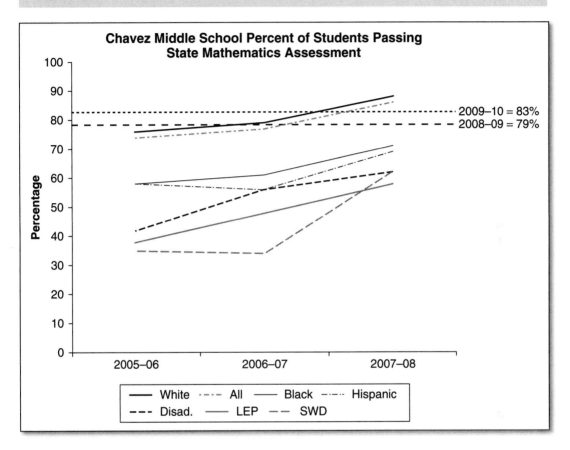

organize much of the information already discussed and begin to make sense of its import. Use Worksheet 5.3 to help plan your strategy for using data to persuade others about the importance of an instructional gap in your school.

A Conclusion That Clearly Identifies the Improvement Area

As you near the end of your Improvement Target Proposal, the logic of your arguments, well supported by data, should be clear and compelling. To cement your ideas in the minds of readers, it is best to remind them of the focal area(s) for instructional improvement that you have identified and supported with student performance and other data. A mechanism for providing this reminder is to begin your conclusion with a rewording of your original thesis. Here is how we would restate the theses for a conclusion:

- Rob: As the LEP population at GWMS grows, addressing their literacy needs across all subject areas becomes even more compelling in the effort to help these students improve their academic performance and achieve adequate yearly progress.

- Laura: The especially challenging student subgroup composed of those dually identified as special education and LEP must have their learning needs addressed in new ways to avoid consigning these students to long-term academic failure.

This type of restatement of the original thesis provides bookends for your discussion of the current situation in your school and reinforces for the reader the importance of the data you have presented. It is a concise statement of the central argument of your entire presentation.

Remembering the keyhole from Figure 5.1, your conclusion should broaden after the restatement of your thesis. The logical direction for looking beyond your thesis is the next step of school improvement planning and the next major performance in the book: the Research Brief. Your investigation into the local situation has undoubtedly opened numerous questions that you are not able to answer with local data alone. It is helpful to preview for your audience the direction you anticipate taking in search of the relevant literature for both a deeper understanding of the problem you have identified and potential solutions. See the following box for our suggested concluding paragraph for Laura's paper.

ROARING BROOK PUBLIC SCHOOLS: CONCLUSION AND NEXT STEPS

The especially challenging student subgroup composed of those dually identified as special education and LEP must have their learning needs addressed in new ways to avoid consigning these students to long-term academic failure. The next step toward a viable action plan requires consulting published research in the fields of both students with disabilities and limited English proficiency. We need to know more about the unique challenges these dually identified students present in classrooms and about strategies that bridge both kinds of needs. It is my hope that the broader experience presented in the research literature will help us understand better the specific situation in Roaring Brook Public Schools and suggest potential solutions that could be adapted to our local needs and circumstances.

Using Tables and Graphics

In this chapter, we have presented four different kinds of graphic communication: (a) the keyhole diagram in Figure 5.1, (b) pie charts to present demographics, (c) a bar chart to present middle school mathematics achievement, and (d) a line graph to demonstrate a trend over time. Each of these graphics was specifically designed to present ideas in a form more compelling and memorable than written narrative. The keyhole was used as a device for reminding readers about a specific structure for written work. The image, once presented and discussed, is then easily remembered by the reader as "the keyhole" and can be referenced by the author with confidence that the reader will remember and understand what he or she is talking about. Pie charts play a somewhat different role. They make vivid the proportion of the total student body of each identified subgroup. The math achievement bar chart in Figure 5.5 provides an easy comparison of student subgroups with one another across 2 years of data. A very quick review of the figure indicates that white students perform substantially higher in mathematics than their minority and other subgroup counterparts. The line graph makes clear that despite gains in the last year, students with disabilities, students in poverty, and LEP students are all performing close to the same level and well below white students. Figures 5.5 and 5.6 have the added feature of the superimposed AYP targets for the following 2 years, helping make the significance of the identified achievement gap even clearer.

Learning which kinds of graphics to present and how to discuss them is often a challenge to our students. Below are four simple guidelines with a few examples.

1. *Charts are generally easier to read than tables.* Consider Table 5.1, the data originally presented by one of our students who wanted to show the relative weakness of seventh-grade math achievement, and Figure 5.7, a chart created with the same data. The intent was to show that student performance in mathematics started out relatively low in seventh grade and improved dramatically in eighth grade. The table shows that the percentage of students failing and performing at the proficient level is greatly reduced and the percentage of students passing at the advanced level is greatly increased, but the information is not as vivid as it could be. The bar chart in Figure 5.7 makes the trend more vivid. Furthermore, by showing the direction of the change (rather than presenting the absolute difference) in percentages—either positive or negative—the point about achievement levels trending positively in eighth grade is clearer.

Table 5.1   Seventh- and Eighth-Grade Math Achievement

Proficiency Level	Seventh Grade (Percentage)	Eighth Grade (Percentage)	Difference (Percentage)
Failing	25	5	20
Proficient	46	22	24
Advanced	28	73	45

Figure 5.7   A New Display of Math Achievement Trends

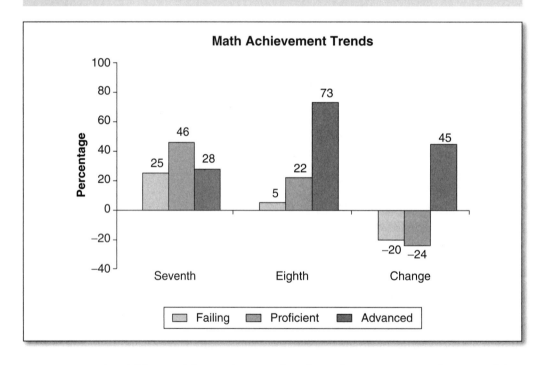

2. *Tables work better than graphs when a large quantity and variety of data are displayed.* Working with bar charts and line graphs, you will likely discover that too much data makes them impossible to read. If you wanted to present the Chavez data for both math and writing over time, for example, then a table would most likely be easier to read than either a bar chart or line graph.

3. *Pie charts are most helpful for observing distributions within a whole.* Reproducing Rob's pie chart of ethnic distribution at GWMS and then comparing it with two alternatives, we can see that there really is no better way to present this data (see Figures 5.8 and 5.9 and Table 5.2).

Figure 5.8   George Washington Middle School Demographics: Pie Chart

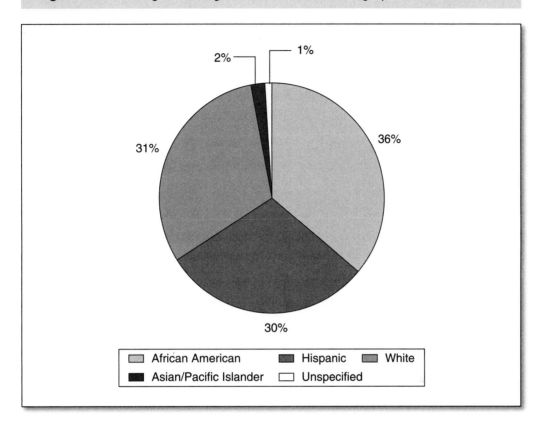

Table 5.2   George Washington Middle School Demographics

Ethnicity	Percentage of Total
African American	36
Asian/Pacific Islander	2
Hispanic	30
White	31
Unspecified	1

Figure 5.9   George Washington Middle School Demographics: Bar Chart

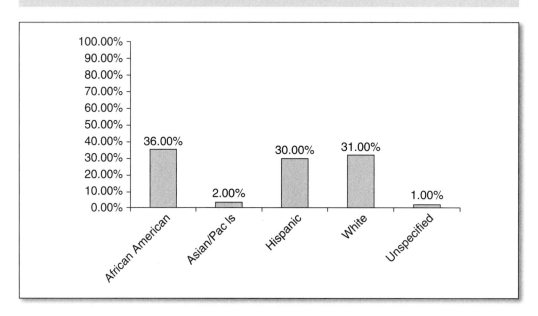

4. *Line graphs work better than bar charts for trends over time.* Figure 5.6 adds a year of data to the bar chart in Figure 5.5. Achievement trends for each group are more vivid when represented as lines over time.

Qualitative Data Displays

Up to this point, our discussion of data display has addressed quantitative data alone. Yet Worksheet 5.3 asks you to collect qualitative data by engaging teachers in informal discussions. Examining and thinking about key data from your notes from those discussions could be a big help in using those data to think about the instructional problem, challenge, or gap that you have identified. We offer two examples below—based on Question 2 in Worksheet 5.3— that can help you organize important qualitative data.

Figure 5.10 presents hypothetical results from informal discussions with teachers at three different grade levels and a specialist. Notes might be quite extensive, yet the matrix helps provide a thumbnail sketch of results. Although students as young as third grade may not have been impacted by their disabilities enough to have Individualized Education Plan (IEP) goals below grade level, the pattern emerges in fourth grade and beyond. A common factor for all students with disabilities is that their teachers perceive them to have difficulty taking standardized tests. Number sense seems to be a problem but maybe not by fifth grade.

Figure 5.10   Qualitative Data Matrix: Brief Text: Teachers' Beliefs About Math Achievement for Students With Disabilities in Grades 3–5

	Below Grade-Level Objectives in IEP	Difficulty Taking Standardized Tests	Weak Number Sense
Third grade	No	Yes	Yes
Fourth grade	Yes	Yes	Yes
Fifth grade	Yes	Yes	Yes/No
Special education teacher	Fourth grade and above	Yes	No

For some reason that ought to be explored further, the special education teacher does not perceive number sense as a difficulty for her students.

The matrix presented above distills qualitative data, which is often unwieldy, into some general patterns. These can be accepted as is, or they can be explored more deeply. Whatever the choice of the leader/researcher, knowledge around the nature of the math achievement problem for students with disabilities is starting to be created. You may believe, however, that Figure 5.10 leaves out too much detail. It would be possible to build the matrix by quoting from the discussions and/or your notes, as in Figure 5.11.

Figure 5.11   Qualitative Data Matrix: Quoted Text: Teachers' Beliefs About Math Achievement for Students With Disabilities in Grades 3–5

	Below Grade-Level Objectives in IEP	Difficulty Taking Standardized Tests	Weak Number Sense
Third grade	Our students have typically been recently identified. Their initial IEPs nearly always have grade-level objectives in math. We often experience difficulty meeting these objectives.	These students have a harder time concentrating than others. Their answer sheets are often messy and filled out incorrectly.	We spend a lot of time on number sense with these students because their foundation is often weak coming out of second grade. We have to push on with basic operations, though.

(Continued)

Figure 5.11 (Continued)

	Below Grade-Level Objectives in IEP	Difficulty Taking Standardized Tests	Weak Number Sense
Fourth grade	Many of these students have failed the third-grade state tests. Third-grade objectives not being met, we must write IEP goals appropriate to their achievement to date.	We're seeing serious test anxiety in many of these children. We try to work with parents to help prepare the kids for testing days.	While most students are focused on multiplication and long division, several of our students with disabilities are still shaky on place value.
Fifth grade	Most students are showing progress, but they are not where they should be according to state curriculum benchmarks. They're getting there, but not at the same rate as their nondisabled peers.	No one likes taking tests, but some of our students with disabilities are beginning to rebel. The most obvious signs are absences on test days and putting their heads on their desks after about 15 minutes of testing.	Whole number sense generally seems okay, but basic operations are weak. Fractions are a difficult concept for many of these students.
Special education teacher	Because they need more time, IEP goals tend to fall below grade level as kids get older.	We help out as much as we can in testing situations. We work hard with our students to help them understand why they are taking the tests and how to approach them. They just really do not enjoy the experience.	I never felt that number sense was such a big issue. We tend to focus more on basic operations. Subtraction and division are the areas of greatest difficulty. When you load fractions in there, forget it!

Figure 5.11 organizes qualitative data in a fashion similar to Figure 5.10, but it preserves much more of the detail. Figure 5.10 demonstrated areas of agreement and disagreement regarding math achievement difficulties for students with disabilities. The more detailed nature of the differing points of view emerges in Figure 5.11. Both matrices improve our knowledge of the problem, and neither is "correct." How you choose to organize your qualitative data is

a matter of professional judgment and personal choice. An important consideration is preserving confidentiality. When you display more detailed data, then individuals may be associated with specific points of view that could have professional consequences for them. It is important to show the qualitative data display you intend to use to those who provided it to let them decide if they are willing to share it more broadly. Whichever path you choose, qualitative data becomes more accessible when the analysis is summarized either through simple representation or through representative quotations.

There are many other ways that qualitative data could be organized. You may find that drawing diagrams that show relationships and sequence of events is more useful than the static matrices above. The goal of these and other displays is to convey meaning from data. That meaning is interpreted by you, which is entirely appropriate when you are in the role of leader/researcher. Those with whom you collaborate may find other meanings in the data, which generates healthy discussion that builds new knowledge.

CONCLUSION

The Improvement Target Proposal presents a compelling set of arguments for addressing a specific instructional challenge, problem, or gap. When written well, it helps focus the attention of multiple constituencies on an area you believe needs to be addressed. This document can help bring others around to your point of view, giving you allies in the work ahead. The biggest test of the quality of your Improvement Target Proposal is how clearly you present data that demonstrates the gap between your school's official aspirations for a group of students and performance to date.

Discussing data is not easy, but vivid graphics help communicate the meanings behind data. The current political climate (see Chapter 1) has placed a great premium on quantitative data analysis that informs educational decision making. Consequently, a change-adept leader will use analysis of such data to help unfreeze key members of the school community regarding a specific issue and will engage others in learning processes that begin with data analysis. Numbers will not tell the whole story, however.

When we talk with our students about data, many of them tell us that they trust numbers more than verbal descriptions. Somehow, numbers seem more concrete than words. This bias in favor of the apparent precision of quantitative data masks much of the subtlety of statistics (see Chapter 8) and ignores the fact that not all important information is quantifiable. There is a strong tendency, particularly in the current educational political climate, to relegate qualitative data to being merely anecdotal. This misses a critical point about how we might come to understand important instructional gaps and their potential solutions. Quantitative data can tell us what the problem is. Figures 5.5 and 5.6 clearly indicate that several student groups' achievement in mathematics has been improving but that a wide gap between them and the majority white population still exists. The quantitative data is silent about *why* the gap persists and *how* these students were able to improve their performance over time. These why and how questions can be answered only by those who experienced teaching and learning in this school over 3 years—the students and their teachers. Future planning depends on a thorough understanding of the reasons why achievement has been improving and the apparent roadblocks that remain. Quantitative and qualitative data go hand in hand to help explain the existence and nature of an instructional problem, challenge, or gap and are therefore both critical to a high-quality Improvement Target Proposal. The nature of each type of data analysis and how they might be used together is discussed in much greater detail in Chapter 8.

REVIEW QUESTIONS

1. What purpose does the thesis serve, and why is it reiterated in the conclusion?

2. In what ways do graphic displays enhance the meaning a reader obtains from your text?

3. How do quantitative and qualitative data complement each other in analysis of the target problem, challenge, or gap?

WORKSHEET 5.1   Writing the Improvement Target Proposal Introduction

This worksheet is designed to help you start writing your Improvement Target Proposal. It walks you through some prewriting thinking and the creation of a thesis to guide your proposal. The final product of this worksheet is a strong introductory paragraph. You may not be ready to work on this worksheet until you have collected at least some data at your site and thought about what it means. It may be best to work on Worksheet 5.2 at the same time you think about how to approach this worksheet, because understanding the difference between espoused theories and theories in use will be critical to writing your thesis.

The introduction to your Improvement Target Proposal is important but *brief*. Your goal should be a one-paragraph introduction that is approximately one-half of a double-spaced page. A thesis is easiest to grasp when it is one sentence without an excessive number of phrases in it. Map out your introductory paragraph by responding to the questions below. Remember, you are setting up your document in the reader's mind. At this point, you are naming what you want to discuss. Details and arguments will come in the body of the Improvement Target Proposal.

1. What are important contextual factors the reader ought to know about the site of your school improvement effort?

   - Are you working on a school-site or district-level issue?
   - Are there relevant historical factors that are important contributors to the current situation?
   - Are there categories of students or instructional problems that have been left out of the improvement planning process to date?

2. How will you narrow the discussion down to a specific thesis?

   - What is your focus area, and what makes it a reasonable choice?
   - How is your focus area a specific case of the general discussion that begins the introduction?

3. Thesis

   - What is the most important point you wish to make?
   - Can this point be broken down into two to four specific parts? If so, what are they?

(Continued)

(Continued)

Using your answers to the questions above, write your introductory paragraph in a clear and coherent manner. Remember as you move on to write the body and conclusion of your paper that your thinking may change as you develop your ideas more completely. You may wish to return to your introduction, and more specifically your thesis, either to revise some portion of the introduction or to adjust your body paragraphs to be certain that they are supportive of the main point(s) you wish to make.

Helpful tip: Keep your thesis in front of you as you write the rest of your Improvement Target Proposal. This helps you keep your writing focused. One strategy is to place the thesis temporarily in the header portion of the file you are creating. This way, you can refer to it at the top of every page as you write. Another possibility is to print out your thesis in large type and attach it to the top of your computer screen for easy reference while you are writing.

**WORKSHEET 5.2   The Difference Between
Espoused Theories and Theories in Use**

As a means of determining your school's espoused theories—its aspirations for students—copy and paste into a new file all the following that you can find:

- Vision statement
- Mission statement
- Goals and objectives for the current academic year

After studying these statements of aspiration, think about the various student subgroups that are present in your school and ask if the school is achieving its aspirations for students in each case. Some suggested categories to investigate:

- Majority ethnic population
- Specific ethnic minority populations
- Students whose first language is not English
- Students in poverty (as defined by eligibility for free or reduced-price meals)
- Students with disabilities
- Transient students
- Students who fit into more than one of the above categories

Those groups of students for whom the school may not be meeting its aspirations provide evidence of a gap between what is desired (espoused theories) and what is occurring (theories in use). You need to decide at this point which group or groups you wish to address in your school improvement effort. Before choosing, think about your own passions and expertise and think about what would be appropriate for a manageable project.

WORKSHEET 5.3   Making Your Case

Building on the work you did in Worksheets 5.1 and 5.2, start from your hunches about which group needs the most help and why, and build your case using data.

1. What do the aggregate testing data indicate to you about the greatest instructional needs of the subpopulation you have selected? Where can you find this data?

   - How should the data be refined and/or enhanced to make your case more clearly?

   - Which data displays will enhance what you write and present your case more vividly?

2. What are teachers' current beliefs about the instructional challenges for this particular group of students?

   - Engage teachers in informal discussions (being certain to keep notes), possibly based on questions such as the following:

     o Do standardized tests appear to measure what these students actually know and are able to do? If not, what other evidence of their ability is available?

     o If students know more than they can show on standardized tests, what are some effective ways of bridging the gap between their knowledge and their test taking?

     o Are there specific skills and/or knowledge gaps that show up consistently for this population of students?

     o Are these students likely to succeed at the next grade level? Why, or why not?

3. After following the steps above, check your thesis.

   - Is the thesis still valid?

   - In what ways could the thesis be strengthened?

   - Can you make it more specific and/or explicit?

PART III

BUILDING A DEEP UNDERSTANDING OF THE PROBLEM

The three chapters of Part III focus on helping you as a leader build a deep understanding of the problem you identified in Part II. In Chapter 6, we introduce the concept of root-cause analysis, which allows you to discover the underlying causes of the instructional challenge, problem, or gap you have identified. Step-by-step procedures are provided for engaging in root-cause analysis, which includes accessing existing knowledge about causes through examination of the published literature and conducting inquiries locally to harness available information and tap into the craft knowledge of teachers in your school. Chapter 7 is a detailed guide on how to find valuable literature and how to make sense of it once you have it. We begin with how to think about or approach the literature and provide practical steps for using online databases. Chapter 8 discusses research design, both quantitative and qualitative. With a deeper understanding of research design, the literature you read will make more sense to you and you will have a clearer sense of your sources' trustworthiness.

BIG IDEAS: BUILDING A DEEP UNDERSTANDING OF THE PROBLEM

1. "Building a deep understanding" of a problem requires questioning causes—not simply jumping to solutions.
2. Identifying causes is a systematic research activity that involves consulting existing knowledge from published work and conducting a local investigation.

(Continued)

(Continued)

3. Leaders who seek to impact significant issues related to the improvement of instruction benefit from knowing how to access research knowledge from various sources of published work.

4. To be a critical consumer of published work, leaders benefit from having a working knowledge of some principles of research design.

5. Triangulation → Trustworthiness.

Taken together, the three chapters in this part of the book provide the means for you to make sense of research—both the action research you conduct in your own site and the published research you find in the 21st-century equivalent of the library. The final product of this part is a Research Brief, a document that helps you organize your own thinking and communicate the essence of relevant research to others (see the figure on the following page).

There are two assignments we include for the academic audience in this part of the book. The first we title Annotated Bibliography, since it is modeled after the act of accessing published work and using a format much like a traditional annotated bibliography to organize what you glean from this literature. Instead of using the customary format for an annotated bibliography, however, in the context of school improvement planning, we suggest that students use the format presented in Worksheet 6.1 to organize notes related to potential causes of the problem found in the literature. This purposeful sifting through the literature brings students a step closer to completing root-cause analysis. Later, in Chapter 9, we present a similar format for mining the literature for potential solutions. Suffice it to say that as students examine published research, it is worthwhile to establish a systematic format for recording information that will assist them and their team in understanding possible causes and the kinds of solutions that would serve to lessen these causes.

Second, the Research Brief is built using, in part, the literature found while doing the annotated bibliography, coupled with the results of any local inquiry focused on causes of the problem. For our purposes, a research brief is a short *literature review* or thematic summary of both published work on a topic that summarizes and evaluates what is known on the topic and themes discerned from local inquiry into the causes of the problem. The Research Brief is written for a *practitioner audience* (e.g., your principal, a school leadership team). As discussed in Chapter 7, this document may be best considered a review *for* research, rather than a review *of* research; in other words, it is not intended to be an exhaustive summarizing of what is known but, rather, a purposeful argument using research that moves your team toward an intended action.

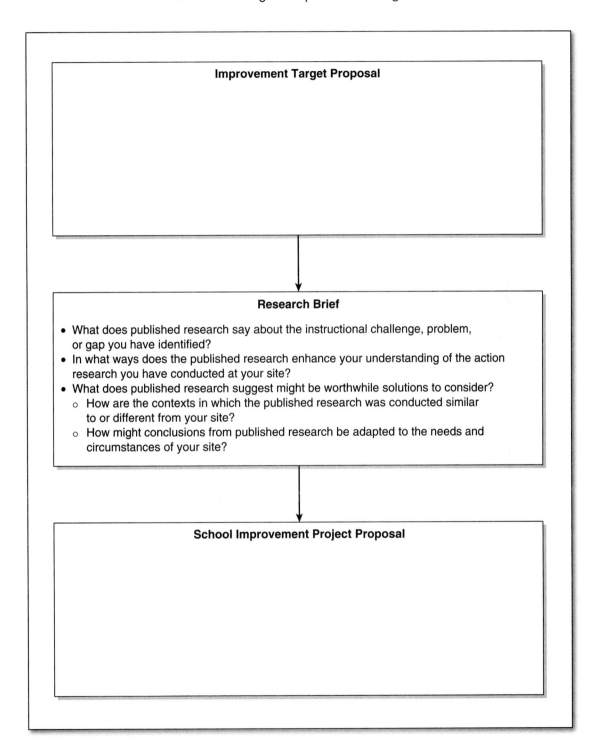

Improvement Target Proposal

Research Brief

- What does published research say about the instructional challenge, problem, or gap you have identified?
- In what ways does the published research enhance your understanding of the action research you have conducted at your site?
- What does published research suggest might be worthwhile solutions to consider?
  - How are the contexts in which the published research was conducted similar to or different from your site?
  - How might conclusions from published research be adapted to the needs and circumstances of your site?

School Improvement Project Proposal

Annotated Bibliography Description and Rubric

Overview

As emerging leaders in your schools, you need to develop the skills associated with accessing the knowledge base on questions that are important to the understanding and improvement of teaching and learning. An *annotated bibliography* provides you with the opportunity to learn how to sift through existing research on a question that interests you and to begin to organize the knowledge that you are gaining by reading this literature.

Task

1. Connect your research to the topic identified in the Improvement Target Proposal. Base your selection on your review of relevant data and on discussions with leaders in your school concerning the areas that reflect current and future improvement priorities for the school.

2. From this selection, state your focus as a research problem. For the purposes of reviewing the literature, your problem can be formulated by completing the sentence, "What is known about…?" (e.g., "What is known about why adolescent boys drop out of school?").

3. Find a number of *research articles* (original research or syntheses) that speak to the question you selected. You will first be interested in building a deep understanding of the problem and the kinds of factors that are thought to cause problems like this in schools like yours and, later, to identify actions that have been found to be effective strategies to deal with these causes. This is an iterative process; as you examine the literature, you will narrow your search as you learn more about the problem. You might identify several articles that are review pieces or syntheses of the literature themselves, but you should also concentrate on identifying primary research (i.e., papers that present an analysis using quantitative or qualitative methods to contribute to the knowledge base on the question). Most of your research can be accomplished on the Internet, with support from your school library, the public library, and/or university libraries.

4. Prepare your Annotated Bibliography using *at least five (5)* of the most important papers you found. An annotated bibliography is a list of articles (or books) that includes a *brief description of the work* and *an evaluation of its usefulness*. The purpose of an annotated bibliography is to provide information about the relevance, utility, and quality of the source *for your purposes*. *Note:* Instead of writing traditional annotated entries, you may use the format presented in Worksheet 6.1 to journal about the literature you are finding in relation to learning about causes of the achievement gap you seek to address.

5. Your Annotated Bibliography should include a *statement of the topic* and research question you are investigating, five annotated entries, and a *reference list* showing the papers you consulted (around 10 sources). Citations must be in APA format.

Annotated Bibliography Assessment Rubric

Criteria	Exceeds Expectations	Meets Expectations	Approaching Expectations	Falls Below Expectations
Statement of problem (ELCC 1.2) Weight: 10%	The paper begins with a clear statement of the topic or problem, which specifically relates to an improvement area identified using assessment results, demographic data, and analysis of school and community needs (Paper 1).	The paper begins with a statement of the problem, which relates generally to a performance area identified using assessment data.	The statement of the research problem is evident but is vaguely worded or poorly spelled out. It is difficult to discern a clear focus for the research.	The statement of the research problem is missing or wholly inadequate.
Bibliographic entries: content (ELCC 6.1) Weight: 40%	Annotated entries provide a clear and concise summary of each research source. Each entry includes an overview of the research (including method and findings) and an assessment of its utility.	Annotated entries provide a summary of each research source. Each entry includes a brief overview of the research and an assessment of its utility but may be lacking in specificity.	Annotated entries provide a general overview of research sources but lack detail or are missing significant elements needed to make the entries useful.	Annotated entries are severely lacking in detail, rendering them of little use.
Bibliographic entries: focus Weight: 10%	All entries clearly and specifically relate to the research question.	Most entries relate clearly to the research question.	Most entries relate only generally to the research question.	The connection between annotated entries and the research question is difficult to discern.

(Continued)

(Continued)

Criteria	Exceeds Expectations	Meets Expectations	Approaching Expectations	Falls Below Expectations
Bibliographic entries: quality Weight:10%	Sources are well balanced, including original research and synthesis pieces from high-quality, credible sources.	Entries are included from quality sources but are dominated by synthesis pieces; original research is not evident.	One or more entries are included from questionable sources, reflecting largely opinion pieces rather than original research or syntheses of research.	Entries are dominated by material from questionable sources; a review of research is not evident.
Bibliographic entries: quantity Weight: 10%	Five annotated summaries are presented, along with a detailed reference list of about 10 sources consulted.	Five annotated summaries are presented, but a reference list of fewer than 10 sources consulted is included.	Four or five annotated summaries are presented along with a reference list of sources consulted.	Fewer than four annotated summaries are presented along with a reference list of sources consulted.
References Weight: 10%	References are complete and presented in APA format.	References are in APA format, but a few (one to three) appear incorrect or are in improper format.	The document contains numerous incorrect or incomplete references.	References are omitted entirely.
Mechanics Weight: 10%	Entries are nearly error-free, which reflects clear understanding and thorough proofreading.	Entries contain occasional grammatical errors and questionable word choice.	Entries contain errors in grammar and punctuation, but spelling has been proofread.	Entries contain frequent errors in spelling, grammar, and punctuation.

Research Brief Description and Rubric

Overview

A research brief is a short *literature review* or compilation and thematic summary of published work on a topic that both summarizes and evaluates what is known on the topic. The main difference between a research brief and a formal literature review is the intended audience: Address your research brief *to a practitioner audience* (e.g., your principal, a school leadership team).

Use your Annotated Bibliography and the sources you collected to provide a synthesis of the knowledge base and to identify what is known, what is not known (gaps in the literature), and what is missing (unanswered questions) in the extant research. (Note: the material you presented in the annotated bibliography is a minimum—you will likely need more sources to do a good job here! Remember, you are trying to present a trustworthy document that school leaders will rely on to formulate actions.) Augment this material with a thematic discussion of any local inquiry you conducted to identify causes of the problem.

Note that you should be crafting your argument toward a potential course of action you might use in your school improvement project. Remember, to get the most out of your efforts, you should use the literature and your own investigative work to identify likely *causes* of the achievement gap and ways to reduce or eliminate these causes as the action you might take.

Task

1. Write a clearly worded, *one-sentence research question* that describes the purpose of your investigation. This should be a reformulation (if needed) or restatement of the question you framed for your Annotated Bibliography, related to the problem you identified in the Improvement Target Proposal.

2. Using the research literature you collected to prepare your Annotated Bibliography, along with any additional sources you might identify, write a *review of the literature* on the question. This review should begin with an introduction that defines your research question and *its importance*. The body of the document should summarize the existing research. Remember that this is *not simply a listing of the research cited*—your review adds value by organizing various studies, comparing them, and identifying strengths and weaknesses of established work. To help organize your review of "what is known," recall that you are informing readers about the nature of the problem, its causes, and later what is known about potential ways to address the problem in schools such as yours.

3. Conclude the paper with a section that presents *your recommendation* based on the available research. For instance, if your question was, "What is known about why adolescent boys drop out of school?" and the research focuses your attention on causes related to student engagement and then remedies such as increasing the availability of extracurricular programs or enhancing the rigor and relevance of the curriculum, you might recommend that your school's improvement team work toward such an objective. *The tone of this paper is persuasive*—this recommendation will connect to your school improvement proposal.

(Continued)

Research Brief Assessment Rubric

Criteria	Exceeds Expectations	Meets Expectations	Approaching Expectations	Falls Below Expectations
Introduction: research problem, overview Weight: 15%	The paper starts with a clear and concise statement of the research question and an introduction that provides a clear road map for the reader, foreshadowing what the paper is intended to provide in the way of information and situating this information in the context of the school's general improvement goals.	The paper starts with a brief introduction that alludes to the research question and provides a general foreshadowing of what is to be included in the document.	An introduction is provided that provides only the barest hint about the research question or the information to be shared.	The paper lacks an introduction entirely, or the introduction fails to provide useful information that is linked to the research question.
Body: application of research to school improvement (ELCC 2.3) Weight: 40%	The body of the paper presents a systematically organized synthesis of research directly relating to the question. Analysis is provided that reflects an awareness of and judgment about the quality of published work.	The body of the paper provides a loosely organized synthesis and analysis of published work related to the research question.	The body of the paper describes published work generally related to the research question but provides a limited synthesis or analysis of published work.	The synthesis and analysis of published work is wholly missing or inadequate.

Criteria	Exceeds Expectations	Meets Expectations	Approaching Expectations	Falls Below Expectations
Conclusion and recommendation (ELCC 2.2) Weight: 20%	The paper concludes with a clear and concise summary of research directly related to the research question and a recommendation and rationale advocating for a possible course of action that could effectively result in the desired improvement(s).	The paper concludes with a general summary of research on the research question. A recommendation advocating for a possible course of action that could effectively lead to desired improvement(s) is presented in general terms, but the rationale for the recommendation is not entirely persuasive.	The paper concludes with a general summary of research on the research question. A recommendation advocating for a possible course of action is not evident.	The conclusion is missing or wholly inadequate; the paper ends abruptly.
Quality of research support (ELCC 6.1) Weight: 15%	Research cited is well balanced, including original research and synthesis pieces from high-quality, credible sources.	Research is cited from quality sources but lacks specificity or is loosely developed.	General supporting research evidence is referenced but appears dominated by opinion pieces or material from questionable sources.	Few solid supporting ideas or evidence from research are included.

(Continued)

(Continued)

Criteria	Exceeds Expectations	Meets Expectations	Approaching Expectations	Falls Below Expectations
Organization of paper Weight: 5%	The paper is powerfully organized and fully developed.	The paper includes logical progression of ideas aided by clear transitions.	The paper includes most required elements but lacks transitions.	The paper lacks logical progression of ideas.
Mechanics Weight: 5%	The paper is nearly error-free, which reflects clear understanding and thorough proofreading.	The paper contains occasional grammatical errors and questionable word choice.	The paper contains errors in grammar and punctuation, but spelling has been proofread.	The paper contains frequent errors in spelling, grammar, and punctuation.

CHAPTER 6

GETTING TO THE ROOT OF THE PROBLEM

Explanations exist; they have existed for all time; there is always a well-known solution to every human problem—neat, plausible, and wrong.

—H. L. Mencken

LEARNING OUTCOMES

Readers who grasp the most important ideas from this chapter will be able to

- understand the concept and value of root-cause analysis;
- begin to develop a logic of action that describes primary causes of the instructional problem they identified; and
- lead their teams in conducting a root-cause analysis using published research and action research in their school.

Suppose for the moment that you arrived for a scheduled appointment at your physician's office, having called this morning complaining of a persistent cough. Upon checking in at the reception desk, you are handed a prescription for an industrial-strength cough elixir and invited to phone back next week if the condition persists. Sound odd? Would you be likely to continue to consult with this doctor when you feel ill?

Although we are exaggerating for the sake of making a point, this example illustrates the central premise of this chapter and, indeed, one of the most important themes represented in this book: It is impractical, unwise, and inherently ineffective to move from problem identification to solutions and actions without first carefully examining the root causes of the problem. In the medical context, we would be aghast if our physician skipped the diagnostic phase of our care regimen and simply prescribed treatment based on an accounting of symptoms. The persistent cough that brought you to the doctor in the first place may have been caused by the common cold or an allergen, or maybe it is evidence of the early onset of a much more serious condition. If there is a serious problem, treating it with cough syrup might alleviate the symptoms, but it will also mask the disease, leading to potentially dire consequences. A thorough diagnostic process might produce much more satisfying long-term results.

SOLUTIONS TOO SOON

Too often, though, our experience has been that once leaders have identified the problem or performance gap based on an examination of data, even if they have done a wonderful job triangulating their investigation and are convinced the problem is real and quite important, they step into a trap that discourages learning and limits innovation—namely, they jump to an obvious solution. It is a natural and almost automatic temptation that is enshrined in our understanding of leadership: A leader is someone who acts decisively and with authority to blot out problems in his or her organization. Perhaps you recognize this as an outdated notion about heroic leadership. Nevertheless, even in cases when collaborative leaders take great pains to distribute leadership, we may end up with precisely the same problem, albeit generated by a team. After a bit of dialogue (sometimes), there is an overwhelming tendency for school planning and problem-solving teams to jump to a solution: "What should we do about this?" The temptation is natural; we have a bias for action, and many times leaders and leadership teams feel more than a bit of urgency about solving the problems in their school, for moral as well as pragmatic reasons. They may also be under a great deal of time pressure (often to submit a completed plan). Unfortunately, this can lead to huge mistakes.

The reason this is problematic is that identifying the problem does not, in itself, suggest why the problem exists in your school. Consider an example: Suppose you have determined that in your high school, a significantly greater percentage of male Hispanic students drop out of school some time during their ninth-grade year when compared with students in other subgroups. The data are very clear to you. Now suppose that your ninth-grade team begins to discuss what you should do about this problem. Perhaps you would assume that there is a transition problem with students coming from middle school . . . but then, why would the impact on this subgroup be different from other student subgroups? Or maybe you would assume that it has to do with something related to the home experience of these students or an issue related to student engagement or curricular relevance. Where would you start? What actions would you take? What do you actually know about why male Hispanic ninth-graders drop out of school, in general or in the particular case of students in your school?

This example is similar to one tackled by a student of ours, who, after a thorough examination of the literature and a discovery of some otherwise unnoticed school climate data collected by leaders in his school, determined that among the causes of the drop-out problem in his school was a disproportionate rate of bullying experienced by Hispanic males as they made the transition to high school. Fundamentally, many of these students did not feel safe at school. Had the team in this school jumped to an "obvious" solution, perhaps related to student engagement or curricular relevance, they may have done some very admirable things to enhance programs and practices at the school, but it seems unlikely that they would have done much to erase the problem. Unless the primary cause(s) of the problem is erased, the problem will persist.

The evidence we use in schools to identify a problem or opportunity for improvement—such as testing data—reveals symptoms of underlying conditions that reflect a gap between where we are and where we want to be as a school. Rushing to implement the first or most easily adopted program or practice may help treat the symptoms or lead to some temporary improvement. But until we work to discover the underlying causes of these performance gaps (i.e., the reason why students are not learning at levels we have deemed successful), we are unlikely to see circumstances improve consistently over time. Indeed, if we reflect on our most persistent instructional problems, it would not be a stretch to suggest that their very persistence is an indicator that we may not have dealt with the most important of their underlying causes.

WHY ROOT-CAUSE ANALYSIS?

At a workshop for school-level administrators, we presented Dr. Brazer, school improvement consultant par excellence (conjuring up images of Johnny Carson playing Carnak the Magnificent), and then invited members of the audience to identify a persistent instructional problem in their school, which he would then solve. First, Dr. Brazer was asked about what to do in an elementary school that has a high percentage of students who are not reading at grade level. After pondering for a split second, Dr. Brazer suggested that the school could deal with this by instituting an after-school tutoring program for at-risk students. Next, a high school principal asked what to do about students who were chronically absent or tardy, and the school improvement whiz suggested that an after-school tutoring program that sought to help these students make up for lost instructional time would be just the thing. Someone then asked about problems associated with wide-ranging differences in teachers' instructional approaches, and the suggestion was to institute—you guessed it—an after-school tutoring program so that teachers could observe other teachers using effective strategies. Like Oz himself, the great and powerful Dr. Brazer had a solution for any problem, though it was the same solution regardless of the nature of the problem and was very much independent of any knowledge about the local school or school community.

The audience giggled a bit; some grimaced (appropriately). Our goal, though, was to raise an issue that impairs our effectiveness at tackling our school improvement goals and that serves as the most important reason we stress root-cause analysis as a step in improvement planning. Consider the number of times you returned to school after a summer break and were met by a new program or practice and wondered (sometimes aloud), "Why are we doing this?" or "What are we trying to accomplish here?" or "What happened to the program we started last year? I thought it was working." At times, it seems we have solutions in search of problems rather than the other way around.

Not-So-Rational Decision Making

As we first mentioned in Chapter 4, this reality is so prevalent in organizations in general—not just schools—that Cohen, March, and Olsen (1972) referred to the phenomenon in their "garbage can model" of organizational choice. These scholars were trying to reconcile the fact that while classic decision theory presumes that leaders engage in a highly rational, step-by-step process connecting problems, choices, and solutions, classic theory cannot explain the seemingly irrational choices that result in decision-making instances when there is a great deal of uncertainty or ambiguity involved. To summarize, they observed that quite often, problems and solutions are somewhat disconnected from one another and that solutions seem to have a life of their own. Some solution choices have proponents who advocate for them or who are attracted to a course of action quite independent of the problem involved. Realization that a serious problem exists may generate a rational search for solutions. In a parallel manner, however, "choice opportunities" may arise periodically quite independent of the discovery of a problem, when a program or practice might be adopted regardless of a need. And further, they noted that participants come and go in the decision-making process, and these participants may have favorite or pet problems or solutions they bring with them. Putting this all together, we can imagine choice opportunities as garbage cans in which problems and solutions are swirling around—situations in which solutions favored by participants are chosen and are in search of a problem to solve, much as the after-school tutoring program was attached to any of a variety of very real problems offered by the audience in our scenario earlier.

This is a brief synopsis of a very rich theory, and much may be lost in translation. The theory highlights, though, that we sometimes encounter solutions that are adopted quite apart from a careful analysis of a problem and certainly without any consideration of the specific causes of the problem in the context and at the time that it exists. The adoption of the "research-based practice *du jour*" in all schools in a district in one fell swoop often has this feel to it. So, too, do some policy preferences proffered by politicians as cures for the real or imagined failures of schools. There are causal assumptions lurking behind solutions such as dissolving low-performing schools or instituting merit pay schemes for teachers—assumptions that may hold for some, or even many, failing schools. But as Rothstein (2004) observes, these preferred solutions share a narrow view of what causes persistently low achievement for some groups of students, placing the onus squarely on schools while ignoring issues relating to the social and economic conditions of students' lives.

Digging Deeper

As we will discuss in the next chapter, one of the primary reasons we need to consult the published literature is to learn what there is to learn about likely causes of the problem or issue you believe needs to be addressed in your school and work toward selecting solutions that will serve to eliminate one or more of these causes. This is a step we often ignore or skip, grabbing the list of ready-made "best practices" touted by peers, central office administrators, the popular and trade literature, and your own prior experience. But jumping to the first readily available solution may lead you astray.

Chances are, the problem you identified has a multitude of causes, some obvious and some not so obvious. An effective approach to remedying the problem necessitates that you aim your actions at eliminating *causes* rather than treating *symptoms*. And that list of ready-made solutions that everyone knows will work? Well, the truth is that some best practices describe more effective methods to realize the gains you seek. But *every best practice has embedded in it a logic of action regarding the causes of the underlying problem it is intended to improve.* The leader's role, quite simply, is to deeply understand the nature of the problem in his or her school at this time and with the teachers and student body that currently exist so that an effective decision can be made regarding what action to take to improve student learning. Ultimately, which best practice to adopt depends on matching what we know about the causes of the performance gap with what is known about which strategies work under what conditions with which kinds of students and teachers and with what kinds of resources in support of the effort.

ACTIVITY 6.1   Roundtable Discussion: What Are the Root Causes?

To emphasize the reality that all instructional problems have multiple causes, take the time to engage in discussion with a group of critical friends about one of the following scenarios:

- You teach in an elementary school with 560 students in Grades K through 5. Results from the state's mandated end-of-course test show that 35% of your third-graders are not reading on grade level. What are some possible reasons?

- You teach in a middle school with 780 students in Grades 6 through 8, with 28% of the student population classified as limited English proficient (LEP). Of these students, 72% qualify for free or reduced-price meals. The high school your students attend in ninth grade complains that your LEP students drop out in ninth grade at a rate that is roughly three times the school's overall average. What are some possible causes?

- You are a counselor in a high school that serves 2,300 students in Grades 9 through 12. In one of the department's regular monthly meetings, the chair reports that the incidence of absences and tardies among ninth-graders this year is much higher than in previous years. What are some possible reasons?

In your exploration, discuss which causes you believe the school might have an opportunity to impact and which seem beyond your control. You might also make a list of questions you would like answered in order to do a better job brainstorming causes—what sort of information would help you have more confidence in your deliberations?

WHAT IS ROOT-CAUSE ANALYSIS?

Earlier in the book, we commented that very often our students describe instructional problems in terms of test scores: (Some subgroup of) students in (such-and-such a grade) score low in (some subject). Our response is to point out that test scores are not the problem; rather, they are a symptom of some problem. Symptoms are the visible, surface-level manifestations of a gap between the *real* and the *ideal*—where you are versus where you want to be. They serve as a red flag that draws attention to an issue that is in need of attention (Preuss, 2007). A root cause is an *underlying reason* a problem exists. Most instructional problems have a variety of causes; the business of teaching and learning is a complex social phenomenon that is dependent on a great many things, some of which the school controls but a great many that it does not. The process of root-cause analysis, in our experience, involves mining what is known (the published literature as well as local craft knowledge) to discover the most likely reasons why a problem exists in our school with our students at this time and then determining which causes we can influence or manipulate. As Preuss summarizes, the notion is that if we can treat or "dissolve" the root cause(s), the problem may be eliminated or substantially reduced.

The concept of root cause is depicted in Figure 6.1. Very simply, symptoms represent the visible, surface-level warning signs that suggest to us that there may be a need for change. Thus, the fact that 30% of fourth-graders do not score at a proficient level on their end-of-term reading comprehension exam is a symptom of an underlying problem. This result, in and of itself, says nothing to us about *why* these students are not succeeding. Suppose, for example, our fourth-grade teachers met as a faculty and spontaneously adopted a new reading series to deal with this problem or that they decided to create an after-school tutoring program (perhaps after attending a session with the aforementioned school improvement guru) or that they agreed on different student grouping patterns or determined that next year they would spend more time on reading comprehension strategies or agreed that the third-grade curriculum needed to change to better prepare students for the rigors of fourth grade. Or maybe a particularly persuasive teacher leader convinced everyone that students' vocabulary skills were weak and contributed to students' comprehension difficulties or that the real reason this happened was that the students who failed did not have adequate reading material at home. Without root-cause analysis, it is possible to get trapped in a shotgun approach to solving school problems. Suppose we adopted the perspective advocated by the most persuasive teacher among us and adopted a "word of the week" strategy to improve vocabulary. This may be of value, but

Figure 6.1   Why Causes Are So Important

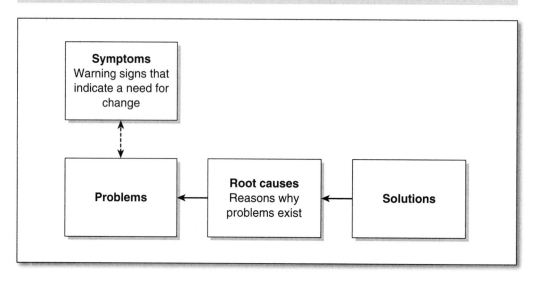

it also seems that the leap to action would be based largely on the need to do something, almost anything, as quickly as possible. When we consider the possibilities outlined above, many actions seem plausible answers to the symptom. Which would be most effective?

Our plea, quite simply, is to take the time to investigate thoroughly the various kinds of causes of the underlying problem, basing this investigation on available literature and evidence; engage in a systematic analysis of which causes the school can truly influence; and craft solutions that seem most likely to eliminate one or more of these causes. Complex, long-standing problems are seldom erased by one action, but continuous improvement necessitates eliminating causes that we have some power to eliminate. Over time, through a process of analysis and reflection, it is quite possible to create lasting improvement by removing underlying causes of the instructional gaps you identified.

Developing a Logic of Action

The process we suggest resembles, in several regards, the one outlined by City, Elmore, Fiarman, and Teitel (2009) in their book on the use of instructional rounds to improve teaching. Borrowing from the work of Argyris and Schön

(1978), they remind us that leaders who confront complex instructional problems in their schools need to develop a coherent *theory of action* to describe a causal story about how they believe things work. "The more concrete the theory and the more it relates to the specific context in which participants work," City et al. write, "the more likely it is to be useful" (p. 43). Participants in the City et al. study often started with abstract theories of action, connecting fairly general ideas and processes, but an iterative process of making the theory more concrete and specific to the problem at hand served to make it more useful. They go on to say,

We encourage people to state their theories of action as if-then proposi-tions, in part to stress the causal nature of the statements and in part to reinforce that these are testable propositions that should be subject to revi-sion if the goal is improved learning. (p. 42)

A NOTE ON CAUSE AND EFFECT

We have been talking about root-cause analysis throughout this chapter—indeed, from the outset of the book—as if the principles associated with cause and effect are widely understood. Well, in a sense they are. In our everyday usage, we under-stand that if I trip and skin my knee, this action "caused" a rip in my pants and some immediate pain, perhaps even the lingering stiffness I experience the follow-ing morning. Such attributions are relatively simple. In contrast, though, what "caused" third-graders as a group to score poorly on an end-of-course reading test is another matter.

Kenny (1979), in his book *Correlation and Causality*, describes in great detail the requirements for making a causal attribution, which we will summarize here. First, any causal statement has two components: a cause and an effect. Second, three conditions need to be present to be able to say that a cause produced an effect:

Time precedence: For A to have caused B, it must have happened beforehand. Until or unless time travel becomes common, causal relationships must have a very spe-cific temporal order: The cause must precede the effect.

Relationship: In a statistical sense, we say that for A to cause B, the two variables must have a relationship, in contrast to being independent. As Kenny (1979) observes, two things are independent if knowing something about one tells you absolutely nothing

(Continued)

(Continued)

about the other. If variables are related, knowing something about one tells you something important about the other. In statistical terms, we might say that the factors are associated or correlated; tests of "statistical significance" can affirm this.

Nonspuriousness: This criterion is a bit harder to explain, and in practice it is a lot harder to affirm. As Kenny (1979) writes, "For a relationship between X and Y to be nonspurious, there must not be a Z that causes both X and Y such that the relationship between X and Y vanishes once Z is controlled" (p. 4). So, to cite a classic example, there is a strong *correlation* between shoe size and verbal ability in young students (i.e., as youngsters' feet grow, their verbal ability also improves). But to claim a cause-and-effect relationship here would be faulty, since it ignores the fact that both phenomena may be explained by a third factor, getting older.

One reason it is so important to probe deeply into the question of what causes the instructional problems identified in schools is to adequately account for the many factors that may need to be considered as contributing to the problem (i.e., to more deeply understand the nature of the problem and create your theory of action—your model of what's going on and why—so that change efforts can be most effective).

In a similar fashion, the process of root-cause analysis involves crafting a proposition that describes what you believe about the specific causes of the instructional problem you discovered in your school. We use the term *logic of action*, rather than *theory of action*, to convey the idea that your propositions should try to explain the reasons the outcomes or processes you are trying to explain happen in your school and why. The "logic" you are proposing is a cause-and-effect rationale to explain the reality in your school. This serves as a bridge to discovering possible actions you might take to promote improvement. As City et al. (2009) put it, this provides a story line that allows you to focus activity on changes that matter most in terms of the instructional improvement you seek; it makes both your vision and strategy concrete and explicit. Later, as you consider how you will plan and then evaluate your actions, a clear logic of action makes it possible for you to deliberately test your propositions about what's going on in your school and why, promoting the kind of learning from your research that promises to generate continuous improvement.

ACTIVITY 6.2   Roundtable Discussion: Finding the Logic of Action

Consider the study described below, and with one or more critical friends, see if you can discern the logic of action embedded in the study. You might draw a concept map to depict these ideas—a flow chart that labels the significant concepts or *constructs* that are important to the study and their presumed relationships.

> This study involves examining the effectiveness of a mentoring program for new principals. For this study, each of five countywide school systems is hiring their own staff of coaches, who are being trained in a very particular coaching model that involves focusing leadership on instructional improvement. Each coach is being trained in the model. Each coach will work with between five and eight new principals.
>
> Of the five counties involved, two are urban, two suburban, and one rural. During the first year, each urban district has 10 new principals, one suburban district has 17, one has 12, and the rural district has 4 new principals. There are 8 high schools, 12 middle schools, and the remainder elementary school sites.
>
> The rationale for doing this project is that often, new principals are left to themselves to learn the ropes, and nationwide, the retention rate for new principals is of great concern. Research has shown that turnover is costly and disruptive to the learning environment. Further, new principals often get absorbed in the administrative demands of the job and seem to pay less attention to instructional leadership. It is believed that the presence of a mentor to help support new principals will result in improved supervision and thus better teaching and, ultimately, better student performance.

Discuss each of the following:

- What is the program, or *treatment,* that is being studied?

- What *outcomes* (i.e., dependent variables) are being studied?

- What are the attributes that we believe will impact the outcomes (i.e., what are the *independent variables*) that we might be interested in measuring?

What kinds of things might confound our understanding of the relationships between the independent and dependent variables? What additional attributes might we need to account for or control?

STEPS TO COMPLETE ROOT-CAUSE ANALYSIS

The actual process of conducting a root-cause analysis was popularized in education and other fields as a critical step in the problem-solving progression associated with total quality management (TQM). Bonstingl (1992), for instance, includes among his "seven traditional tools" for TQM several techniques for generating ideas about root causes and then analyzing the degree to which these causes contribute to identified problems. Ishikawa (1985) associates the "analysis" phase of quality circle activities with "probing into causes" (p. 147), which is a critical bridge between assessing the current situation and discovering solutions or "corrective measures" en route to promoting continuous improvement. (Ishikawa, incidentally, is credited with developing one of the most often-used structured brainstorming techniques used in root-cause analysis, the fishbone diagram, which we will introduce below.)

To reiterate some points we have already made, we believe that the first important step needed to begin to develop a deep understanding of your problem is to have one or more guiding questions—that is, to be very clear about what knowledge you seek to gain as well as the purposes you have for your inquiry and to ensure that your problem statement is not stated as a solution. Using your questions as a springboard, take a balanced approach that is informed by what others have found and represented in the published literature and field-based work you and your colleagues conduct in your school. We suggest that you may start at any point, but be certain to include in your root-cause analysis process consulting the literature, having targeted conversations with colleagues at your school, and further probing available evidence at your school.

Returning to the point we made earlier in this chapter, an important part of the goal here is to create a definite logic of action that spells out the nature of the original problem and your hypotheses about why the problem exists (in terms of the causes you isolate as most important) and then work toward a course of action and a rationale describing why taking that course of action has a high likelihood of remedying the problem. The root-cause analysis and your subsequent identification of one or more solutions are informed by published research, balanced with local knowledge amassed by teacher leaders.

Consulting the Literature

Surprisingly, there is little mention in the management or problem-solving literature about consulting the existing knowledge base as a part of conducting root-cause analysis. We advocate that your inquiry into the root causes of the problem you identified include consulting the extant literature to learn about the topic and discover what is known about why problems such as yours tend to exist in schools. As such, we suggest that the first focusing question for your review of literature should be,

"What is known about why (this problem) exists in schools such as ours?"

This question provides specific focus to the initial inquiry and would serve to direct you to literature that has the greatest relevance to your school improvement efforts, at least in the initial stages of your inquiry. How to approach the literature as a critical consumer is discussed in detail in Chapter 7.

As you read the literature, maintain a log or diary to record potential causes as you learn about them. It is important that as you do this, you record sufficient detail about the nature of the problem (is it much like the problem in your school?), the setting in which the study took place (is it similar to your school?), what the authors suggest as important causal factors, and the logic of action suggested (why do they believe that these factors caused the problem?). Note, too, any information that might be available about the boundary assumptions of the cause-and-effect claim (are there certain conditions under which this claim is made that might be important?). For instance, might it hold only in urban schools or in elementary schools or for Hispanic students? Record, as well, any reflections you may have related to the trustworthiness of the source and why you believe the hypotheses you recorded are credible. These reflections will be especially important if you find, as we often do, that there are conflicting claims made in the research. Use Worksheet 6.1 as a model for keeping your journal.

Searching for Causes in Your School

The literature is a vital part of your causal inquiry. But root-cause analysis is not a process that can be informed solely by published literature. In the best-case scenario, the literature can help you develop a coherent logic of action based on a trustworthy body of research conducted in a variety of sites, preferably schools much like yours. Studies of schools similar to yours that have problems such as the one you identified will inform your inquiry and suggest hypotheses about likely causes of the problem. However, no two schools are the same, and nothing in the literature can replace the professional judgment and collective knowledge of the teachers and leaders in your school about your local problem and what causes the situation you seek to change with your students at this point in time.

There are many tools that you can use to structure your local inquiry into the causes of the problem you are seeking to address, most of which involve some form of brainstorming with stakeholders at the school. The technique you use to compile ideas about causes will depend a lot on the problem itself, whether it is a long-standing issue for the school or a relatively new one, and the scope of the problem. Regardless of your approach, though, an important first question involves who you will consult as "local experts" on the problem.

A Panel of Experts

A general tendency we observe is that causal inquiry often includes only those individuals whom you have ready access to in your professional life. It is extremely important, though, to be strategic in your inquiry. As a general rule, *consult the stakeholders whom you believe to have the most pertinent direct information about the nature of the problem.* For instance, if you were seeking to understand the causes of poor attendance at parent conferences, you might bring the question up at a grade-level team meeting with your colleagues. This will yield some good information. But as with all other kinds of inquiry, creating trustworthy results requires that you go beyond the obvious or easy sources and triangulate your investigation. With just a bit more effort, you could elect to involve school leaders, teachers, and parents in your investigation. You might refine this strategy by focusing first on those school leaders who are responsible for scheduling and organizing conferences; teacher leaders who have some history in the school and who might provide some perspective on trends over time; and a mix of parents, including those who have missed conferences. The latter group will be especially difficult to reach, perhaps, but they will also have the information that bears most directly on your inquiry: Who better to ask about why parents miss conferences than parents who missed conferences?

Let's take this example just a bit further. In Chapter 8, we discuss some elements of research design that will help you structure an inquiry in a more reliable fashion, but an inquiry such as the one just described need not live up to the same standard as a peer-reviewed research article or a commissioned study. Suppose you and three or four of your grade-level colleagues each agreed to phone parents of five of your students to ask whether they attended conferences, and if not, why? (Better yet, suppose you could identify parents you know did not attend conferences recently.) In a very short time, you would have evidence from 20 to 25 parents to contribute to your inquiry. The point here is a simple one: Not every inquiry needs to involve web-based surveys of hundreds of parents to be useful to you in your investigation of likely causes;

you may be able to add some very worthwhile evidence to your discussion with just a bit of effort. Worksheet 6.2 will help you lay out a plan for who you might involve and how you would involve them in your local inquiry.

Why Does the Problem Persist?

There are a few structured brainstorming activities that we have used that may help your inquiry into causes. The first is a technique from TQM called "the five whys" (Bonstingl, 1992; Preuss, 2003). Assume for the moment that any problem that you have identified has both surface-level causes and some deeper, root causes—fundamental reasons why the problem persists. The "five whys" is founded in the notion that only by repeatedly asking the question "why" will the fundamental causes of a problem be revealed.

Preuss (2003) offers an interesting example of how this might work. To paraphrase, suppose our original problem is an increase in the number of disciplinary referrals for tardiness at our high school:

- Why so many tardies? Students don't have enough time to get from class to class.

- Why don't students have time? The school reduced passing time this year.

- Why did the school reduce passing time? To reduce time students have in the halls between classes.

- Why did the school want to reduce time students have in the halls? To reduce disciplinary problems associated with goofing around between classes.

- Why did the school want to reduce disciplinary problems? To improve school climate.

Preuss (2003) observes that this example reveals not only the value of repeated "why" questions but also the fact that using the "five whys" helps reveal unintended consequences of past actions, such as trying to reduce disciplinary referrals presumably caused by having too much time in the halls resulting in an increase in referrals for tardies. In our experience, it doesn't always take "five whys" to develop a deeper understanding of the root causes of a problem, but likewise, stopping at the surface-level discussion of causes seldom reveals all you need to know.

Another structured brainstorming activity that is useful, particularly with decision-making groups, is the affinity diagram. Technically, constructing an affinity diagram is a generic technique that may be used any time you would like to mine the knowledge of a group and reduce many ideas to a relative few. The steps you can use as applied to causal analysis are as follows:

- Frame the question clearly for the group: What are the likely causes of (the problem) in our school?

- Provide each group member five or so sticky notes (or index cards), and invite them to think carefully about the problem and write one idea they have about the cause of the problem on each sticky note.

- Collect the notes—these are your "raw data."

- Assemble the group around a table or, if using sticky notes, alongside a blank wall on which you can place the notes.

- Read each proposed cause one at a time and place them on the table or wall. As you read, if an idea requires clarification, you may ask for the author to clarify, but as a brainstorming technique, it is important that the group not debate, argue, or advocate for one idea over another. The goal here is to see if there are patterns across people that reveal a degree of consensus about the probable causes of the problem.

- Place like ideas alongside each other so that you create groupings or "stacks" of ideas that relate to the same underlying cause.

When you are done placing all ideas, see if you can develop a thematic hypothesis about each grouping as a cause of the problem. Using Worksheet 6.3, which we developed as a generic tool for recording brainstormed causes, you might take each of your themes and formulate your hypothesis about how each one relates to the original problem, then record evidence you may have available to support this assertion.

A graphic organizer that you can use to facilitate brainstorming causes is the fishbone diagram. The fishbone diagram, developed by Kaoro Ishikawa, got its name because of its general shape (Bonstingl, 1992). The fishbone can be used as an organizer for brainstormed ideas you have gathered or as a group process technique. Using the generic format presented in Figure 6.2, write the problem statement as the effect—it is the outcome you are trying to explain by indentifying causes. The larger "bones" of the fish are represented by broad categories or themes, and the smaller bones are contributing causes that fit into the theme. In the original formulation in the context of TQM in industry, quality circles often started with the four "M" themes: man, machine, method, material. In a school context, Preuss (2003) suggests curriculum, instruction, student demographics,

Figure 6.2   The Fishbone

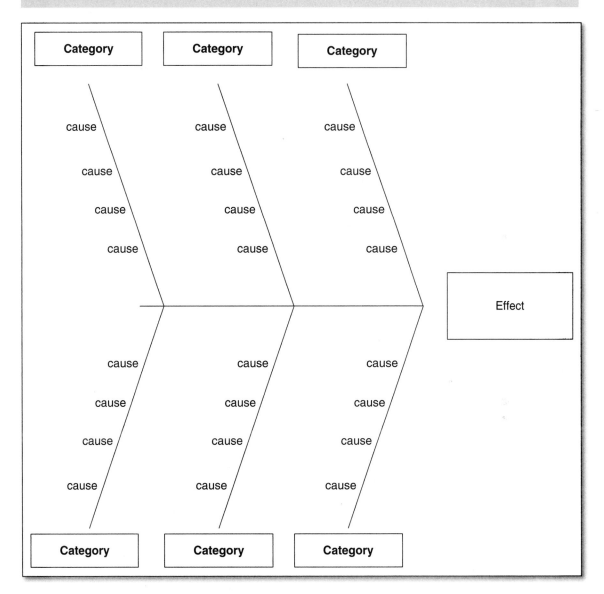

and system processes. Our preference would be to develop the themes inductively, depending on the nature of the problem you are addressing. Although the fishbone can be used as a stand-alone activity for groups, we would suggest using it together with an activity such as the affinity diagram—draw your fishbone on butcher paper; you can array the sticky notes thematically as "small bones" and develop themes based on your collective wisdom about the nature of the problem. A completed fishbone, then, would array your team's ideas graphically and result in a visual representation of the thematic causes of the original problem.

Putting It All Together

Having consulted the literature and conducted a thorough local inquiry into the likely causes of the problem you identified in your school, you may be awash in ideas. As we noted earlier, few instructional problems have just one or two likely causes. But asking why the problem persists puts you a great deal closer to constructing a solution that has a chance to create lasting improvement. Two additional steps will help you proceed.

First, at the outset of this chapter, we implored you to take the time necessary to investigate the various kinds of programs, processes, and practices that may serve as causes to the problem you identified, basing this investigation on available literature and local evidence, and then to consider which causes the school can truly influence. Assuming that you have used Worksheet 6.3 to assemble your list of causes, along with brief statements of your hypotheses about how each cause contributes to the problem and the evidence you have available to support the claim, ask the following question about each: To what degree can the school influence this cause? Many factors that affect student learning, such as family upbringing or genetic factors, are well beyond the reach of the school. It makes no sense investing time and energy trying to alleviate these causes. Discuss with your team which of the causes you believe the school can truly influence (but do not spend a lot of time debating this yet). Create a fresh list, using the same worksheet format, including only those causes you feel you can influence.

Next, we suggest you and your team conduct an informal Pareto analysis for the remaining causes. Vilfredo Pareto, an economist, suggested that for any problem, there are relatively few causes that are responsible for the majority of a problem. The quality management guru Joseph Juran (1992) used his research to formulate the Pareto Principle, noting that for any problem, there are a "vital few and trivial many" (p. 68) causes. Quality experts might suggest that you create a Pareto chart, which involves collecting data on the frequency of various causal factors and arrays this information graphically to show which causes are among the "vital few." In our experience, though, few instructional problems lend themselves to this kind of precise accounting. However, this does not lessen the importance of the question: Among the remaining causes you believe your school can influence, which are most potent, representing the "vital few" factors that account for the majority of the problem?

Our suggestion, then, is that as a last team activity, you engage in a dialogue about the relative import of the remaining causes, focusing on developing a rank order of these causes in terms of their contribution to the problem. Using Worksheet 6.4, reorder the causes in terms of the percentage contribution you estimate they make to the problem, such that the total contribution is 100%. Record, as well, the evidence you used to come up with your ranking (which may include published literature, craft knowledge gleaned from stakeholders, data you consulted and collected, and so on).

We acknowledge that this ranking process is far from a precise science, but consider what you will have accomplished by engaging in this stage of the analysis: You will have developed a deep understanding of the nature of the problem you identified using research literature; tapped into the collective wisdom of stakeholders who know your school, your students and staff, and the community; explored data that you collected related to the problem; and synthesized this knowledge to develop a series of hypotheses about the most significant causes of the problem. You are poised now to approach the process of identifying actions, or solutions, that serve to lessen or eliminate one or more of the significant causes of the problem, thereby creating significant improvement in teaching and learning in your school.

REVIEW QUESTIONS

1. What is the difference between problem articulation and root-cause analysis?

2. How might discovering root causes help with the articulation of a logic of action for your school improvement project?

3. What are some useful sources for determining root causes?

WORKSHEET 6.1   Journal of Causes Found in the Literature

For each article you find that helps you identify possible causes of the problem, use the following guide questions to record your reflections:

Full bibliographic citation:
What is the problem being studied?
What is the cause(s) of the problem?
What is the logic of action—why is this thought to be a cause?
What are the "boundary assumptions" (i.e., conditions under which the cause-effect relationship is thought to hold)?
What are your thoughts about the trustworthiness of this claim? Any limitations?

WORKSHEET 6.2   Planning Your Local Inquiry Into Causes

Statement of the problem:

Stakeholders Who Have Direct Knowledge of the Problem	Method for Involving Them in the Inquiry

WORKSHEET 6.3   Recording Potential Causes

Statement of the problem:		
Cause	**Hypothesis (This is a cause because . . .)**	**Evidence to Support This Claim**

WORKSHEET 6.4   Informal Ranking of Causes

Statement of the problem:

Cause	Percentage Contribution to Problem	Evidence to Support This Claim
	Total: 100%	

CHAPTER 7

FINDING SUPPORTIVE LITERATURE

LEARNING OUTCOMES

Readers who grasp the most important ideas from this chapter will be able to

- articulate their research problem and guiding questions;
- grasp the nature of the task of searching published research for root causes and potential solutions;
- understand the differences among various kinds of published research sources; and
- use various databases and websites to locate important published work.

The first application of research used to lead school improvement involved accessing information about your school to begin to identify issues that warrant attention—gaps between the *real* and the *ideal*. Having thought deeply about these unique situations at your school and having accessed a variety of data to triangulate your inquiry and build trust in your initial conclusions, the next steps involve a different kind of inquiry: discovering what others have learned and written about these kinds of issues and how they affect teaching and learning in schools. In the last chapter, we discussed root-cause analysis as a critical step that includes two components: accessing what is known about such problems in schools similar to yours by exploring published literature and conducting action research in your own school focused on discerning likely causes. In this chapter, we will review how to conduct "library" research in support of the problem, challenge, or gap that you are interested in addressing as a leader in your school.

The word *library* is in quotations in the previous paragraph because, while we think of accessing the formal knowledge base as library research, with today's information technologies, the library is typically at your fingertips, connected to you through a keyboard, computer screen, and high-speed Internet connection. Thus, it may be more appropriate to think of published literature as residing in a "knowledge base" that exists in both print and electronic media, rather than a physical library. The ready availability of information is a powerful gift; the quality and quantity of knowledge available to us at the click of a button is literally breathtaking compared with what might have been accessible a short time ago. This gift, however, is not entirely cost-free; ready access to huge volumes of information brings new meaning to the term *caveat emptor*. With access to high-quality, published resources comes access to material that is offered by well-meaning people with an agenda, information that is intended to persuade and convince, advertisements masquerading as published work, and sometimes, flat-out lies.

Our goal in this chapter is to provide you with some systematic ways of thinking about the kinds of sources you might use to inform your decision making and how to go about finding them. We will spend considerable time focusing on building trustworthiness (i.e., strategies that ensure that the information you collect is reliable). By the end of the chapter, you will learn some tactics to apply to unearth the literature that will help you diagnose and articulate the causes of the achievement challenge you have identified, and you will learn some first steps toward identifying potential solutions.

ACTIVITY 7.1   Perusing the Web

While it seems unlikely in this day and age that readers need much of a demonstration of the vast resources available electronically, it is nonetheless worth a few minutes to explore both the virtues and the potential land mines that reside at the other end of Internet search engines.

With one or more critical friends, conduct an Internet search to try to find a clear and compelling answer to one of the following questions. En route, discuss the relative merits of the sources you uncover.

1. What are the likely benefits and costs to reducing class size in all grade levels of a school system?

2. Should states take steps to increase the number and variety of charter schools?

3. Should students who fail to demonstrate proficiency on state-mandated assessments be retained and repeat the same grade until they demonstrate proficiency?

4. In your state, what percentage of school-age students are home-schooled? What are the most common reasons parents elect to home-school their children?

WHY ACCESS THE LITERATURE?

As we discussed in the previous chapter, having identified with reasonable certainty a problem or issue you believe needs to be addressed in your school, the temptation is to jump to a solution, to decide on an action that you believe will "fix" the problem. This temptation is exacerbated by a pool of all-purpose solutions touted by peers, neighboring schools, popular literature, and your own practical experience. Jumping to the first readily available solution is problematic on a number of levels. First and foremost, an effective approach to remedying the problem necessitates that you aim your actions at eliminating *causes* rather than treating *symptoms*. Second, even if you are reasonably certain of the causes of the problem, a multitude of possible solutions may be available, some of which may suit your situation much better than others. A solution may fit better for a variety of reasons: It may be more efficient or effective than others; some may better complement existing programs and practices; the physical, human, or fiscal resources may be readily available to ensure success for some solutions but not others; and so on. Additionally, there may be considerable evidence available on how effective various solutions are apt to be and under what circumstances these solutions might work best. Ignoring this information seems foolhardy.

Consulting the knowledge base, then, has two distinct purposes for leaders interested in improving their schools. First, researching what is known about the problem you have identified allows you to learn about the kinds of factors that are known to cause the problem in schools such as yours. Suppose, for example, that you discovered that sixth-grade boys were performing significantly lower than girls on your state's criterion-referenced math examination. Gaining an understanding of what is known about why an achievement gap might exist between sixth-grade boys and girls in mathematics will help you better understand the nature of the problem and may also help you craft more precise questions about programs and practices in your school. As you deepen your understanding of the problem and the nature of why problems like this tend to exist, consulting the knowledge base on the kinds of programs and practices that are effective at eliminating the root causes will also help you select appropriate actions that have the greatest likelihood of success.

THE RESEARCH BRIEF AS A REVIEW *FOR* RESEARCH

To find relevant and trustworthy literature and to assess this literature critically, leaders need to develop the skills associated with accessing the knowledge base on questions that are important to the understanding and improvement of teaching and learning. In the process, you will use the sources you collect to provide a synthesis of the knowledge base, a document we call the Research Brief, which we presented in the introduction to Part III. For our purposes, a research brief is a type of *literature review* or compilation of published work on a topic that both summarizes and evaluates what is known on the topic. Strictly speaking, there are many kinds of literature reviews—there are reviews that are intended to be stand-alone documents that pull together what is known on a subject or question; literature reviews that are part of research proposals, theses, or dissertations that are intended to highlight aspects of research related to a study and/or to propose a conceptual framework for the study; and reviews that serve to situate research findings within what is known on a subject (*What Is a Literature Review?* n.d.).

In a debate over the merit of different approaches to the literature review in doctoral research, Maxwell (2006) makes a distinction that informs our application here: There is a difference between reviews *of* research and reviews conducted *for* research. The former focuses on coverage, being "encompassing," and summarizing a field for a wider audience. Indeed, there are scholarly journals devoted to this kind of review with papers designed specifically to pull together all the research that informs us about a specific question or topic. The latter, in contrast, is intended to inform a planned study or action to create a focus and justification for a question, position, or course of action. The key element in this type of review is relevance to the intended purpose, rather than being all-encompassing or exhaustive. It is this type of purposeful review that we suggest.

Another big difference between our Research Brief and a formal literature review is the intended audience: As a school leader, you need to address your discussion of research to a *practitioner audience* that is interested in participating with you in some activity aimed at improving your school. Thus, we suggest that you write your Research Brief with your school's improvement team in mind as the audience, informing members of the team about what is known on the topic you selected and ultimately persuading the team regarding an approach to the problem.

ACTIVITY 7.2   Reading Research I: A Discussion Protocol

As you begin to access the extant literature, it is important to develop a degree of familiarity with the way research knowledge is communicated, to become comfortable with the genre, and ultimately, to develop the capacity to read critically. In this chapter, we will suggest several "Reading Research" activities, which would ideally be done in groups, to help you in this endeavor.

(Continued)

(Continued)

For the first Reading Research activity, work with a group to select an article on a topic that you have agreed is a high priority for your schools or that at the very least focuses on a topic of general interest to your group. For an initial activity, select something from a particularly accessible source—for instance, *Educational Leadership* or *Phi Delta Kappan*. (Make sure the piece is intended to communicate research findings, either original research or a synthesis on a topic of interest.)

Each member of the group should read the article and identify a small number of quotes from the article that captured something important—an important theme of the work, an idea that appealed to him or her, or perhaps something that was troubling. Complete the following steps together:

- Pick someone to be the presenter. The person on his or her right will serve as timekeeper.
- The presenter takes *3 minutes* to share his or her quotes and speak briefly (THREE minutes, timekeeper) about why these quotes were selected.
- Going in a clockwise direction, each member of the group then has a *1-minute* opportunity to respond to the presenter's comments. Feel free to agree, disagree, add to, or dispute something you heard (respectfully, of course).
- Members of the group LISTEN TO but do NOT RESPOND as each person speaks. (Don't let this become a debate.)
- When everyone has spoken, the original presenter takes an opportunity to respond to the group's comments for *1 minute*. Focus these comments on what you learned from others' comments.

Repeat this protocol in your group until everyone has had a chance to speak.

To debrief, discuss your collective reactions to the piece, how members of your group decided what was important to share, and what conclusions (if any) you were able to make based on your reading of the piece. What did you learn? How, or in what ways, might you consider the article to be trustworthy?

Practicing What We Preach: A Brief on Writing a Brief

While the performance of writing a research brief is somewhat different from doing an academic literature review, to write this chapter, we approached our task by practicing what we preach: We consulted the published literature on writing research syntheses. Primarily, this literature provides advice on writing literature reviews for academic audiences; so we will be selective in drawing from this literature, being careful to interpret the guidance provided for our specific purposes. Nonetheless, our efforts provide a reasonable model for the work we suggest you do to access the literature to inform your work.

1. We clarified our purpose and started with a clear guiding question: What does published work suggest we do to access current research literature to produce a synthesis of what is known on a topic of interest to school leaders?

2. We devised a strategy for accessing different kinds of literature. In our case, after considering our options and doing some brief legwork, we determined that a reasonable strategy would be to rely primarily on websites posted by university research libraries, augmented by a small selection of research texts already in our personal libraries. Although these research texts and academic publishers offer some guidance for our task (including books written specifically as guides to writing literature reviews), even a cursory investigation reveals that there is a tremendous wealth of up-to-date and highly accessible information on the task of writing a literature review provided via the web from highly knowledgeable and credible sources: research librarians.

3. We used online databases to search the web for useful information to inform our synthesis. Given the huge amount of information on the topic, we scanned available resources and selected exemplars that we will use to inform our work. Note that our goal was not to "cover the universe" or to review all that is known on the topic. Just as we suggest that the goal of your Research Brief be a purposeful rather than an exhaustive review, ours is to inform a set of recommendations for action. It is not important that we "cover" every available source but, rather, that we select trustworthy sources and craft our report in a fashion that is highly informative and usable for your purposes.

4. We read the material we collected, dissected what we felt to be most important, and crafted the following.

THE LITERATURE: WHAT AND WHY?

What is a literature review?

- Review of research vs. review for research
- "What is known about (insert your research topic)?"
  - What are some likely CAUSES of the problem cited in the literature?
  - What kinds of treatments or interventions are most often cited as effectively addressing the underlying causes of the problem?

(Continued)

(Continued)

Purposes: Consulting the knowledge base has *two distinct purposes* for leaders interested in improving their schools:

- Researching what is known about the problem you have identified allows you to learn about *the kinds of factors that are known to cause the problem in schools like yours.*

- Consulting the knowledge base on the kinds of programs and practices that are effective at eliminating the root causes will help you *select appropriate actions* that have the greatest likelihood of success.

Why do we bother?

- To document *what is known* on a topic

- To *justify the need for action* (identify what is known about the subject, prevalence of the problem, reasons why the problem is important)

- For your school improvement projects, to help you *identify causes* of the gap between your school's performance and goals and to eventually help you *identify actions* (solutions)

How?

- Start with guiding questions:
  - What is known about why [this problem] exists in schools like ours?
  - What actions have been shown to effectively eliminate the causes of [the problem] in schools like ours?

- Devise a strategy for accessing the literature
  - Keywords
  - Identify likely sources

- Access literature and sift through available evidence
  - Using online search engines
  - Trustworthiness and the World Wide Web

- Read, dissect, synthesize

We encourage you to use our guidance as a starting point and to take a lesson from our strategy: Take advantage of the resources readily available to you locally. If you are enrolled in a leadership preparation program while using this book, you have ready access to the college or university library, research librarians, your college or university's writing center, and so on. If you are a practicing school leader, use professional library resources provided by the district, local or regional higher education institutions, or the public library. Augment what we offer with what you can find doing a search similar to the one we did: Use available search engines to identify up-to-date guides for completing your tasks, including sources that inform you on how to write a research brief as well as those that point you to sources of knowledge to inform your topic.

To foreshadow an important point we will make below, we live in an age that is distinguished by the pace of knowledge creation itself, as well as the immediacy with which knowledge is shared, making it feasible for your present inquiry to be based on a wealth of information that may not have been available just a short time ago. There is great opportunity here if you learn to use it well. There is also peril, for another distinguishing feature of the means available to share knowledge through the web is huge variability in the quality of work that is available at the click of a mouse. This makes it vitally important that you learn to use good judgment in culling information you use to inform your decisions.

Start With Guiding Questions

Creswell (2009) writes, "Once the researcher identifies a topic that can and should be studied, the search can begin for related literature on the topic" (p. 25). The first step we recommend for writing your Research Brief is implied in this statement: Start with one or more guiding questions. In short, be very clear about what knowledge you seek to gain to inform your perusal of current research as well as the purposes you have for your inquiry. Although this seems like a simple matter, there are some pitfalls to avoid.

For formal literature reviews such as those done for dissertations, Creswell (2005) distinguishes between research topics and research questions. In this context, a topic may be thought of as the broad issue a study is about, whereas research questions define what you want to learn about the topic by conducting your study. Quite literally, by stating the questions, you define what it is you seek to know about the topic you are studying.

An obvious point about selecting a research topic is that researchers should select topics that are important to them and that they care about or believe deserve systematic attention. The selection of a topic provides broad focus for a researcher's work; within this topic, the researcher will define more specific issues or questions around which she or he will craft a position or thesis that will be the focus of the research study. Maxwell (2005) makes the point that a research problem "identifies something that is going on in the world" (p. 34), something that *justifies* the research being undertaken by defining what we need to learn more about to figure out how to deal with it. Graduate students who are required to conduct research studies often have a very difficult time defining their topic or problem, generally because their personal experiences, frustrations, or reading of existing research provides them with many possible ideas. You may encounter a similar problem, because there are many aspects of your school that require immediate attention. Therefore, articulation of guiding questions helps focus your investigation into the knowledge base on a topic relevant to you and your school.

Even after landing on a topic, another problem that plagues many doctoral students is defining questions that are researchable. Sometimes, students select questions that are trivial—they can be answered with a simple statistical inquiry. For example, if my topic of interest was "school dropouts" and I posed research questions such as, "What is the dropout rate for male students?" my work could be completed in a nanosecond with a well-targeted search. In contrast, some students phrase research questions that are too broad, making it hard to craft a study. For the same topic, for instance, suppose my question was, "What should we do about the dropout rate?" How would I design my study around such a question? Where would I start? This question is far too general.

As we already established, though, the task before you is very different from the task facing a graduate student writing a dissertation or thesis or a scholar crafting a research study. For one thing, scholars conducting original research face very different evaluative criteria—when we sit down with doctoral students or face a group of our peers as researchers, our work is judged on not only its technical quality but also on the degree of relevance (Who cares?) and its originality (What's new here that adds to the knowledge base?). For your work, technical quality is important, too, but relevance is localized (addressing a problem in your school) and originality is not important—in fact, leaders for today's schools are consistently admonished to ensure that actionable ideas are well connected to already published work.

In our experience, it is important for you to be clear about your topic and define guiding questions for your inquiry into the literature. One clear advantage you have is that for your work as a leader in your school, selecting your topic amounts to understanding the broad nature of the problem you identified through examination of data about your school. In contrast to a doctoral student facing a blank page and many years of intensive scholarly inquiry, your topic is local in nature and well defined by data available from your school or district.

We have already established the vital importance of root-cause analysis and the notion that one primary reason to consult published literature is to discover what is known about why problems like yours tend to exist. We suggest that the first focusing question for your review should be,

"What is known about why [this problem] exists in schools like ours?"

Thus, as an example, a clear focusing question might be, "What is known about why Hispanic males drop out of ninth grade in large, suburban high schools like ours?" This question provides specific focus to the initial inquiry and would serve to direct you to literature that had the greatest relevance for your school improvement efforts, at least in the initial stages of your work.

Recall that root-cause analysis is not a process that is solely informed by published literature. Indeed, to build a deep understanding of the nature of the causes of the problem you identified in your school, your inquiry needs to take a balanced approach that is informed by what others have found through disciplined inquiry and represented in the extant literature and field-based work you and your colleagues have done in your school. This is not necessarily a linear process; you might start by consulting the literature or by having targeted conversations or, as our student interested in the dropout problem did, by looking at school climate data. What is important to recognize, though, is that the likelihood of developing a deep and rich understanding of the problem facing your school is greatly enhanced by taking this kind of balanced approach. We have found that too often, leaders are constantly reminded to examine student performance data of varied kinds systematically, as if identifying the problem accurately is an end in itself. This is an important step, of course, but one that would best be construed as a step in a more involved process that leads to solutions and actions through systematic causal analysis that is informed in the fashion discussed above.

Identifying likely causes of the problem you are seeking to address is not an end, either. Your inquiry into the published literature starts with a guiding question about root causes, but your goal as a leader is informed action. The published literature has something significant to say about potential solutions, so it is important that you frame a question related to understanding and identifying the kinds of actions that have been shown to be effective in eliminating the causes of the problem you seek to eliminate. We suggest, therefore, that your second guiding question be,

"What actions have been shown to effectively eliminate the causes of [the problem] in schools like ours?"

Notice that we recommend that you probe the literature for solutions that have been shown to eliminate causes effectively. This might seem to take you far afield from your original problem statement, but the logic is consistent with the overall process we suggest: Problems are eliminated when their causes are addressed. So, to extend the example introduced earlier, if we find that male Hispanic students are dropping out of school because they do not feel safe as a result of being bullied, a solution needs to deal with student safety and the prevention of bullying. Indeed, this mirrors the case we introduced in Chapter 6, and in this instance, our student's team used the literature to identify a bullying prevention program that had been well established through systematic research to impact this problem in secondary schools, and the program was launched with the enthusiastic participation of members of the ninth-grade team at the school. Problems are eliminated or reduced by impacting their causes (not merely their symptoms).

By crafting two specific, targeted questions and using these to guide an inquiry into the causes of a problem revealed through the examination of student performance data, a definite logic of action was established that spelled out the nature of the original problem, a course of action, and a rationale describing why taking that course of action had a high likelihood of remedying the problem. The root-cause analysis and identification of an action or solution was informed by published research, balanced with local knowledge amassed by teacher leaders.

ACCESSING DIFFERENT KINDS OF RESOURCES: UNDERSTANDING RESEARCH SOURCES

Definition of a research topic and subsequent identification of specific guiding questions help identify a place to start the search for relevant work to inform the Research Brief. However, crafting an approach to search the literature requires a basic understanding of what's out there and how to evaluate critically what constitutes material that is worthwhile and trustworthy for your purposes. In short, an informed consumer of research knowledge has a strategy in mind defining where to start and how to cull through the mountain of available work "out there" that may serve as a guide toward action. To start, it is helpful to consider a few basic categories of available literature along with the advantages and disadvantages of relying on knowledge embedded in resources of these types.

Primary vs. Secondary vs. Tertiary Sources

The literature that you review comes into existence in a very specific way (*What Is a Literature Review?* n.d.). Typically, research literature is work written by scholars for scholars, at least in terms of work published in scholarly journals or in research reports written for funders of scholarly work. Researchers build on the work of others, adding to what is known on a topic by addressing questions that reflect the state of what is currently known. Thus, a first distinction that is useful in categorizing literature is whether a work is primary, secondary, or tertiary in nature.

The Purdue University library resource (*Writing a Research Paper,* 2010) observes that these terms refer to the "distance" to the original research topic. "A primary source is an original document or account that is not about another document or account but stands on its own." A primary source, then, is original, raw data or a firsthand account by the actual subjects of work done to advance knowledge on a specific research topic or question. In the humanities, primary source materials might include original accounts of historic events, diaries, or memoirs; in the sciences, primary material might include lab notes, results of experiments, and so on. Secondary sources would then include interpretation, analyses, or commentary of primary sources, including books or journal articles reporting about the findings of original research or work summarizing or criticizing others. A tertiary source would include such things as encyclopedia entries, digests, or textbook entries. These are intended to provide a general introduction to a topic or question.

The categorization of sources as primary vs. secondary can get a bit confusing since the distinction is somewhat field-specific. For our purposes, the distinction made on the Ithaca College library web resource (*Primary and Secondary Sources,* 2010) provides useful guidance:

> In the natural and social sciences, the results of an experiment or study are typically found in scholarly articles or papers delivered at conferences, so those articles and papers that present the original results are considered primary sources. (para. 1)

Secondary resources include any papers or articles that are written about primary resources, including review articles or papers that are written to evaluate or criticize original work (e.g., a book review). Thus, a review of literature on a question or topic would be considered a secondary source, since papers of this kind are intended to either provide a synopsis of what is known about a research topic or question or to advance an argument or position on a topic supported by reference to the current research literature.

It is often extremely useful to start a search for relevant research literature by working backward from tertiary or secondary sources to primary sources. Thus, a digest or textbook section relevant to a research topic may help better define the important themes associated with the inquiry and may also help direct you to high-quality primary sources. The idea here is to mine the reference list in the secondary or tertiary source and begin to identify scholars who are generating useful knowledge on a topic. While there is no replacement for your own judgment on this, if scholars or journalists who are writing on your topic consistently refer to certain scholars' work or identify a specific study or research report as critical to an understanding of the topic, this represents important data for you in your search for relevant material. Nevertheless, stopping your literature search with tertiary or secondary sources is ill advised; doing so delegates the judgment about what represents relevant and useful research knowledge to others, whose purposes may not align with yours and who certainly do not share an understanding of your specific problem or school context.

Scholarly Journals vs. Popular Magazines

The web resource on the University of California-Berkeley website (*Critical Evaluation of Resources,* 2009) describes scholarly research as work that is published "by and for experts." Before publication, a paper that is submitted for consideration for publication in a scholarly journal goes through a peer-review process. Peer review involves having a number of acknowledged experts in the field review each paper submitted for consideration to determine the paper's technical soundness, originality, and value to the field. This process is typically (though not universally) done as a "double-blind" exercise, such that the authors do not know the names of the reviewers, and the reviewers do not know the names of the authors; only the editor of the journal has this information, thus ensuring a measure of objectivity or, at the very least, safeguarding the process from favoritism or bias. The Wesleyan University library resource describes the process this way:

> When a scholar submits an article to an academic journal . . . the editors . . . will send copies to other scholars and experts in the field who will review it. The reviewers will check to make sure the author has used methodologies appropriate to the topic, used those methodologies properly, taken other relevant work into account, and adequately supported the conclusions, as well

as consider the relevance and importance to the field. A submission may be rejected, or sent back for revisions before being accepted for publication. (*What Is Literature*, n.d., "Publishing the Literature," para. 2)

Academic journals will prominently identify if they are peer reviewed in print and on the journal's website (if they maintain one) and outline the process they use for review. They will also include a list of members of their editorial board, which provides those thinking about submitting for publication and readers an opportunity to get a sense of the credentials of the individuals who do the lion's share of the reviewing. (Most journals also invite guest reviewers as a means of recruiting future editorial board members and to ensure that papers are reviewed by experts on the specific topic of the submission or who are well versed in the methodology used.)

Popular magazines may include widely read publications such as *Time* to publications the Cornell University library resource calls "substantive news," such as the *Economist* or *Scientific American* (*Distinguishing Scholarly Journals*, 2009). In some cases, articles in these publications are written by staff or freelance writers who are not typically experts on the topic, and articles are shorter and directed toward a general audience. In other cases, articles may be written by scholars with acknowledged expertise in the field, but papers are not presentations of original research. Regardless of source, articles in popular magazines are *not* peer reviewed, they are editor reviewed, meaning that decisions about publication are not vetted by an expert panel but, rather, are made by the publication's editor(s).

Some publications that fall within the genre of popular magazines are a bit harder to categorize because they publish work that clearly intends to communicate research findings. On the one hand, these publications are not directed to a general audience, and articles often contain some footnotes and a list of references. On the other, articles seldom have other components that typify original research papers, such as a clear description of research methodology, and they are editor reviewed. Prominent publications that fit within this category in our field include *Phi Delta Kappan* and *Educational Leadership*.

In contrast to papers published in scholarly journals, scholars writing papers for these publications more typically describe their research or summarize important themes that they believe a more general (often practitioner) audience would find interesting and useful. Some papers in these forums provide secondary descriptions of an original study; some papers are reviews of literature on a topic or question; others may be descriptions by scholars or practitioners about programs or practices that appear to work well in authentic school contexts. As an example, papers published in *Phi Delta Kappan* are often written by top scholars in our field, but they are best described as syntheses or summaries of original work that have been reworked to communicate research findings to practitioners and policymakers. A small number of references may be provided in these papers, directing readers to the original work published in a more scholarly venue.

ACTIVITY 7.3   Reading Research II: Discussing Original Research

In the first Reading Research activity, we suggested that you begin to access research knowledge by examining a paper from an accessible source such as *Phi Delta Kappan*. Ultimately, though, it is important to include papers from academic, peer-reviewed journals that publish findings from research studies and/or research reports made available through think tanks, funders, or government sources.

For the next Reading Research activity, select an article on a topic that you have agreed is a high priority for your schools, this time from a reputable academic journal (e.g., *Educational Administration Quarterly, Journal of School Leadership, American Educational Research Journal*). Again, make sure the piece is intended to communicate findings from an original research study, rather than presenting a literature review or synthesis.

To develop your skills, this time prepare an annotated bibliography entry based on your reading of the piece. With one or two partners, exchange your bibliographic entries and provide some constructive criticism of each other's work.

- What did each of you think of the paper? What criteria did you use to assess it?

- What were the authors' purposes in conducting the study? What were the central research questions addressed?

- What, exactly, was the method used to answer these questions? (What kinds of issues are included in the methods section?)

- What were the primary conclusions?

- Did you find the paper convincing? Why or why not?

To debrief, discuss your collective reactions to the piece, how members of your group decided what was important to share, and what conclusions (if any) you were able to make based on your reading of the piece.

- What did you learn?

- How, or in what ways, might you consider the article to be trustworthy?

- In the final analysis, what makes a "top-tier" journal top-tier?

Just as we advocated starting with tertiary or secondary sources, a useful strategy for searching the research literature may involve starting with articles in more practically oriented outlets such as trade or association magazines (e.g., *American School Board Journal, NASSP Bulletin*). These articles are especially helpful in suggesting practical applications of original research (i.e., in connecting research to practice) and thus may be worthwhile places to start a collection of materials relevant to your Research Brief. As noted, they often provide venues for top scholars to communicate research findings to broad audiences and may also provide references that can be accessed directly in subsequent searches.

For a number of reasons, though, there is no suitable replacement for identifying and accessing original journal articles in your research efforts. First, as described above, the peer review process ensures that work published in academic journals meets a high standard of quality; building your Research Brief on such work helps ensure confidence and trustworthiness in your arguments. Second, while syntheses or digests can provide thematic summaries of research work, they may not provide enough detail for you to judge how relevant a research finding might be to your school's situation or context. As we will discuss in greater detail in Chapter 8, it is important to understand the specific research questions addressed in a study and to at least skim a journal article's methods section to understand how a research study was done, the context in which the work occurred, who the participants were, and so on, all of which is valuable in understanding if the findings are pertinent to your school's context and your problem. This may be especially relevant when you get to the stage of reviewing research on specific solutions or practices that you might implement in your school—knowing where and how a program was judged to be effective may make all the difference in your decision about recommending a course of action. Finally, scholarly research articles will be much clearer about the limitations of the original research, information that is much less likely to be featured in a digest or review article that deals with many studies. Understanding these details will help you judge how relevant individual studies are for your purposes.

Journal Articles vs. Conference Papers, Proceedings, or Dissertations

There are a variety of ways scholarly work reaches readers, some of which we have already discussed. Publication in scholarly journals is only one way researchers report their findings, though, and it is increasingly possible for users of online search engines and information retrieval services to access far more than print or online journals. Among the most important of these include distribution of papers that have been presented at scholarly conferences, proceedings published as a result of a scholarly meeting, and completed dissertations.

Many scholarly organizations and associations sponsor research conferences or annual meetings for the express purpose of creating a venue for the exchange of ideas among individuals who are knowledgeable and actively working on similar research topics. In education, for instance, the Annual Meeting of the American Educational Research Association (AERA) occurs every spring, usually in April, and attracts literally thousands of scholars, policymakers, and students in all disciplines related to the advancement of knowledge in an education-related field. At present, AERA is organized into 12 divisions representing major areas of study and more than 200 special interest groups, smaller collections of scholars who share an interest in much narrower research areas (e.g., charter schools research, classroom assessment, organization theory). At AERA's annual meeting, scholars and students present their work in an assortment of forums, ranging from large keynote presentations to smaller paper discussions, poster sessions, and symposia. To present a paper at AERA, authors must submit a proposal that is blind reviewed so there is some assurance of research quality, although in contrast to submission to a peer-reviewed journal, an abbreviated abstract is reviewed rather than a completed research paper. Very often, an abstract describes work in progress or nearing completion, and it is fair to say that papers presented for feedback at the conference are more likely to be in midlife or an advanced developmental stage toward submission to a journal rather than completed and well-polished work.

AERA provides an example of an extremely large and diverse association that sponsors an annual research meeting. In addition to AERA, there are smaller regional and state research associations that sponsor annual meetings (e.g., Mid-South Educational Research Association), which are also peer reviewed, and there are many more narrowly focused scholarly associations and learned societies that sponsor annual forums for the discussion and exchange of research knowledge (e.g., International Reading Association, University Council for Educational Administration, National Council of Teachers of Mathematics). Many of these organizations publish proceedings following their meetings, which are often peer reviewed. Proceedings from research conferences may provide abstracts of papers and contact information so that an interested party can request a copy of a full paper from an author, or they may feature full text of a selected number of papers from the conference, or both.

Doctoral students completing a PhD or EdD generally produce a dissertation based on original research they have conducted to investigate one or more significant research questions in their chosen field. A dissertation must be presented to the graduate faculty at the student's college or university, and the student defends his or her work orally before it is accepted. Although dissertations are sometimes available only at the university library where the student graduates, a significant percentage of dissertations are indexed in online search engines and may be available online or through interlibrary loan. For instance, while writing this chapter, we conducted a search for dissertations online through ProQuest, a search engine to which our university library subscribes (www.proquest.com), and discovered that we could access 389 dissertations that were completed in the past 5 years on the topic "educational leadership." Of these, 378 were available online in full text.

Value Added

We already made a case for why it is important to use peer-reviewed journal articles as a cornerstone of any search for research knowledge. However, conference papers and dissertations represent additional sources of research information that deserve inclusion in your work. One of the drawbacks of the peer review process used by top research journals is that the process takes a long time; it is not unusual for work to take months, sometimes years, to reach readers of academic journals. The use of electronic means to submit and process papers through the review process speeds things up considerably compared with just a few years ago, but the fact remains that the time elapsed between a researcher conducting his or her investigation and results of that work appearing in print can be quite lengthy. The same work often appears in the form of papers presented at conferences or in conference proceedings well before it might be accepted in a journal. Research presented at conferences provides a chance for the consumer to see work "in process" and to identify scholars who are currently working on questions of importance to your school improvement efforts. Additionally, many papers presented at conferences deal with program evaluations or descriptions of projects or programs in authentic educational settings. These may be extremely useful sources for information about both the causes of problems similar to the one you are investigating in your schools or possible solutions as you move to that phase of your inquiry.

A similar set of arguments might be made in support of accessing dissertations that were recently completed on a topic of interest. This represents work that has not yet been published in journals or in a book, and the author may be a scholar-practitioner who, like you, faces challenges related to the topic in an authentic school setting. One particular advantage of dissertations is the requirement that students writing them be very clear about the research they use as a foundation for their work; most dissertations contain excellent reviews of research literature and, thus, provide a source of identifying journal articles and scholars who are writing on your topic. This also helps determine how to situate the dissertation in the field and may aid in judging how trustworthy the dissertation is as a source of research knowledge.

The primary caveat with conference papers and dissertations, compared with peer-reviewed work appearing in scholarly journals, has to do with quality. While conference papers and dissertations go through a variety of peer reviews, the fact is that only a small proportion of this work will make it into a scholarly journal. As mentioned earlier, it is no secret that papers presented at conferences are often not completely developed, and the purpose for presenting them is to get feedback from knowledgeable parties well before submission to a journal. Not all that feedback will be positive, and some of it will result in significant shifts in research procedures. Some associations, particularly regional and state-level ones, purposefully structure their conferences to encourage dialogue on work that is in an early stage; it is quite valuable for scholars who are developing research areas to hear themselves communicate about their research and to receive feedback from others. Also, many associations encourage papers that represent positions or opinions on a topic; these may be valuable to encourage dialogue on a topic or to stimulate research ideas, but they do not represent research.

Quite simply, the range of quality at many conferences can be pretty wide. Consider the typical acceptance rates at conferences compared with many scholarly journals as an indicator. It is not unusual for state or regional conferences to accept well more than half of all proposals, and national associations generally accept between a third and half of all proposals. Top journals may accept something closer to 10% to 15% of all submissions. Similarly, not all doctoral programs are the same, and standards associated with dissertation research vary. Thus, as we will describe in more detail later in this chapter when we discuss using the Internet to identify and access research sources, it is important to consider the source carefully when using conference papers and dissertations, and it is especially important to triangulate sources when relying on these types of research to ensure confidence in your conclusions.

Additional Sources of Research Knowledge

In the sections above, we have considered a variety of different categorizations for sources of research knowledge that can be applied to your search: primary vs. secondary vs. tertiary, journal vs. magazine, journal vs. conference paper vs. dissertation. One reason to provide the above information is to help you, as a consumer of research, understand some of the benefits and liabilities associated with various kinds of source materials.

Before turning to the question of how to go about collecting research publications using the Internet, it is worth mentioning that we ignored some obvious sources of research knowledge in the above discussion—for instance, books. Books that are relevant to your topic may be quite worthwhile; for one thing, book-length treatments of a topic can go into much greater depth than journal articles or can cover a wider scope of material related to your research topic. Consequently, a book on your topic might provide you with a better sense of the history of investigation on the topic or a better understanding of the controversies in the field. One factor to remember, though, is that the runway for publication of a book is even longer than for a journal article, and the vetting process for books is quite different than for research journals. Research-focused books are often published for the purpose of persuading the field about a position on a topic, advocating for adoption of a program or practice, justifying findings of a funded project, or supporting the adoption of a policy. It is therefore important to examine the espoused purpose of the book, get a sense of the tone, and be aware of the balance of the presentation of material. Books that are intended to present research findings should include a systematic discussion of methods, strengths and limitations of the research approach, a review of relevant literature, and a list of references that empowers you with the opportunity to investigate source materials. It is useful to consider the reputation of the author(s) (e.g., is the author recognizable as an authority based on other work you have been perusing?) and the prominence of the publisher (e.g., university presses often publish quality research, some learned societies publish work in their fields).

Book-length research reports are increasingly available to the public through foundation websites and search engines. In much the same sense as a research book might be thought of as a much longer journal article, a research report might be thought of as a book-length conference paper. Research reports are vetted in the sense that a funder has reviewed the work and accepted it, but most such reports are not peer reviewed in the same sense as a journal article. Similar to conference papers, the main value of a research report is that it affords the reader a chance to see firsthand results of systematic inquiry soon after completion of a project. But like conference papers, the quality of the work reported may vary greatly. Some foundations commission studies and/or reviews of literature on hot topics in their fields of interest, often by prominent scholars, and make these available in full text on their websites. As with all your work, it is prudent to be a critical consumer here, since foundations may have very particular positions to support. Likewise, think tanks with specific political agendas make advocacy and position pieces readily available, and these show up through electronic searches along with more objective material. As we will discuss below, all such searches require judgment on your part, though many of these sources will end up being worthwhile additions to your work.

Finally, another source for research knowledge might be faculty at a local university (perhaps the one in which you are currently enrolled or the one from which you received your degree), administrators or policymakers, or other experts in the field. With electronic access to prominent scholars through e-mail, it is increasingly possible to go straight to the sources of research or policy knowledge; similarly, as you begin to look for solutions to your problem, it might be possible to contact vendors who have conducted some evaluation work on a program or practice they sell to schools. While it would be foolish to rely only on personal contacts or anecdotal discussions with local experts, you would be equally mistaken to ignore such sources for your purposes. If, for instance, you were aware of a faculty member at a local university who was working on a project in your area of concern, it would seem efficient to discuss your problem with him or her or ask for direction in your work. Similarly, if an acknowledged expert on a topic works in your school system, it would seem worthwhile to pick his or her brain on the subject.

Summary

It should come as no surprise at this stage of the discussion that we believe that the most relevant, current, and trustworthy *research knowledge* on the problem you identified in your school that may inform your thinking is likely to be represented in scholarly journals. However, especially if your question deals with a relatively new or novel topic, conference papers and dissertations in the field will also likely be useful, and these sources may be augmented by books, research reports, or even personal contacts with experts. As a rule, your goal is to provide a trustworthy answer to your guiding questions related to the likely causes of the problem you identified and a persuasive argument for a course of action backed by available research knowledge. Creating your explanations and arguments will require focus, persistence, and balanced use of available knowledge. Much of this work will come to you via the World Wide Web; hence, we will now turn to the question of how to evaluate work found via electronic searches.

COLLECTING RESEARCH KNOWLEDGE: USING ONLINE DATABASES

Creswell (2009) provides useful advice on the steps to take to locate research material to conduct an academic literature review. Again, although this advice is offered primarily for aspiring scholars rather than leaders embarked on crafting a proposal for a school improvement project, much of this advice is on point for your work:

1. Begin the process by identifying a set of keywords that will be used to search for material using electronic databases or an online catalogue in a library. A helpful strategy is to identify keywords contained in or suggested by your guiding questions. Keywords may also be obvious to you based on your thinking about how to frame your problem, though it is often the case that search terms you begin with may be rather broad (e.g., dropout rate) and thus lead you to a large number of sources, only a small percentage of which relate to your specific topic. Do not despair; deriving useful search terms is an iterative process that is informed by your initial searches. As you identify useful literature, you will be able to successively identify more useful key terms.

ACTIVITY 7.4   Keyword Searches

Developing a keyword search list that you can use to start your examination of the literature is an iterative process. As you begin to access search engines and databases, you should use the results you obtain to add to or refine your list.

To start, with one or more critical friends, create a list of possible search terms by considering answers to the following:

1. What is your "problem"—write a clear statement of the original issue you identified in your Improvement Target Proposal.

2. Consider the nature of the problem you identified:
   - What instructional areas are involved?
   - What student groups are most affected?

3. What are some characteristics of your school that might help refine the search (e.g., suburban, Title 1, elementary)?

4. What other factors might delimit your search (e.g., types of sources, years searched)?

2. Access electronic databases and conduct initial searches using the keywords you identified. The searches may be conducted from any Internet-connected computer, though it may be useful to consider starting your search at a library, either at a local university or at a branch of a public library. The advantages of starting at a library include available assistance from research librarians and the opportunity to access any subscriptions the library has to computerized databases (see below).

3. Identify an initial set of sources that appear to be on target for your topic. Creswell (2009) suggests placing a priority on research articles or books, which would be a necessity for a doctoral student starting his or her work. For purposes of identifying relevant research knowledge to inform a school improvement project proposal, the strategy outlined earlier should prove useful: Begin by identifying tertiary or secondary research sources, particularly articles that are intended to review the state of the research on your topic. As you become more familiar with the research, move to primary research articles in peer-reviewed publications.

4. Procure this initial group of sources, many of which will be available in full text online but some of which will require access to library resources. Quickly skim these to get a sense of the appropriateness of the articles for your purposes. As you become familiar with the sources, refine your keyword list for subsequent searches and be sure to identify themes that appear to be prominent in the literature. Additionally, make note of the scholars whose work is cited repeatedly on the topic and mine the bibliographic references included in the articles.

5. As you identify sources that appear to be especially relevant or representative of the knowledge base on your problem, begin to draft summaries of these sources, using the format for an annotated bibliography discussed in Chapter 6.

Creswell (2009) also discusses the notion of designing a literature map or visual picture to help organize ideas in the literature. Concept mapping is a familiar teaching technique to many educators; in this case, the notion is to draw a picture connecting the many unearthed concepts that relate to the topic of your search. Since your initial efforts will be directed at understanding research knowledge that informs why problems like the one you identified in your school tend to exist (i.e., the causes of the problem) and your later efforts will be directed at identifying possible solutions, it would be useful to think about constructing two such concept maps: one that depicts how various causes relate to your problem and another that shows how various solutions address important causes of the problem and thus reduce or eliminate the problem. As we discussed in Chapter 6, this may be helpful in clarifying the *logic of action* you use to explain why you believe enacting the program or practice you recommend will lead to achievement of the educational improvements you identify, thus reducing or eliminating the problem you identified.

What's Behind the Search

Before beginning the search, it may be useful to step back and consider how search engines work. There are two broad types of search engines: automated "crawler-type" engines and human-powered indexes. A crawler-type engine creates its listings using an automated computer program, or "spider." The spider accesses a webpage, follows pages that are linked to it, and then creates an index or catalogue based on the content of these webpages. One important feature of automated search engines is that when webpages are changed, the catalogue is updated with the new information. When a search is conducted, the program searches the pages that have been catalogued to find matches and rank them based on relevancy. It is important to note that while crawler-based search facilities are generically the same, there are differences based on the programs used to run the systems (*How Search Engines Work*, 2007). For instance, Google's PageRank algorithm is a patented automated system that yields the page rankings it returns when each search is conducted (Strickland, n.d.). Barlow (2004) points out that while some search engines index every word on a webpage, others index only parts based on some defined algorithm. Unless authors of webpages define keywords for their documents, users may be dependent on the search engines to accurately identify key terms. The differences between search engines based on these subtle variations suggest that it is worthwhile to use multiple automated engines to conduct your search, in effect triangulating search results.

Human-powered indexes depend on people to create their listings. The Educational Resources Information Center (ERIC) is a good example of this type of database. Whereas crawler-type systems automatically troll the web and periodically update newly posted or changed webpages and use automated means to identify keywords and create indexes of web contents, human-powered systems rely on descriptions that are submitted to the index. Searches thus result in a list of matches based on a review of the descriptions or listings provided by authors. This ensures that search terms authors believe to be most associated with their research are linked to their work. Services such as ERIC publish a thesaurus of descriptors used to index papers, which may be perused in preparation for conducting a search to ensure accuracy and target a search. Additionally, each listing returned through an ERIC search includes a list of the keywords associated with each paper, which may be used to refine future searches and access papers on like topics.

The text box on the following page features a listing of some places to start searching for research on the Internet. We include a number of free, open-access search engines; subscription databases that may be available through a university or public library; and web resources made available through government agencies, learned societies, associations, and/or think tanks. Consistent with the strategy discussed above, we recommend using multiple types of search engines, taking advantage of resources that help you identify published work; unpublished conference presentations and/or dissertations; and work sponsored by foundations, government agencies, or associations.

Managing Your Search

The University of Queensland library offers some additional advice for managing the search for research literature (*Making Sense of the Literature*, n.d.). First, decide on a system for organizing your search, including a means for keeping track of your keyword search strategy and for recording bibliographic information and some reflection on the utility of various sources. One approach that works for us is keeping a journal, which can be done in a spiral or loose-leaf notebook (the latter affords the flexibility of inserting copies of material printed as a result of a web search).

Once you know how you will record your progress, take a "first pass" at the literature: "When you first come to an area of research, you are filling in the background in a general way, getting a feel for the whole area, an idea of its scope, starting to appreciate the controversies, to see the high points, and to become more familiar with the major players" (*Making Sense of the Literature*, n.d., para. 4). As noted earlier, restrict your first searches to the most recent sources and focus on identifying some review pieces that serve to outline the themes associated with the area you identified. Use these sources to get a feel for the important questions, conclusions, and controversies; identify the "heavy hitters" in the field, scholars whose work is recognized as prominent or who have informed policy and practice; and refine your keyword searches using descriptors associated with papers that appear to you to be especially promising. As the Queensland material suggests, "This begins your first step in making sense of the literature. You are not necessarily closely evaluating it now; you are mostly learning through it" (para. 7). In the early stages of your search, focus on getting a broad sense of what's out there, refine your search approach, and begin to amass some understanding of how you might best evaluate work on the topic you are investigating. And remember, focus initially on understanding the nature of the problem and its likely causes, only later shifting to a search for solutions or programs that may be useful for promoting improvement.

SEARCHING FOR LITERATURE USING THE INTERNET

Free Search Engines

In addition to general-purpose search engines such as Google and Yahoo that have become a part of daily life for anyone connected to the Internet, the freely available search utilities that may be useful to identify educational research include the following:

- Google Scholar (http://scholar.google.com) provides access to research in a wide variety of scholarly fields. Resources may include scholarly journal articles, conference papers, or unpublished papers made available from foundations or research centers.

- The Educational Resources Information Center (ERIC; www.eric.ed.gov) is sponsored by the U.S. Department of Education. ERIC includes access to journal articles, conference papers, research reports, and policy documents. Materials have been indexed in ERIC since 1966, and many sources are available in full text. The ERIC website includes access to a thesaurus of descriptors used to index papers, which may be useful in generating a keyword list.

Commercial Databases

Libraries purchase licenses to access commercial research databases in disciplines that are relevant to scholarship in a variety of fields. The databases available through specific libraries are often listed on their websites, as are holdings accessible through the database. Some important commercial databases include the following:

- ProQuest provides access to a wide range of databases, including ERIC and Digital Dissertations, as well as the ProQuest Research Library and index of academic journals.

- EBSCO Host provides access to Academic Search Complete, Education Search Complete, and Educational Administration Complete, among other indexes in their holdings.

- JSTOR provides access to full text of a wide range of scholarly journals in education and other disciplines.

Note that web links are not provided here since access to these sources is restricted based on license; thus, these services generally require either a password associated with registration at a university or accessing the services from within the library.

(Continued)

(Continued)

Other Sources of Educational Research

A wide variety of associations, think tanks, and government and research organizations provide access to original research and/or syntheses of research in education. Many of the search engines highlighted above might bring you to resources on these sites, but it may also be worthwhile to peruse them directly. Some of the sources that may be of interest include the following:

- The U.S. Department of Education (DOE; www.ed.gov). The DOE provides an enormous amount of material that may be useful, including links to the What Works Clearinghouse and ERIC. The DOE website is well worth perusing. Among the places worth noting is a web resource providing links to "other online educational resources," which can be accessed at the following URL: www2.ed.gov/about/contacts/gen/othersites/index.html.

- Regional Education Laboratories (http://ies.ed.gov/ncee/edlabs). The regional labs are funded by the Institute of Educational Sciences, U.S. Department of Education. They each have websites of their own, linked to the above URL. The mission of the regional labs is to help policymakers and practitioners address educational problems. Consequently, each lab conducts research and provides technical assistance to educators in its region.

- Education Commission of the States (ECS; www.ecs.org). The ECS is dedicated to helping states create effective policy and promote quality practices to improve schools. The ECS website provides access to a listing of topics of importance to ECS, which are linked to resources on these topics.

- The following membership associations are each deeply concerned with applying research to improve leadership and schools; thus, each provides access to research briefs and summaries on its website as well as access to association-sponsored publications:
  o National Association of Secondary School Principals (www.nassp.org)
  o National Association of Elementary School Principals (www.naesp.org)
  o American Association of School Administrators (www.aasa.org)
  o Association for Supervision and Curriculum Development (www.ascd.org)
  o Phi Delta Kappan (www.pdkintl.org)

- Various university departments and centers may make original research available via their websites. Generally, a researcher would be connected to these via one of the above-mentioned search engines (e.g., ERIC, Google Scholar), but some may be worth perusing. Among those that may be useful are the Wisconsin Center for Education Research (www.wcer.wisc.edu) and the Consortium for Policy Research in Education (www.cpre.org).

Becoming a Critical Consumer: Evaluating Sources

Eventually, of course, it is important to become a critical consumer, to evaluate the worth of the literature you are collecting and determine the degree to which you trust the information offered as guidance for understanding and addressing your problem. We have no sure-fire, step-by-step guide to becoming adept at this but tend to agree with the Queensland site's observation that "you learn to judge, evaluate, and look critically at literature by judging, evaluating, and looking critically at it. That is, you learn to do so by practicing" (*Making Sense of the Literature*, n.d., para. 8). Research library web resources offer a lot of useful guidance on evaluating research sources. Since virtually anyone with a minimal amount of technical knowledge can publish material on the Internet, much of this material is focused on evaluating webpages. In this section, we will review some general guidelines on evaluating published work, some of which applies to both print and electronic sources, and then we will turn to the specific problem of knowing whether to trust material presented on a website.

A common fear is that it is impossible to understand published research without an advanced degree in statistics. While we do not agree with this sentiment entirely, in Chapter 8 we provide some guidance on understanding some fundamental issues associated with research methodology that is useful for becoming a good consumer of work published in peer-reviewed journals. Some of what we will share may be called "technical knowledge," but a good bit of it is common sense.

On balance, as the Queensland material says,

> In critically evaluating, you are looking for the strengths of certain studies and the significance and contributions made by the researchers. You are also looking for limitations, flaws, and weaknesses of particular studies, or a whole line of enquiry. (*Making Sense of the Literature*, n.d., para. 9)

While you may not have a doctorate in research methods, do not consider this a liability. Remember that your purpose as a leader is to access research knowledge to inform your decision making and guide your actions, and your specific goal at this juncture is to provide a synthesis on what is known about the causes of problems like the one you selected to focus on in your school. Trustworthiness will come from triangulation of the available research; your case will be strengthened if you build your rationale and logic of action around a variety of work that you believe to be relevant to your school context, the identified problem, and your specific goals.

Evaluating Published Sources

Engle and Cosgrave (2009) provide useful guidance on some initial steps readers can take to evaluate published sources, first by examining bibliographic listings and then by reviewing content. They suggest that initially, even before looking at an article, readers examine the following:

- *The author.* What are the author's credentials, institutional affiliations, educational background, and/or areas of expertise? Is the author associated with a prominent college or policy institute, for instance? What are the values or agendas associated with the institution?

- *Date of publication.* When was the work published, and how current is this information? If your topic is relatively new or developing, material may become irrelevant quickly.

- *Publisher or journal title.* Note the publisher for books or the journal title for an article. Is the book published by a reputable publisher, such as a university press, or an advocacy group that may have a political agenda or a for-profit company seeking to prove the worth of a program or product? Is the journal prominent in the field, or is the piece in a popular or trade magazine?

Initially, it may be hard to know what the prominent research journals are in a field associated with your school improvement topic, but as you begin to scan the literature, this will become clearer. In terms of some questions to ask as you peruse the content of articles you selected, consider the following (Engle & Cosgrave, 2009):

- *Intended audience.* Who is the article written for, primarily? A scholarly audience or a practitioner audience? Is the work too simplistic or too technical for your uses?

- *Objective reasoning.* Is the material presented fact, opinion, or propaganda? The late Senator Daniel Patrick Moynihan once quipped, "Everyone is entitled to his own opinion, but not his own facts." The important distinction here might be best characterized as determining whether the work is presenting well-researched ideas and conclusions supported by evidence rather than biased or one-sided information intended to persuade, or worse, to deceive.

- *Coverage.* Does it substantially cover the topic, or is the connection limited? Does it add to what you already know on the subject or provide you with additional ideas, conclusions, or references?

- *Writing style.* Is the paper well written?

Advice offered on the University of Washington-Bothell web resource adds that it is worth assessing the reference or bibliographic information provided by a source (*Evaluating Sources*, 2010). We have already commented on the importance of triangulating information contained in reference lists, especially early in your search as you are becoming familiar with the literature. Examining reference lists will inform you about who the significant scholars are in a field. As you become more knowledgeable, the reference list may also be important in helping you identify additional resources, determining how a piece is situated in relation to existing work in the field, and judging whether a piece offers new insights or is largely redundant with work you have already collected.

Evaluating Internet Sources

As we noted earlier, Internet resources pose a special challenge. While the web affords unprecedented access to full-text articles from peer-reviewed sources, original and summarized research reports and policy documents, and databases of interest, with a click of the mouse, you may also be directed to evaluations of programs intended to sell you a product or service, opinion pieces, partial truths, and misinformation. Kirk (1996) summarizes the dilemma well:

> When you use a research or academic library, the books, journals, and other resources have already been evaluated by scholars, publishers, and librarians. Every resource you find has been evaluated in one way or another before you ever see it. When you are using the World Wide Web, none of this applies. There are no filters. Because anyone can write a webpage, documents of the widest range of quality, written by authors of the widest range of authority, are available on an even playing field. Excellent resources reside alongside the most dubious. The Internet epitomizes the concept of Caveat Lector: Let the reader beware. (para. 1)

Of course, much of the material available on the Internet *has* gone through rigorous review—for instance, material available through electronic portals providing access to full-text offerings from traditional print journals, peer-reviewed electronic journals, and so on. The difficulty resides in the fact that amid these more trustworthy materials may be articles, reports, and other kinds of documents that have not been subject to any kind of quality control measures. Particularly when you turn to the question of identifying programs and practices that may offer solutions to the causes of the problem on which you are working, you are apt to find products or services being touted by parties interested in selling you something, evaluations produced by parties with an interest in showing how well something worked, or summaries highlighting the benefits of an approach while minimizing either the costs or difficulties associated with supposed success.

"On the Internet, nobody knows you're a dog."

Source: Reproduced from Steiner (1993).

Learning More About Electronic Resources

There are abundant resources available to guide researchers to become good consumers of electronic resources; in our review, we relied on advice offered by the University of California-Berkeley (*Evaluating Web Pages,* 2010) and the

Johns Hopkins University (Kirk, 1996) websites as representative of the best advice available. Synthesizing this advice, we recommend the following steps in evaluating the trustworthiness of web resources but also recommend examining these and other available resources at research libraries.

1. Examine the web address.

   - The UC-Berkeley library advises that readers examine the URL for each webpage, looking for information on **authorship**. Does the web address suggest that the page is a personal page (i.e., does it include an individual's name, or is the page housed on a commercial provider's site?)? Personal pages are not inherently problematic, but this may suggest that material posted has undergone little or no outside review. What is the domain type? This information is associated with the suffix of the primary portion of the web address (e.g., .edu, .org, .gov, .com). Is the domain appropriate given the information you expect from the source? For instance, if you believe you are accessing a government report and the domain is .com, might this suggest that you are actually accessing only a portion of the original or worse?

2. Scan the webpage.

   - The UC-Berkeley library suggests that an initial scan might reveal a link or text box that provides information about **authorship** (e.g., "About us" or "Background"). Similarly, the Hopkins library recommends seeking out an answer to the question "Who wrote this?"—both in terms of the specific author and in terms of understanding the nature of the organization sponsoring the website. The UC-Berkeley material advises that if a specific author is not obvious or if the sponsoring organization is not clear, it may be possible to truncate the web address to find this information (i.e., eliminate all information in the web address except the text between "http://" and the first backslash). The notion here is to be sure of who claims responsibility for the material posted to the site. Consider the criteria suggested earlier: What are the author's credentials, institutional affiliations, educational background, and/or areas of expertise? Is the author associated with a prominent college or policy institute or a think tank, association, political party, or lobbying group? What are the values or agendas associated with the sponsoring institution? Is the organization a respected leader in the field or perhaps a for-profit start-up trying to gain a foothold in the market?
   - Examine the page to determine **currency**. The Hopkins library suggests that for many types of material, currency may be obvious (e.g., the page

may indicate clearly when it was posted or last updated, it may include a copyright). However, for some webpages, currency is extremely hard to determine. It may be possible to draw some conclusions based on a scan of a reference list or factual material presented (e.g., census or other kinds of data). Consider the importance of this criterion for your search; if you are looking for historical information, it may be less important than if you are trying to determine the most current thinking on a topic.

3. Examine tertiary indicators of website quality.

   - What is the look and feel of the website? For instance, is the page professional in appearance or amateurish? Are there advertisements on the site or pop-up windows?

   - Websites typically contain links to other relevant resources. What are the links provided on the site, and do they seem sensible given the subject matter? Are the links well organized and documented, and are these links to reliable and trustworthy sites or do they suggest a hidden agenda or bias? Do the links work? The latter issue may be an indicator of currency of the site.

   - Is bibliographic or reference information provided? Just as an examination of reference material in a journal article provides information about the quality and currency of the research knowledge offered, so too does the reference material on a website provide a sense of the seriousness of the work, its quality, and how to situate the material in the field. Similarly, the UC-Berkeley library suggests a careful examination of any reproduced information such as tables or graphs: Are sources carefully noted and permissions evident? Is there a link to the original source material, especially if this material resides on another website? The reader should be able to verify information provided from other sources.

4. Determine the point of view.

   - The Hopkins library notes that information presented in any form is seldom neutral. Even the most objective work involves a choice process involving researchers selecting some questions over others, particular methods, and types of information they will bring to bear in their investigation. Scholars have favored theories or perspectives. Nonfindings (i.e., research that shows that a program or treatment did not work or that a presumed statistical relationship appears nonexistent) are often harder to get into print than statistically robust findings. It is prudent to remember that scholars have opinions about the subjects they study. This is especially important when examining Internet sites. As the Hopkins site admonishes, "The popularity of the Internet makes it the perfect venue for commercial and sociopolitical publishing. These areas in particular are open to highly 'interpretive' uses of data" (Kirk, 1996, para. 4). Thus, as you examine the material on a website, triangulate the information gleaned by taking the steps suggested above with your reading of the tone and purpose of the text. Is the piece primarily aimed at informing or advocating for a position? Is the organization lobbying for a position or trying to convince policymakers and practitioners of the efficacy of one path of action over another? Is the presentation fair and even-handed, noting both the strengths and limitations of a piece of research or the advantages and disadvantages of a course of action? Consider the tone of the presentation, and think about the author's reason for posting the webpage.

5. Does it all make sense?

   - In the end, as the Hopkins site asks, does the material presented add up? Here is where triangulating information you have already discovered from highly reliable sources tends to pay off handsomely. Is the material you discovered as credible as material already collected? How do the conclusions compare with other sources? If the material were presented in a print journal or even a magazine in the field, would it seem believable?

Finally, it is often useful to take full advantage of the electronic age we live in to gain the confidence you need in a source you find potentially important to your work: E-mail the author or the organization that posted the material in question, or Google the person to find additional materials he or she has written or sponsored. The Berkeley library also suggests using Alexa (www.alexa.com) to learn valuable information about website sponsors. Entering a URL into Alexa's search box returns a wealth of material about website sponsors, including information on the organization, website traffic, related Internet sites, and websites linking to the organization.

CONCLUSION

Our goal in this chapter was to provide you with some systematic ways of thinking about the various sources of research knowledge you might access to inform your understanding of the problem you identified as the focus of your school improvement project and your decision making on what action to take in your school. Our focus has been helping you amass trustworthy information using a variety of strategies that ensure that the information you collect is reliable. Your specific performance goal for the research you come to understand is to write a research brief for your school's improvement team with the goal of informing members of the team about what is known on the topic you selected and ultimately persuading the team regarding an approach to the problem.

In this chapter, we modeled the approach we advocate in our own presentation. That is, we took steps much like the ones we advocate for you to prepare a synthesis on how best to approach the literature to provide source material for your Research Brief. To reiterate:

1. We clarified our purpose and started with a clear guiding question: What does the literature suggest we do to access extant research literature to produce a synthesis of what is known on a topic of interest to school leaders?

2. We devised a strategy for accessing different kinds of literature. In our case, we determined that high-quality, trustworthy sources existed on websites posted by university research libraries, hence we relied primarily on these sources, augmented by print materials we were already aware of based on our experience.

3. We used online databases to search the web for useful information to inform our synthesis. Our goal was not to "cover the universe" or to exhaustively review every single source but, rather, to inform a set of recommendations for action. Thus, we selected trustworthy sources and crafted our report in a fashion that is highly informative and usable for your purposes.

4. We read the material we collected, dissected what we felt to be most important, and organized the material in a fashion that we believe to be helpful.

For your work, we suggested that there are two important guiding questions to focus your inquiry. The first involves discerning the likely causes of the problem you identified as a focus for your work: "What is known about why [this problem] exists in schools like ours?" Answering this question is intended to help you build a deep understanding of the nature of the problem you identified in your school. This investigation requires a balanced approach that is informed by what others have found through disciplined inquiry and represented in published literature and field-based work you and your colleagues have done in your school. Second, your inquiry into the published literature shifts to identifying the kinds of actions that have been shown to be effective in eliminating the causes of the problem you seek to eliminate. We suggest, therefore, that your second guiding question should be "What actions have been shown to effectively eliminate the causes of [the problem] in schools like ours?" Using these questions to guide your inquiry is intended to help you build a clear logic of action that spells out the nature of the original problem, a course of action, and a rationale describing why taking that course of action will have a high likelihood of remedying the problem.

Using the guidelines presented in this chapter, we suggest you begin by building a keyword list associated with your identified problem and start the search for an answer to the question "What is known about why [this problem] exists in schools like ours?" Look for secondary and tertiary syntheses or reviews of literature on the topic initially. If it is possible to identify a digest or review piece on the topic, particularly one that was recently written, it will be possible to identify significant themes in the research. Likewise, well-done syntheses will provide bibliographic references that can be mined—take special note of the scholars who are prominently featured. Many times, searching for work written by these authors is the key to quickly and efficiently locating important information. During the initial stages of the search, scan the material you collect in the fashion outlined earlier, assessing the worth of various sources and using successive search results to direct you to the most useful resources. Be a critical consumer along the way, focusing on moving to peer-reviewed work to inform your judgment.

At the risk of repeating ourselves, ultimately, your persuasiveness as a leader is dependent on having crafted an argument that is both compelling and well supported.

To ensure *trustworthiness* in your work, it is important that you *triangulate* your search by using a variety of highly reliable sources of varied types.

REVIEW QUESTIONS

1. In what ways could you use a tertiary or secondary source to guide your reading of primary sources?

2. What are some of the advantages and disadvantages of using non-peer-reviewed, published work?

3. What are some nontraditional sources that might inform your selected problem, challenge, or gap?

4. What are some of the most effective ways to use online databases of research?

CHAPTER 8

UNDERSTANDING RESEARCH
DESIGN AND ANALYSIS

LEARNING OUTCOMES

Readers who grasp the most important ideas from this chapter will be able to

- understand the major components of a typical research article;
- recognize the differences between quantitative and qualitative research;
- align appropriate research design with different kinds of research problems and questions; and
- criticize the quality of research in terms of its usefulness for their school improvement projects.

The previous chapter focused on finding literature that informs your thinking about the problem you have identified by first finding root causes and then solutions for the instructional challenge you are addressing. However, you may have found that some of the research you read was difficult to understand or to trust because the methodology was unclear or difficult to decipher. Most of us have a natural tendency to read the introductory portion of an article that presents the research questions to be addressed, then skip or skim everything until we get to the conclusions. Much of what is in the middle seems hard to grasp and somewhat irrelevant to our purpose in reading the article. However, it is far from irrelevant, because that material in the middle is critical to the reader's sense of whether the research was well done and truly relevant to her or his own work setting. Our mission in this chapter is to help make research design accessible to you to the extent that you can understand more than just the questions and the conclusions of most published articles. Our goal is to help you judge whether published work is trustworthy and relevant for your purposes. By trustworthy, we mean that the questions asked are appropriate and researchable, the findings are supported by credible evidence, and the conclusions follow logically from the findings.

This chapter complements earlier chapters because it clarifies what the authors you have encountered were attempting to accomplish through their research designs. It should also help you assess the quality of the published research you have found so that you can cite the sources that you believe to be most powerful. Two final benefits from this chapter are that it will help you think about how you may wish to conduct action research regarding the nature of the problem you have chosen and will help you select appropriate methods to use in the process of evaluating your project.

Typical Components of Published Research Papers

- Statement of the problem, including the purpose and significance of the study
- Research questions
- Conceptual framework
- Methods
  - Research design
  - Participants, setting
  - Data collection, instruments
  - Data analysis
  - Limitations
- Presentation of findings
- Discussion of findings and implications

While the form of research papers will differ somewhat depending on the nature of the study being presented, we organize our discussion in the sections that follow by looking at issues related to each of the main components of a typical research paper (see sidebar). Perhaps the most important point to stress at the outset is where we start: A high-quality research paper must be designed to answer specific, well-formulated research questions.

FORM FOLLOWS FUNCTION

There are a wide variety of possible research approaches. Generally speaking, the approach chosen to pursue a line of inquiry must "fit" with the questions the researcher purports to address. For example, if I seek to inform the question of how satisfied third-grade teachers in my school district are with their pay or benefits, I am asking a descriptive question that could be answered quite simply by using an attitude survey to collect opinions and analyze the responses by reporting simple patterns (e.g., the percentage of teachers who are very satisfied, somewhat satisfied, and so on). If I am interested in understanding if new principals' job satisfaction is related to their sense of work overload, I might employ a design that seeks to provide a statistical measure of association between measures of these two concepts. Alternatively, if I wanted to understand more about the nature of this relationship, I might instead decide to interview a number of new principals to understand more about this relationship in context. If, instead, I am researching the question of how implementation of a new program for teaching Algebra I affects student performance on a criterion-referenced, end-of-course assessment, my design would need to be quite a bit more involved to glean trustworthy results.

At the outset of the vast majority of published research papers, just after a short introductory vignette and well before the methods section, authors typically provide the first relevant information you need to judge the trustworthiness of the research: They outline the research problem or questions they intend to address and provide a synthesis of the conceptual underpinnings of the work. Since the choice of research design must serve to provide credible evidence to answer the questions posed, understanding the author's aims and perspectives is critically important to judging the trustworthiness of the research.

STATEMENT OF THE PROBLEM

Articles usually begin with a discussion of the research problem in a manner that narrows down to specific research questions. A typical pattern is to begin with a statement of purpose, what the author wishes to learn. Gersick (1989), in a landmark study of small-group decision making, wanted to know how time pressure affected group behavior. She had two purposes: (a) to follow up on field-based research she conducted previously and (b) to figure out whether laboratory simulations of group work behavior were worthwhile. Here is how she states her dual purposes:

> This article discusses a study conducted to follow up on my original research by exploring the cognitive and behavioral links between pacing and development. A laboratory simulation was designed to permit both close observation of groups working and close questioning of participants on how they thought about their work. Using this previously untried design with the field-based model dictated a second purpose for the study: to assess the suitability of laboratory simulation as a research tool for the phenomena of interest. (p. 275)

Authors may choose to discuss the research and/or practical significance of their study either before or after presenting research questions. Our preference is generally to explain significance prior to getting into questions; so we present it in that order. Significance refers to the importance of a study and addresses one of our favorite questions: "So what?" It is generally a more involved explanation than purpose and is supported by citations that situate the work in the existing knowledge base and help make the statement of significance persuasive. Discussion of significance helps explain why the author pursued the study and ought to motivate the reader to read it. Articles are not always written with the structure that we might prefer, however, and Gersick (1989) chose to diffuse her discussion of significance as she presented the relevant literature. Here are two excerpts:

> For groups with creative assignments and the responsibility to invent their own work processes, pace is a complex manifestation of group members' speed in managing their own interaction and their interaction with outside stakeholders, solving problems, and discovering and developing new ideas. Understanding what such groups do to accomplish those ends by a deadline overlaps importantly with understanding what they do to create a product at all.

> However, it was not clear whether patterns observed in naturally occurring teams could also arise under artificial conditions and drastically shorter time limits. As McGrath (1987) pointed out, we currently have no theory of how laboratory time translates to real-world time. An important issue for the study, then, was to see if the field-observed patterns appeared at all or appeared in distorted form. (pp. 275–278)

Gersick's main interest was determining if laboratory experiments were more revealing of work-group decision making than more naturalistic studies completed in the workplace. If you happened to find this article and discovered that what the author thinks is important about the study has nothing to do with your own instructional problem, challenge, or gap, then you might want to stop reading at that point.

With purpose and significance clearly established, the author is then ready to present research questions. These questions are both general and specific enough to convey what the author wishes to understand as a result of conducting the study (Maxwell, 2005). They make the statement of purpose concrete, and they should align with significance. Here is how Gersick (1989) chose to present her research questions after her discussion of significance (note that we have cut her elaboration in an effort to focus on the questions themselves):

The current study addressed three research questions. The first was if transitions occurred, and if they did, how they worked. . . . The second question addressed how groups paced themselves throughout their life spans and what was special about their temporal midpoints. . . . The third research question was what happened when the midpoint of a group's allotted time passed without the team's completing a minimally successful transition by closing its Phase 1 agenda and agreeing on a new basis for Phase 2 work. (p. 278)

The research questions that Gersick poses in this article are clearly qualitative in nature. She is seeking the details of what happens in small-group decision making and *how* groups handle time pressure. The methods she discusses later in the article involved observations and interviews, two key tools of qualitative research that help reveal the kinds of details she sought.

In an article that uses quantitative methods, it would be customary for the statement of purpose and/or research questions to identify something about the specific factors that are involved—for instance, using the example posed earlier, "The purpose of this study is to determine the relationship between new principals' job satisfaction and their sense of work overload." A quantitative study would often also include specific research hypotheses about the relationships tested and a description of criteria used for judging whether these hypotheses are supported. Hypotheses are used to guide the investigation and the discussion of results.

CONCEPTUAL OR THEORETICAL FRAMEWORK

Empirical research commonly employs a conceptual framework, sometimes referred to as a theoretical framework. The primary purpose of a conceptual framework is for the author to explain his or her perspective on the research problem and hunches or hypotheses about what is happening inside the research setting (Merriam, 2009; Miles & Huberman, 1994; Yin, 2009). Authors typically present their conceptual framework after their statement of the problem and before discussion of methodology. This makes sense because the conceptual framework helps focus research questions in a specific area and helps indicate the kinds of categories into which data will fit.

The conceptual framework tends to be a popular section for readers to skip because it is abstract and seems to have little to do with the findings. This result often stems from poor writing in which the author ignores the conceptual framework after establishing it. As discussed in Chapter 2, though, the conceptual framework is important to gleaning how the authors connect theory to the research they are conducting and situate the study in terms of its connection to problems of practice. When it works well, the framework guides understanding of findings and helps the reader grasp the scope of the author's vision of the research—what was included and what was left out.

Sometimes, authors will adopt a previously published framework for their study. This is the case with Conley, Fauske, and Pounder's (2004) study of teacher work-group effectiveness:

> In examining models of team effectiveness, Vinokur-Kaplan (1995) noted that contemporary models have progressed beyond early "laboratory and T-groups–based models" that focus on the "internal dynamics and development of groups" to provide more attention to the "organizational environment in which teams are established and must perform" (p. 306). This "ecological perspective" on group effectiveness emphasizes such issues as how work teams interface with such organizational structures as "reward and boundary systems," as well as the organization's role in "supporting or undermining" a work group's performance and effectiveness (Vinokur-Kaplan, 1995, p. 306). For these reasons, Hackman and Oldham's (1980) work group effectiveness model was selected as the study framework because it represents one of the more comprehensive conceptualizations of work group effectiveness. (p. 665)

Conley et al. go on to explain what the Hackman and Oldham model is and how they apply it to their own study. Notice in the above excerpt that Conley et al. are also placing or situating their study in a larger literature. This helps lend legitimacy to their choice of the Hackman and Oldham model.

Many authors choose to build their own conceptual frameworks from scratch, so to speak, by borrowing concepts from a range of published work and putting them together into a unique model or elaborate hypothesis that fits their specific study. However the conceptual framework may be established, reading it helps you know the theoretical bases for the author's analysis and adds an important component to your understanding of whether or not a particular article is useful to you. This point is clarified by a classic debate. If your project involves improving language arts achievement for special education students, then you are likely to find some articles that use phonics theory as the basis of their conceptual framework, while others use whole language theory. Understanding the author's chosen perspective is important as you consider the findings and how they relate to your own school.

METHODS

The methods section of a research article, generally speaking, provides information to the reader about how the study was conducted. It provides, in brief, a blueprint for understanding what the researcher(s) did to obtain credible evidence to answer the research questions posed. Although methods sections vary somewhat depending on the research designs employed, certain questions should be answered that will help you determine whether the study is trustworthy for your purposes:

- *What research design was employed in the study?* As we already mentioned, the research design used must "fit" with the purposes, questions posed, and conceptual framework. Having already learned about these purposes and questions, the author(s) should spell out, in detail, the specific steps taken to conduct the research. Design refers to the general structure of the research and influences all subsequent aspects of the methodology.

- *Who was involved?* Social research involves collecting evidence from human beings in some social setting. Thus, there are really two questions here: In what settings was the research conducted, and who were the participants? Even if the research involves mining data already compiled, as a study using large-scale federal data sets might do, knowing the kinds of schools participants attended or other information related to the sample employed is critical to understanding how relevant the research might be to schools like yours.

- *What information was collected?* To answer the research questions posed, the researcher must collect some evidence from participants related to the concepts involved in the study. To understand the trustworthiness of the research, it is important to know what information was collected and how it was collected.

- *How was the analysis conducted?* Whatever information was collected from participants must be analyzed in order to draw some conclusions about the answers to research questions. How this analysis was conducted should be spelled out by the author(s).

The methods section should clearly lay out the research design employed to collect credible evidence to answer the research questions. There are three broad categories of research designs: quantitative, qualitative, and mixed methods. Creswell (2008) provides a brief summary of the distinction between quantitative and qualitative traditions:

Quantitative research is a type of educational research in which the researcher decides what to study; asks specific, narrow questions; collects quantifiable data from participants; analyzes these numbers using statistics; and conducts the inquiry in an unbiased, objective manner. *Qualitative research* is a type of educational research in which the researcher relies on the views of participants; asks broad, general questions; collects data consisting largely of words (or text) from participants; describes and analyzes these words for themes. (p. 46)

Quantitative studies tend to involve testing specific relationships, propositions, or theories (e.g., is there a relationship between job satisfaction and the intention to leave one's job?) or seek to describe some known attributes of a phenomenon (e.g., what percentage of elementary principals intend to leave their jobs?). Qualitative studies tend to seek to provide a detailed exploration or understanding of a phenomenon that we know less about. A premium is placed on discovering the lived experiences of participants in order to build a deeper understanding of some phenomenon and, from this understanding, develop propositions or theory. Mixed methods designs combine elements of both quantitative and qualitative research. For example, we might utilize a mixed method design to learn first about some phenomenon (qualitative) to develop a survey instrument and then use this instrument to collect data to learn if our understanding generalizes to a broad group of people (quantitative). Or we might conduct a survey of a group (quantitative) and conduct a number of focus group interviews later to help understand why the pattern of results might have emerged (qualitative).

From the very first time we ask the question, "What is the level of student achievement?" we are drawn to quantitative measures, typically state-mandated standardized test scores. These indicators of student achievement are readily available and, in some ways, easy to understand. The current policy context tends to favor one type of quantitative design, the randomly controlled experiment, in the sense that this design provides more credible or rigorous evidence concerning the claim that a reform initiative "causes" an impact on student learning. Indeed, there are certain advantages to the true experimental design in producing trustworthy answers to research questions that have to do with the efficacy of a program or treatment in relation to student outcomes. However, as we will discuss below, not all research deals with questions about program efficacy, and a great deal of work provides useful information for researchers and practitioners about the nature of reform programs, the conditions under which problems and their solutions exist, and what types of factors represent potent causes of persistent problems.

It is useful, then, to understand both the virtues and limitations of various designs in order to be able to judge whether research you encounter is useful for your purposes. In the sections that follow, we will review some basic issues that are important to understand dealing with design, settings and participants, data collection, and data analysis. Because approaches to these issues tend to differ substantially for quantitative and qualitative studies, we will deal with these questions separately for each of these two traditions. The following subsections discuss specific aspects of methodology that are common to most research articles. Our intent is to give you enough description and discussion so that methodology sections of research articles will make more sense to you when you read them and to provide some reasons for you to read this kind of material carefully.

Types of Quantitative Research Designs Discussed

Experimental

- Experimental designs
- Quasi-experimental designs

Nonexperimental

- Descriptive designs
- Correlational designs
- Causal-comparative or *ex post facto* designs

Quantitative Research Design

There are a number of different types of quantitative designs, which we will review briefly in two broad groupings: experimental designs and nonexperimental designs (see sidebar).

Experiments

The current political and policy context influences what might be considered credible evidence, particularly in terms of identifying actions or solutions that are thought to produce improvements in student learning. As Goldring and Berends (2009) comment, "The U.S. federal government became involved in debates regarding education research because it had a relatively high level of discomfort about both the quality and impact of the research on education" (p. 165). Unlike other professional fields such as medicine, it was asserted that the research base in education is "soft" and "evidence often consists of poorly-designed and/or advocacy-driven studies" (U.S. Department of Education, 2003, p. iii). Much of the angst about educational research is focused on claims about solutions (i.e., claims that implementing a program or strategy will produce an improvement in school operations, the learning environment, and/or student learning). No Child Left Behind (NCLB) calls on educators to use "scientifically based research" to inform decisions about interventions or solutions.

In *Identifying and Implementing Educational Practices Supported by Rigorous Evidence: A User-Friendly Guide*, the U.S. Department of Education (2003) provides a synopsis of the policy set forth in NCLB that asserts that "well-designed and implemented randomized controlled trials are considered the 'gold standard' for evaluating an intervention's effectiveness" (p. 1). Indeed, promoting evidence-based research is one of the foundations of NCLB, and in the years since adoption of the law, the government has followed up with funding that credentials *randomized controlled (i.e., experimental) designs* above other kinds of research (Schneider, Carnoy, Kilpatrick, Schmidt, & Shavelson, 2007).

Schneider et al. (2007) explain, "Research designs are defined by the types of questions asked. In the case of randomized controlled experiments, the question is: What is the effect of a specific program or intervention?" (p. 9). Goldring and Berends (2009) explain further, "An experimental design is a research design where a *treatment*, or in our case an intervention or strategy, is given to subjects or participants to measure whether the intervention causes a change in behavior" (p. 169). The experimental design is, quite simply, the most appropriate and strongest design to promote internal validity—that is, the claim that a causal inference is true.

There are many variants on the experimental design, but the defining element of a *true* experiment is random assignment of participants to groups. Trochim (2001) explains that the idea here is to create groups that are probabilistically equivalent; random assignment assures that each member of a sample has an equal chance of being assigned to the treatment and control groups, so we may expect with reasonable certainty that any effect produced by participating in a treatment is attributable to the treatment and not some other, unrelated attribute of the situation or group. The goal of such a design is to show that an outcome is a result of a particular program *and* that this outcome does not occur when the program or treatment is not given. "If you randomly assign people to two groups, and you have enough people in your study to achieve the desired probabilistic equivalence, you can consider the experiment strong in *internal validity* and you probably have a good shot at assessing whether the program causes the outcome(s)" (p. 193).

Consider the following simplified example. Suppose you wanted to know if a new reading program was effective in terms of promoting student achievement in reading comprehension for third-graders in your school. You randomly assign third-graders to one of two groups and provide the new curriculum to one group (the treatment group) and the existing curriculum to the other (the control or comparison group). Using a reliable assessment of comprehension, you conduct a pretest of all students before implementing the programs and then a post-test afterward and compare the groups in terms of their growth. Since participants had an equal chance of being assigned to either group, you could have some confidence that a greater degree of growth for the treatment group is due to the new program. Essentially, random assignment limits the degree of potential bias.

Goldring and Berends (2009) note that a prudent consumer of research knowledge will consider three factors when assessing experimental work: random assignment, which we already discussed; a comparison group; and pre- and post-measures related to outcomes. They note, additionally, that the time frame or duration of the study may also be important: "The optimal time to determine if an intervention has an effect is at least one school year" (pp. 170–171). It is useful to know if the study has been replicated and whether similar results have been found in alternative iterations of the treatment. Finally, they note, the reader can typically place more stock in a study conducted by a third party than in one conducted by the developer of a program or intervention. Consistent with advice we have already provided, publication of results of a study in a peer-reviewed journal would be far preferable compared with finding such results on a commercial website, for example.

Cautionary Notes

It is important to recognize that even when random assignment is possible, many things can foil an experimental design, including such things as not having a sufficiently large sample or experiencing attrition during implementation of the program (Trochim, 2001). Experiments conducted in authentic school settings might suffer from a variety of threats to internal validity claims associated with factors that are beyond control. For example, Trochim discusses social threats to validity resulting from interaction between group members. One such threat is termed the *diffusion* or *imitation threat*, which occurs when members of the control group learn about the treatment by visiting friends or chatting at lunch time, for instance. Comparison group members might take up or imitate certain aspects of the treatment, thus threatening the true post-test performance of that group. Another social threat is *compensatory rivalry*, which involves members of the comparison group becoming competitive with the treatment group because they are receiving special considerations. "As long as people engage in applied social research," Trochim concludes, "you have to deal with the realities of human interaction and its effects on the research process" (p. 186).

The biggest problem with experimental design in social settings such as schools, though, is that they tend to be intrusive and hard to implement effectively. Put simply, the more a researcher tries to control factors that could threaten the internal validity of a cause-and-effect claim, the less likely the program is implemented well in a setting similar to a typical school or classroom. In the extreme, we could conceive of the optimal condition for assuring internal validity as a laboratory setting, where all external influences that might otherwise affect the differences between a control and treatment group are erased save for the impact of the treatment itself. Of course, results from this extreme design would hardly be generalizable to a normal school setting; hence, *external validity* would be sacrificed. You could have little confidence that similar results would occur in a classroom under typical school conditions.

Additionally, random assignment is not always practical. Considering the example posed above, the school or school system may have compelling reasons to purposefully group students, for instance, or parents might object to their children being randomly placed—those whose children are in the treatment group might object to their children being used as "guinea pigs" to try out a new program, and those whose children are in the control group might object to the fact that the other group is gaining access to a new program. Typically, when random assignment is not plausible, researchers will use already existing groups to test whether a program or treatment leads to a hypothesized outcome. So we might implement our new reading program in half of the third-grade classrooms and compare indicators of student achievement across classes to gain an insight into the effectiveness of the new program.

An experiment that does not include random assignment is considered a *quasi-experiment*. Researchers who use quasi-experimental designs may attempt to match groups on as many characteristics as possible to account for important differences in groups (e.g., prior achievement levels, demographic characteristics), but pre-existing groups are often used for convenience and to accommodate the realities of the social situation. Attributes of group members can be measured and accounted for statistically and generally are to determine the "pure" effect of a treatment. But it is important to remember that treatment and control groups may differ systematically due to factors associated with nonrandom assignment, and the ways in which these groups may differ is sometimes very hard to discern. Groups may differ in terms of prior knowledge, motivation, a variety of demographic factors, home environment, engagement in school, and on and on. As an example, one class may have special education students assigned to it, while another may have students who speak English as a second language; the school might systematically separate these two groups to simplify teaching and to help with the logistics of providing specialized teachers in specific classrooms. The virtue of random assignment is that we can assume within reason that such attributes are distributed throughout treatment and control groups (i.e., they are probabilistically equivalent) and, thus, impact the outcomes of these groups consistently. When random assignment is impossible, it is difficult to be sure that the program or treatment produced the outcome instead of some attribute of the group or situation. Internal validity is threatened.

Nonexperimental Quantitative Designs

There are a variety of nonexperimental, quantitative designs that appear in the literature, generally presented in studies that do not seek to judge or prove the efficacy of a program or treatment but, rather, seek to establish the viability of a theoretical proposition or shed light on the nature of relationships between some phenomena of interest. Three families of nonexperimental, quantitative studies are likely to be encountered: descriptive, correlational, and causal-comparative designs.

Briefly, descriptive designs are likely the most familiar type of quantitative study. In a descriptive study, sometimes referred to as a survey design, researchers seek to discover patterns of responses or trends in large groups of people. For instance, a study that seeks to answer the question, "What proportion of high school students were truant this month?" or "How satisfied are parents with their child's school?" would lend itself to descriptive designs. Typically, a survey would be used to collect data to answer such questions (Creswell, 2009) and to discover trends or response patterns for target groups. These types of studies answer "what is" questions; for instance, we may discover that 22% of all high school students in our district were truant this month or that 35% of parents are "very satisfied" with their children's school, whereas 25% are "somewhat satisfied" and the remainder are "somewhat dissatisfied." This type of study would be considered a cross-sectional design, in that responses were collected at a single point in time. If we collected these data repeatedly, we would be using a longitudinal design, which would allow us to compare trends over time. Descriptive studies are especially useful for discovering how subjects think or feel, discovering the degree or level of a measure of interest across a group of people, or comparing perceptions of levels between groups (e.g., the percentage of students absent and unexcused in 9th, 10th, 11th, and 12th grades). A limit of the descriptive design is that once we have described subjects regarding the phenomena of interest, we have very little information about why they answered the way they did, what kinds of things might be associated with this outcome, or what might have caused the response pattern we discovered.

Correlational designs are also quite common in the social science literature. Creswell (2009) sums up this family of quantitative designs well:

> Correlational designs are procedures in quantitative research in which investigators measure the degree of association (or relation) between two or more variables using the statistical procedure of correlational analysis. The degree of association, expressed as a number, indicates whether two or more variables are related or whether one can predict another. (p. 60)

Extending the example used in the previous paragraph, we might want to know if the percentage of students cutting class in high schools across our district is associated with the size of the school. We would measure both variables for each high school and compute a statistic called a *correlation coefficient* to determine the degree of association between these two measures. In actuality, there are a number of statistics that are based on the concept of correlation, including regression analysis, path analysis, and analysis of variance (to name but a few). Regardless of the statistic used, these designs get at the same type of question: Is there an association between some outcome (referred to as the dependent variable) and some factors that are thought to be associated with, or to predict, this outcome (independent variables)? By computing a correlation coefficient or any of the various statistics associated with procedures based in correlation, we can tell whether an association between variables is statistically significant (i.e., due to chance or "real"), the strength of this association, and the nature of the relationship (i.e., the direction—a positive correlation implies that as the independent variable increases, the dependent will also increase; a negative correlation means that as the independent variable increases, the dependent decreases).

Correlation ranges from +1 to −1. A +1.0 correlation means that a one-unit change in one variable will correspond with a one-unit change in the other (in either a positive or negative direction). For example, one might find that for every minute of additional review time prior to a test, a calculus student's test score will improve by one point. A −1.0 correlation shows that a one-unit change in one variable will correspond to a one-unit change in the other in the opposite direction (e.g., each additional assignment of a 1-hour detention is associated with a reduction of one unexcused absence). "Perfect" correlations at or near the value of +/−1.0 are relatively rare. If each hour of additional class time spent on writing expository essays has a 0.40 correlation with standardized writing test scores, this suggests that a 1-hour increase in time spent will produce a 0.40-unit increase in test scores. A correlation at or near zero means that a change in the value of one variable tells you practically nothing about the likely value of the other (i.e., that they are independent). Figure 8.1 presents graphic representations of three types of correlations.

Figure 8.1   Three Types of Correlations

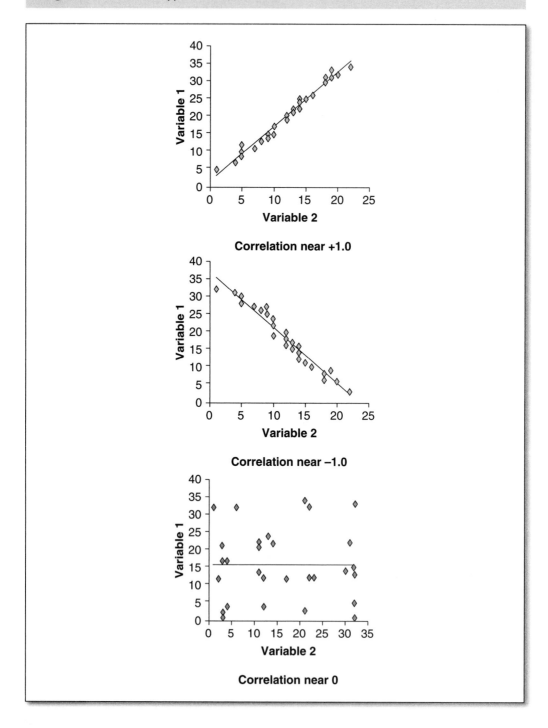

It is quite common to measure the degree of association while controlling for the effect of other factors (e.g., the correlation between absenteeism and the percentage of students who passed the high-stakes graduation exam last year while controlling for school size). When quantitative research "controls for" a specific influence or factor, this means that the researcher is statistically removing the influence of that factor, thus allowing for the examination of other effects with this influence "held constant."

Cautionary Notes

Correlational designs are often used by researchers to test research questions that are related to a theoretical proposition or question about whether some cause-and-effect notions may be sound. We may have a notion that class-cutting behavior is affected by the size of the school in a causal manner (i.e., there will be greater class cutting in larger schools because they are larger). A statistically significant correlation would lend some support to this notion, but it is a common error to use correlation to support a causal attribution. Put bluntly, correlation can never prove causation. Recall that in Chapter 6, we introduced the three criteria that must be met for a causal claim to be supported. One of these criteria was that to claim that A causes B, there must be a relationship between A and B—that is, there must be a correlation. However, all three criteria must be supported, not just one. Specifically, we must also be able to say that A came before B and that there are no other factors that may in fact explain the relationship between A and B.

Repeating an example from Chapter 6 may help make this clear. Suppose we discovered a sizable, positive correlation between knowledge of vocabulary and shoe size among elementary school students in our school. Does this imply that shoe size causes an enlarged vocabulary or that learning new words causes one's feet to grow? Of course not. A third variable, namely age, is related to both—as children get older, their vocabulary knowledge tends to grow, as does the size of their feet. Though we have no special knowledge of podiatry, we are betting that the mechanisms that "cause" these quite independent kinds of growth are unrelated. Correlational studies are often used in theory building and as support for models that may one day be tested by more rigorous means to support claims of cause and effect, but in and of themselves, they cannot be used to "prove" such a claim.

A final type of quantitative design that is sometimes used to lend credence to a claim of cause and effect is the *causal-comparative* or ex post facto study. In this kind of research design, the researcher creates two or more distinct groups related to some independent variable—for instance, one group that received a program and another that did not—and tries to decipher after the fact whether experiencing the treatment may have produced an outcome. We might examine data after the fact to see if a reading program we put in place 3 years ago seems to have yielded greater pass rates on a reading assessment for different groups of students. The causal-comparative design is similar to an experimental design in that the researcher is comparing groups based on exposure to a treatment or program, but it is quite different in that the comparison is done well after the treatment is provided. Controlling for the plethora of factors that might have influenced the outcome through random assignment and other controls related to implementation is not possible in an ex post facto study. Any variables not controlled remain possible explanations for why the outcome produced came about, which may offer alternate explanations or possible causes for the outcome. Thus, if we find support for the assertion that our program produced learning differences, the best we can say is that there is an association that suggests a possible cause-and-effect relationship. Though the claim to cause and effect is not as strong as it might be with a true experiment or even a well-constructed quasi-experiment, this type of design allows us to learn something useful about the effects of a program already implemented, thereby making good use of archival data. Additionally, as compared with a true experiment, the method is relatively nonintrusive, making its use more practical in most circumstances. It is also a popular method used to mine information from already collected data sets—for instance, any of the wide range of national data sets collected over time by the U.S. Department of Education or those assembled by various state education agencies.

Setting and Participants in Quantitative Research

A second category of information you should be able to glean from reading the methods section has to do with the subjects of the research study. The question of who was involved in the research and the kinds of schools or other research settings that were involved is important to your judgment about external validity (i.e., whether the results are generalizable to people and places similar to those you seek to impact). Put simply, even a rigorously done study involving primary school students in elite private schools may have very limited utility if you are trying to design an intervention for at-risk juniors and seniors in large, urban public high schools.

SOME CONFUSING ISSUES . . .

However gentle our introduction to research design might be, there is a good deal of potentially confusing jargon. Indeed, learning about research is akin to learning a new language. Below, we have isolated a few of the more confusing terms along with their definitions.

External Validity vs. Internal Validity

Validity refers to the relative truth of a proposition, inference, or conclusion.

External validity is related to *generalizing*. So external validity refers to the truth of claims about *generalizations*—it involves the degree to which the findings of a study might apply to different people in other places and at other times.

Internal validity has to do with the truth of a claim regarding cause-and-effect relationships. The key question here is whether changes in an outcome of interest can be attributed to an intervention (i.e., the cause) and ***not*** to other possible causes.

Random Selection vs. Random Assignment

In terms of selecting participants for a study, *random selection* is how you select the sample of people from the population you are studying.

Random assignment has to do with how the people you select are placed into different groups or treatments in your study. So once a sample is drawn in an experimental study, participants may then be randomly assigned (or not) to a treatment and a control group.

Sampling Error vs. Sampling Bias

Sampling error involves the extent to which a random sample differs from the population (e.g., some attribute of the population is underrepresented).

Sampling bias refers to nonrandom differences between the sample and the population that are the result of something the researcher did or didn't do when drawing the sample.

Sampling error is beyond the control of the researcher, though if a sample is truly random (and large enough), it should be minimized. Eliminating or minimizing sampling bias is the responsibility of the researcher.

Where a study takes place is important for understanding the findings. However, setting does not mean just the specific geographic location of data collection; the setting might be better referred to as the context, including important background information such as student and staff demographics, school and/or district neighborhood or environment, and possibly some brief history of the organization or entity being studied. Understanding the research setting is important for any type of design but may be particularly important for qualitative research, discussed in more detail below.

We want you to be aware of the necessity of mining the methods section for any and all available information about setting. Trustworthy work will provide a good deal of information that allows you to judge the strengths and limitations related to generalizability. Because of ethical issues related to confidentiality, though, some information may be withheld so that it is impossible to identify specific research sites or participants. This is essential to the research process and should not be seen as deception or unwillingness to share vital information about settings; indeed, confidentiality is often necessary to protect participants and to ensure that they share their thoughts and feelings fully.

Participants

Similar to the research setting, if you are trying to generalize your situation to that which you have read about, you need a strong sense of whether or not the participants in the study are anything like the people who work and learn in your school. The ways in which special education students respond to particular instructional strategies in Evanston, Illinois, may differ greatly from how students without discernable learning disabilities engage with the same program in Topeka, Kansas.

There is, however, a very different and perhaps more important issue with respect to research participants. You will want to ask yourself, "Did the researchers engage the *right* participants?" One of the great challenges of research is getting the most appropriate people to participate in the study. Adults may be reluctant to be interviewed or observed if they believe that revealing their beliefs or behaviors would jeopardize their professional standing. Children are protected by more restrictive human subjects review rules and require participation approval from parents, which may be difficult to obtain. For these reasons and more, researchers may end up surveying, talking to, or observing individuals who are only indirectly involved in the question that most interests them. As a critical reader, it is important to ask yourself whether or not the researchers obtained information from the individuals who are most knowledgeable about the topic, or at least reasonably so.

Sampling

While the sampling process (i.e., selecting participants) is important for any type of research design, sampling in quantitative research is a highly technical and often overlooked issue in judging the trustworthiness of research. The goal of many quantitative studies is to test the viability of a theoretical proposition for the purpose of generalizing to a broader group or to determine if a treatment or program has had the desired effect. The term *population* refers to the entire group of people a researcher is interested in studying. For example, the population might be all high school students in a district (or, for that matter, all high school students in the state or country). Because it is generally impossible or impractical to involve the entire population in a study, researchers draw a sample from the population. The term *sample* refers to the subgroup of the population who are actually studied. The goal is to employ a sample that is highly representative of the population so that generalizations are seen as reasonable.

Creswell (2009) divides sampling procedures into two types. Probability samples are considered the most rigorous form of sampling, in that they are designed to produce the most representative sample from the accessible (or reachable) population. The distinguishing characteristic of a probability sample is that all units in the population have an equivalent chance of being picked to be a part of the sample. This feature minimizes the potential bias in the ensuing sample and tends to produce a sample that is much like the population. There are many varieties of probability sampling. One example is the simple random sample, which involves selecting a sample at random from the accessible population, having the result of distributing characteristics representative of the population across the sample, thus reducing the likelihood of bias. Stratified random sampling is a technique employed to ensure that an ensuing sample is like the population in some already known way by dividing the sample according to this characteristic. For instance, if we know that 60% of our student population is female and 40% is male, we might randomly select 60 female students and 40 male students, thus ensuring that the resulting sample reflects the population in this regard.

Probability sampling is a preferred method for drawing samples that are much like the population in question, but it is not always possible, practical, or cost-effective to use this method. The second type of sampling Creswell (2009) identifies is nonprobability sampling, which involves identifying participants "because they are available, convenient, and represent some characteristic the investigator wishes to study" (p. 155). The term *convenience sample* literally refers to a sample of individuals identified because of their willingness to be a part of a study. Another type of nonprobability sampling is snowball sampling, a technique that involves identifying people in the population with

desired characteristics and then using information from these people to identify others with desired characteristics.

In point of fact, the goal of any selection process is to produce a sample that
is relatively bias-free. Because natural variability exists, any sample will differ
from the population—methodologists refer to this as sampling error. Sampling
error is inherent in the research process. As Creswell (2009) puts it, if you can
imagine drawing repeated samples from a population and measuring some
characteristic, each time you would get a slightly different result, and this result
would differ somewhat from the "true" population score. In quantitative
designs, using larger samples will tend to reduce the degree of sampling error,
and there are well-trodden formulas for determining appropriate sample sizes
for yielding sufficient confidence in results. All else equal, larger samples yield
more accurate or representative results, though the size of the sample required
depends on a number of other considerations, including the size of the population and the amount of error the researcher deems acceptable. (As an example, if a pollster is willing to accept 3% error and the original population is
10,000 people, a simple random sample of just over 960 people would provide
95% confidence in the results; if the original population were 550, a sample of
around 360 would be needed.) In practice, sample sizes are also determined by
available resources and other practical considerations such as the accessible
sample and availability of accurate e-mail or snail-mail addresses.

Sampling bias refers to systematic error that the research introduces through
the selection process. Whereas sampling error is inherent, sampling bias is not.
In fact, it is no exaggeration to say that the main purpose of researchers' decision
making in selecting participants is to either reduce or be able to explain any bias
that might be introduced by his or her choices in selecting participants. This is
not always a simple matter; Trochim (2001) puts it this way:

> At this point, you should appreciate that sampling is a difficult multistep
> process and that you can go wrong in many places. In fact, as you move
> from each step to the next in identifying a sample, there is the possibility
> of introducing systematic error or bias. For instance, even if you are able
> to identify perfectly the population of interest, you may not have access to
> all of it. Even if you do, you may not have a complete and accurate enu-
> meration or sampling frame from which to select. Even if you do, you may
> not draw the sample correctly or accurately. And, even if you do, your
> participants may not all come and they may not all stay. Depressed yet?
> Sampling is difficult business indeed. (p. 45)

Consider the examples in Activity 8.1 in terms of the decisions made by the
researchers that may or may not introduce systematic bias into the sample.

If the goal is to access a sample that is in most ways similar to the population being studied and, thus, to learn something that would be generalizable to that population, the researcher's task is to try to ensure that procedures used to assemble a sample do not result in favoring participants with certain characteristics. Of course, the flip side of this is that to answer many research questions, it is vital to deliberately select specific participants who exhibit the characteristics under study.

ACTIVITY 8.1   Sources of Bias in Sampling

For each of the following scenarios, discuss the pros and cons of the sampling approach. What are the likely sources of sampling bias?

1. Principal Apple wants to know how parents of children in her elementary school feel about the school's new discipline policy. Her assistant, Mr. Brown, constructs a brief, five-item paper-and-pencil survey, which they decide to give to teachers to give out and collect at back-to-school night.

2. Ms. Charming, the new director of research for the school system, has been asked to assess how effective a new, proposed reading program will be at improving reading comprehension of ninth-graders. She and her cracker-jack assistants determine to draw a sample, at random, of six high schools to pilot the program this year. Within each school, half of the ninth-grade classes will be randomly assigned to pilot the new program, while the other half will use the existing program. Pre- and post-test data will be used to compare student gains in comprehension.

3. Principal Dawkins is eager to determine if students appreciate the new salad bar in the lunchroom. He decides to bring the question up at a brainstorming session of the school's leadership team to find out what teachers, staff, and students on the team have heard.

4. Superintendent Eager and his associates need to get an accurate count of how many students would be likely to take advantage of a new curricular opportunity made available through a unique partnership forged with State University. They agree that they will systematically select every 20th student from a list of all students currently enrolled in Grades 9, 10, and 11 at their high school and phone them next Saturday to find out whether they would be interested. They agreed that they would quit when each had gotten an answer from 20 students.

(Continued)

(Continued)

5. Principal Grant and assistants Jackson and Harding have been assigned the task of constructing next summer's leadership development program for all school-based administrators in the school system. Three programs are available and within budget. They need to decide by next Friday afternoon which of the three to recommend, based on polling administrators who are likely to attend. Using a list of administrators who attended last year's program, they e-mailed principals and asked them to rank-order their preferences. They gave respondents a three-day window of opportunity to respond.

6. Principals Porter, Robinson, and Saturday have decided to conduct the definitive study about the most appropriate time to start the school day. They access school-level data from an existing federal database that includes the following variables: (1) school start time, (2) average student scores on criterion-referenced achievement tests, and (3) student demographic characteristics (e.g., gender, race, family income). They use all the schools in the database to determine if there is a relationship between start times and student achievement for elementary, middle, and high schools in a stratified random sample of schools in the United States.

Data Collection in Quantitative Research

The methods section should specify what data were collected from participants, how they were collected, and why the reader should consider the resultant information to be trustworthy measures of the topics being studied. In quantitative studies, the term *instrument* is used to refer to the means by which researchers measure or record data. Instruments might be used to record performance (e.g., achievement on teacher-made tests), participant attitudes (e.g., questionnaires, survey scales), or observations (e.g., walk-through checklists; Creswell, 2009). Numeric data may also include demographic or factual information, such as characteristics of the sample being studied.

Numeric data are symbols; that is, measurement involves assigning some value to represent an underlying attribute of a concept we are interested in studying. Researchers construct measures to enumerate attributes of some underlying construct so that statistics can be used to manipulate these data and arrive at some inference about the meaning of the construct to subjects or the relationships among concepts for the population being studied. There are different types of quantitative measures, including categorical variables (e.g., male, female); ordinal variables, which have a rank order but the differences between response options have no inherent meaning (e.g., small, medium, large); interval variables, whose responses have a rank order and the difference between responses has meaning (e.g., very dissatisfied, dissatisfied, satisfied, very satisfied); and ratio variables (e.g., real numbers, scales with a true zero value; Trochim, 2001). Different levels of measurement open up concurrent possibilities in terms of the statistics that may be employed to derive meaning from quantitative data. See Figure 8.2 for a summary of the types of measures discussed.

Figure 8.2 Types of Quantitative Measures

Categorical Variables	Categories are labels or names; no order is suggested.	Male or female
Ordinal Variables	Categories are named and a rank order is suggested, but the differences between categories are not meaningful.	Small, medium, large
Interval Variables	Categories are named and ranked, and the differences between categories are meaningful.	Very dissatisfied, dissatisfied, satisfied, very satisfied
Ratio Measures	These are real numbers with a scale that has a "zero" point.	Age in years, weight in pounds

Hoy (2010) points out that in quantitative studies, it is important to understand the relationship between theoretical constructs or concepts and variables being measured—for example, trust or intelligence. There is no universal consensus on what these things mean. Reasonable people differ on what "intelligence" represents. To measure such things, we *operationalize* the concept through measurement, and the resulting value is referred to as a variable. As Hoy describes, "The operational definitions must capture the true meaning of the constructs, that is, be valid, and they must provide a consistent and objective measurement, that is, be reliable" (p. 30). Of particular interest here is *construct validity*, which is the term used to refer to the degree to which a measurement can in fact be said to generalize to the theoretical concept or construct you intend to study (Trochim, 2001).

ACTIVITY 8.2   Design an Instrument

Suppose for the moment that you've just been assigned as an assistant principal of Rene Descartes Elementary School, a brand-new math magnet school. Your principal, Dr. Newton, has asked that you devise a measurement tool that would allow the administrative team to visit classes briefly and get a sense of the quality of instruction going on in the school. In other words, he would like you to create a walk-through instrument. Here are Dr. Newton's requirements:

- Your instrument needs to allow you to record phenomena directly observed.

- The result of your data collection must be a quantitative result. In other words, Dr. Newton wants an accounting of how often or in what percentage of visits you observed "good stuff" going on in classes.

- The implementation of the instrument will involve brief visits to many classrooms. For instance, Newton may visit 10 classrooms in a morning. You know that in some cases, students might be engaged in an activity that does not provide an optimal opportunity for him to observe the teacher in action, but across many classes, he hopes to get a good sense of the teaching that's going on in the school.

Newton insists that you focus your attention on *student behaviors*, not teacher behaviors—he may not know much about pedagogy, but he knows that the students do the learning, and he figures that noting what students are doing will give a good read on the quality of their experience.

With all of these in mind, develop a first draft of your walk-through instrument. (Start with some broad categories. In general, what are some characteristics of the *kinds of instruction you'd like to see* at Descartes? Then, what would students *be doing* if this kind of instruction were going on? In other words, what should you be able to observe?)

With one or more critical friends, design your instrument and discuss the merits of employing such an instrument to collect data on the learning climate of your school. How would you go about collecting these data? What steps would you and Dr. Newton need to take to ensure that your inquiry is trustworthy? What are some potential barriers to ensuring such a result?

Instruments

Researchers conducting quantitative studies related to educational problems and solutions are obliged to provide a good deal of information on the instruments used, their appropriateness for the study at hand, and how measures used relate to the underlying constructs involved in the study. And because of the technical nature of the development process, it is quite typical to find that researchers employ measures that have been validated elsewhere, in which case the author is obliged to provide the name of the instrument, the developer, and information related to validity and reliability for use with subjects like the ones featured in the study. If the measure is a survey scale or test, sample items should be provided and information related to scoring should be provided so that the reader understands what a "high" and "low" score means in relation to the underlying construct. If the researcher modified an established instrument, how and why the modification was made should be described fully as well. Finally, how and when the instrument was administered should be clearly stated, information that may be important to assessing generalizability, a pattern of responses inherent in the findings, or potential bias in the results.

All this information is important for you to judge whether use of the instrument was consistent with its established purpose and reasonable for the purposes stated. You might ask yourself whether the instrument seems reasonable as a measure of the underlying construct. It is both reasonable and important to examine the operationalization to determine whether you agree that the measurement reflects a meaning of the underlying construct that you find reasonable. For example, a well-known reading assessment might be used to measure "reading achievement," and you might know from experience with the instrument that it yields inherently subjective assessments of reading achievement when used with students in the grade levels studied. Or an attitude scale might be used to measure "effective leadership" that reflects a fairly narrow meaning of this concept or one that really does not reflect a meaning that would be useful for your purposes.

On occasion, research studies employ original instruments that were devised specifically for that study. Although it is certainly plausible to create a valid and reliable set of measures for a single study, when we as readers encounter this situation, we are wary. At a minimum, in such a circumstance, the authors need to supply a rationale for creating a new measure rather than using an already established one, and they need to supply ample information about how the instrument was pilot or field tested and revised to determine if it is a valid and reliable measure. Finally, it is useful to have some assessment of how the new measures relate to already established ones, including how and why the new measures provide clear advantages to existing measures.

Data Analysis in Quantitative Research

The methods section should describe in some detail how the data collected for the study were analyzed, including procedures used for scoring and cleaning the data, procedures used for analysis, and criteria used for determining inferences based on the results obtained. Fundamentally, the description of analysis must incorporate all the elements already discussed. Information included in this section must "fit" with the design employed, the subjects included, and the kinds of data collected. It should spell out clearly how the data were manipulated and used to render conclusions about the research questions posed.

It is hard for us to provide much in the way of general guidelines for reading the data analysis section of methodology; the features will differ dependent on the nature of the statistics used. Information presented about how the data were collected and scored, for instance, would simply lay out procedures that spelled out how data were collected from members of the accessible sample and what instruments were used to collect these data. Procedures for actually receiving and cleaning these data would spell out how the instruments were received from subjects and what steps were taken to ensure that these were complete and usable.

Among the common features of the analysis section that would apply regardless of test used is a description of how missing data were dealt with in creating the database used for analysis. Invariably, there are several kinds of missing data in any study. First, some individuals included in the study's sample will not respond at all. Second, some individuals who respond to many or most of the questions posed will leave other responses out, either by choice or by mistake. Creswell (2009) suggests that missing data may be an indicator of a flaw in the study—for instance, questions may have been posed that confused or embarrassed respondents, or a survey layout may have obscured a question. The most conservative response to missing data is to eliminate participants with nonresponses, although this will reduce the ensuing sample and may eliminate otherwise worthwhile data. Several statistical techniques exist for imputing missing data as well. Whatever the method, the study's author should make clear how he or she dealt with missing data, and if there is a great deal of missing data inherent in the study, results should be interpreted with due caution.

As we mentioned early in the chapter, many quantitative studies would employ some delineation of specific hypotheses tested. Without going into all the gory details, hypothesis testing involves the process of stating one or more hypotheses that various statistics are used to test, to either support or refute the stated hypothesis. The tools used for hypothesis testing are referred to as inferential statistics. When engaged in hypothesis testing, it is customary to state a null hypothesis, which infers that the relationship you are hoping to support will not occur. For instance, if we were involved in conducting an experimental study to determine if Reading Program X increased comprehension skills among third-graders, our null hypothesis would be that the difference in growth from pretest to post-test for a treatment and comparison group would be zero. An alternative hypothesis might be that growth for the treatment group would be significantly higher than the comparison group. Statistically, we would be testing whether we have confidence that the gain for the treatment group was "non-zero"—that is, not due to chance.

Statistical significance refers to the probability that our observed difference is due to chance. The asterisks you observe after statistical measures on data tables in papers typically refer to a statistic achieving or exceeding a critical value that corresponds to a "significance level" or probability that the observed outcome was due to change, typically 0.05 or 0.01, meaning that we would be either 95% or 99% confident in the result (i.e., the assertion that the resulting statistic is non-zero).

Because statistical significance is sensitive to sample size, such that a study using a large sample would have a greater likelihood of finding non-zero or statistically significant results even when the actual results are quite modest, an alternative metric referred to as practical significance or effect size may also be used to gauge results of a hypothesis test. Effect size allows researchers to gauge the strength of an outcome literally as a small, medium, or large effect, a conclusion that is not influenced by the sample size. There are a variety of different measures used to gauge effect size, each suitable for different underlying statistical tests (Creswell, 2009). The methods section of a quantitative paper should contain clear criteria used for judging both statistical significance and effect size. Reporting both statistical significance and effect size would yield more information to judge the results of the study and, hence, to our mind, would enhance both the utility and trustworthiness of the work.

ACTIVITY 8.3   Reading Research III: Identifying Components of Research Papers

In the previous chapter, we suggested that you engage in two Reading Research activities to begin to explore the merits of published work. For the next Reading Research activity, we suggest that you once again select an article on a topic that you have agreed is a high priority for your schools from a reputable academic journal (e.g., *Educational Administration Quarterly, Journal of School Leadership, American Educational Research Journal*).

(Continued)

(Continued)

Or, if you prefer, go back to the article(s) you selected for Reading Research II. This time, as you peruse the article, identify each of the following:

- The statement of the problem, including the purpose and significance of the study
- The study's primary research questions
- The study's conceptual framework
- The description of methods; see if you can identify each of the following from the methods section:
  o Research design
  o Participants, setting
  o Data collection, instruments
  o Data analysis
  o Limitations
- Presentation of findings or results
- A discussion summarizing implications of the research

To debrief, discuss what you found and any reactions you have to this material. What did you learn from a more careful examination of the structure of the paper and a more deliberate look at the methods section? Does the method seem to "fit"—in other words, is this method useful to answer the research questions posed? Does this examination help you judge the trustworthiness of the piece?

QUALITATIVE RESEARCH DESIGN

Quantitative measures are without a doubt very useful, but they tell only part of the story. Quantitative studies that you have read are typically asking questions about what happened. For example, it would be possible to ask, "Did students in the limited English proficiency subgroup score lower, the same, or higher than the majority population?" or "By how much do the scores of LEP students differ from those of the majority population?" Discovering that LEP students scored substantially lower (perhaps in a statistically significant way) is important information,

Types of Qualitative Research Designs Discussed

- Case studies
- Grounded theory
- Ethnography

but alone, it may not guide action very well, because the answer to this question conveys nothing about *why* LEP students scored lower.

Qualitative research can be viewed in contrast or as complementary to quantitative research. It is primarily concerned with how and why things happen (Maxwell, 2005). It is neither better nor worse than quantitative research, but qualitative studies tend to have somewhat different purposes, because they start from different types of questions. As we discussed above, randomized experimental research has been elevated by the U.S. Department of Education as the "gold standard" for research. This kind of designation is misleading. Just as there are different and appropriate quantitative designs for different situations, qualitative research reveals information that cannot be found with quantitative methods.

Central themes of this book are the importance of root causes and refraining from jumping to solutions too soon in the school improvement process. In some senses, experimental research may bias readers toward jumping to solutions because they believe that evidence that an intervention works automatically implies that it should be widely adopted. This places the solution prior to an understanding of root causes for the problem purported to be solved by the solution or the context under which the solution works. Qualitative research, in contrast, is well suited to examining context deeply, including revealing issues such as root causes, special circumstances for a school or district, and nuanced perspectives of teachers regarding an instructional problem and past efforts to solve it. Instead of just asking, "What works?" qualitative research focuses on how and why things work (or not) and the kinds of problems people encounter in the daily activity of teaching and learning.

We often find that combining quantitative and qualitative design in a mixed-method study provides the clearest discussion of a particular research problem. You may discover as you search the literature that you will obtain a more informed perspective if you consult both quantitative and qualitative studies. Whether research articles are purely qualitative in nature or employ mixed methods, there are several broad types of qualitatively oriented research you are likely to encounter:

- *Case studies,* perhaps the most common form of qualitative research readers of this book will find, are employed to investigate and describe the details of contexts and situations that are not presently well understood (Merriam, 2009; Yin, 2009). They can be conducted as single-case studies to delve deeply into one situation or multiple-case studies intended to compare a small number of cases in order to draw somewhat broader conclusions. Each case will need to involve multiple participants and a deep understanding of the context in which they work.

- *Grounded theory* turns the theory testing from quantitative research designs on its head. Grounded theory is developed by first collecting qualitative data in a specific setting, then working with the data inductively to construct a theory about what the data means and/or what is going on in the setting (Glaser & Strauss, 1999; Phelan, Davidson, & Yu, 1998). Grounded theory helps researchers think about common situations from new perspectives and may result in our "seeing" new phenomena.

- *Ethnography* is a method drawn primarily from anthropology. This is an intensive approach that focuses on one individual or a small group of individuals to learn as much about their lives and perspectives as possible. Context is important as it affects the individual, but the individual is the focus. A classic, early educationally focused ethnography is *The Man in the Principal's Office*, by Harry Wolcott (2003). When first published in 1973, this book revealed many mundane and surprising details of the work life of a suburban elementary school principal.

Many of the same issues that are important in quantitative research design are reflected in qualitative design but with some twists. In the sections that follow, we explain the major components of qualitative investigations in a manner designed to focus your attention on specific components of qualitative research articles, and we do so in a manner parallel to the quantitative designs discussion.

Setting and Participants in Qualitative Research

Understanding the research setting is particularly important for qualitative research because of its tendency to emphasize uniqueness rather than similarities. To appreciate the usefulness of a case, for example, you would need to know how your school is similar to or different from that particular case. That would be difficult to determine without key details of the setting in which the published case was based. Phelan et al. (1998), in their set of seven case studies of students attending diverse high schools in California, demonstrate the need to understand the context deeply and present it in a readable fashion. The following excerpt also gives some glimpses into the work involved in case study method.

Over the course of 2 years, we spent literally hundreds of hours with [50 high school–age] youths. In addition to conducting four in-depth interviews with each student, . . . we spent more than 80 full days shadowing youth (well over 300 classroom observations) and many hours in hallways, lunchrooms, and on school grounds.

As the students became increasingly comfortable, we spent time with them on a regular basis. We found that their descriptions of teachers and classroom events were inherently more understandable when we observed what they described. As we visited on a more regular basis, the students introduced us to their friends and sometimes their families. We spent time in peer groups comprised of recent Mexican and Vietnamese immigrants; second-generation Mexican and Filipino youth; those involved peripherally in gang-related social activities; [and] youth who went through periods of homelessness. . . . In some cases we got to know the friends almost as well as the participants in our study themselves. (pp. 5–6)

In addition to the above authors' effort to understand their participants' high school and social contexts, they reveal that they sought a range of student experiences to put together coherent research findings about how students experience high schools characterized by racial and ethnic diversity. Similar to quantitative research, Phelan et al. (1998) pursued a specific sample that would be representative of students with similar experiences. Rather than trying to achieve a random sample, however, the authors used purposeful sampling to achieve a level of typicality that would not be possible with random sampling because the sample size is too small (Maxwell, 2005). This strategy is typical of qualitative research, because the purpose is to understand differences among participants and their relationship to lived experiences.

Chances are good that you will work to address the learning challenges of a subset of your school's population. You are engaging in a type of purposeful sampling when you look at one or two subgroups in your school and will be interested in research that has examined a similar purposeful sample.

Data Collection in Qualitative Research

Reading qualitative research, one might conclude that there is little or no data because numerical measurements are not involved in the findings. This is a narrow view of what constitutes data. Qualitative researchers work with data that is observable, if not necessarily measurable. One of our research interests is in the area of decision making. Decisions can be observed as they occur in small groups, but the quantification of decisions is likely to be meaningless in most circumstances. There are, however, specific qualitative data such as the pathways decisions take as they are being made and the contexts in which they are made. The most common techniques for collecting this kind of data are interviewing participants, observing behavior, and gathering documents.

Interviews are most often set up as formal appointments in which the researcher asks a participant a predetermined set of questions designed to elicit the participant's experiences and beliefs. A common variation is to make the interview more open-ended to allow the participant to discuss issues the researcher may not have considered prior to the interview. However the interview is ultimately conducted, it is most likely to be audio-taped and transcribed so that the researcher is able to study the details of what the participant said and compare participants with one another.

It is difficult to know if and how a participant may be filtering or otherwise altering responses to questions. Motivation for doing so might be to make the participant look more virtuous or skilled in the eyes of the researcher than she or he actually is. Qualitative researchers seek ways to corroborate what participants have said by asking similar questions of people who hold similar and different positions; they triangulate their data collection. Additionally, triangulation can be derived from employing a different data source—for example, observation. In *Adolescents' Worlds*, Phelan et al. (1998) invested a great deal of effort in observing the students they interviewed to be able to see firsthand what the students were talking about. Doing so and presenting this data in addition to interview data lends greater veracity to the *Adolescents' Worlds* case studies.

In our research on decision making, meeting minutes provide potentially useful documents that memorialize what decisions were made and who participated in the process. Though not always reliable or consistently kept, such documents provide an additional means of triangulation that allows the researcher to verify what was conveyed in interviews and/or observed during meetings.

The methodology section of any qualitative research study should clearly describe the circumstances under which data was collected. More important, you should be able to see how data collection operationalizes or makes concrete the important ideas that appeared in the conceptual framework for the study. You should be able to visualize what the authors of a particular study did in order to obtain the data that they report.

Data Analysis in Qualitative Research

As you might expect, data analysis for qualitative studies involves more interpretation of ambiguous data than is the case for quantitative studies. The simplest way to think about how data analysis works for qualitative research is that the researcher is the analytical instrument (Glaser & Strauss, 1999; Maxwell, 2005; Merriam, 2009). However, this does not mean that data analysis is completely idiosyncratic. The researcher ought to explain which techniques were used for qualitative data analysis and why.

Qualitative researchers will typically develop a set of codes or labels for chunks of interview transcripts, field notes, and/or documents that convey specific ideas. The reader should be informed about how the codes were developed, what software (if any) was used to code and sort data, and whether or not codes were verified through a process of having more than one person apply codes to transcripts. It is common for codes to be developed from the constructs contained in the conceptual framework. For example, if our conceptual framework for a study of middle school students includes the idea of social networks, we will undoubtedly code interview data with that construct whenever we detect participants talking about how they employ or relate to social networks. However, some researchers prefer to derive codes from reading the data rather than referring to the conceptual framework. This occurred in one of our decision-making studies when a doctoral student was reviewing interview transcripts. She noticed that many of those interviewed were preoccupied with the problem of consistent implementation, and she suggested a code not derived from the conceptual framework to capture all the instances of this concern. Qualitative researchers are free to code their data any way they wish, but they have an obligation to explain to the reader the process they used.

The use of data codes facilitates something called the constant-comparative method in which thorough reading of qualitative data sources yields comparisons of different chunks of data that reveal similarities and differences (Merriam, 2009). Another way to look at qualitative data analysis is as sorting (i.e., putting data chunks in smaller piles of like material) and collecting, or finding common attributes that re-sort the data into larger piles that reveal broader themes. Both the search for differences and the search for common themes are important parts of the process of making sense of large quantities of qualitative data (Maxwell, 2005).

Methodology Summary

We have described something of an ideal set of methodology items to look for in research articles. Unfortunately, space limitations and reader interest often combine to create methodology discussions that are far from the ideal. The emphasis in most articles is on findings and conclusions, as it should be. However, this may lead the reader to feel less well informed about how the study was actually conducted. Nevertheless, we have provided markers for you to seek in methodology sections that may help you avoid skipping them and help you derive more information from them. Reading methodology sections more carefully may also give you ideas to use in your own action research to articulate the problem you intend to address and when you design the evaluation of your project (see Chapter 10).

Biases and Limitations

The one element of many methods sections that we did not yet discuss but that should be of interest to readers eager to understand the inherent trustworthiness of a piece is the discussion of potential biases and limitations of the study. While this section is sometimes relegated to the very end of the article, wherever it is presented, it is common for authors to discuss the inherent issues they could not avoid in constructing their research design and in conducting their study.

The issues raised here may be as different as the topics, settings, and procedures featured in empirical works. In quantitative studies, an author might discuss inherent limitations in the accessible sample, for instance, or issues relating to the use of the instrument employed or the analysis used. In qualitative studies, since the researcher is literally a part of the data collection process, it is quite typical to discuss his or her own potential biases or viewpoints and how these might affect the types of questions posed or the analysis itself. In any case, the critical reader will carefully review the limitations cited by the authors of a study and consider the implications of these acknowledgments.

CONCLUDING SECTIONS

Research articles contain a findings or results section in which authors explain what their data reveals. This may be done in a manner that answers the research questions or hypotheses directly, structures the results in terms of the conceptual framework, or a combination of the two. Quantitative studies typically contain tables and graphs of quantitative data with discussions of these statistics in terms of statistical and/or practical significance of findings. Qualitative studies are much more likely to have quotations from interviews or field notes as supporting material for research. (See, for example, the discussion of quantitative and qualitative data displays presented in Chapter 5.) Whatever method is employed, the author should be building a clear argument for what was found in the research setting by providing a preponderance of evidence using statistical results and/or exemplary qualitative data to support the argument made. The findings section ought to be free of conjecture and opinion so that the reader can think about what was discovered without being biased by the author's interpretations of *meanings* (as opposed to interpretations of *data*).

Finally, at the end of a research paper, it is customary to present a concluding section that seeks to make sense of the meaning associated with findings, often returning to the original research questions and significance. The conclusions section is where authors explain what they believe the research means. They typically return to earlier topics in the article, including why the research is important (significance) and their hypotheses about what was happening in the research setting (conceptual framework). A well-written article will use the research literature cited in discussion of the research problem and conceptual framework to explain how this particular study fits into the larger research picture. Finally, authors often discuss surprises they encountered and why these were surprises, gaps in their own research, and ideas for future research that would build on what they found. The conclusions section ought to stimulate your thinking about your project and how research informs the work you will do.

CONCLUSION

There is no doubt that many of us find the details of research articles to be effective antidotes to insomnia. Nevertheless, when confronted with a substantial, persistent student achievement problem, the search for understanding and meaningful responses to that problem should motivate us to want to understand the specifics of relevant research. In this chapter, we introduced a good deal of vocabulary and many issues associated with understanding research publications by reviewing the most typical sections you will find in papers published in peer-reviewed journals. This will also serve as a guide for navigating papers presented at research conferences, as well as final reports of commissioned studies.

We hope that this chapter has provided a sort of manual for understanding how the purposes and questions posed in a research article connect to a specific research perspective and methods used and that you feel more comfortable reading methods sections in research articles in order to glean critical information that informs your school improvement efforts. Most important, our aspiration is that you will be critical in your reading of research so that you can discern what is helpful from what is not. If you can discover research that informs your thinking about a specific student achievement problem and that helps you think about how to conduct your own action research, then you will be well on your way to becoming a research-informed leader in your school and district.

REVIEW QUESTIONS

1. Thinking about the questions that guided your search for published literature relevant to your problem, challenge, or gap, which type of research methodology do you believe is most appropriate? Why?

2. What are some of the sampling challenges presented by your specific problem, challenge, or gap?

3. How is sampling likely to differ for a qualitative study as compared with a quantitative one?

4. In what ways would a mixed-method approach to your focus area reveal a variety of information?

5. What are the various strengths and weaknesses in the research you have found searching for published literature relevant to your focus area?

PART IV

COMPLETING THE JOURNEY: SOLUTIONS, ACTIONS, AND IMPLEMENTATION

The remaining chapters put all the hard work you have engaged in up to this point to good use. In Chapter 9, you will identify an action that you will take to reduce or eliminate the causes of the problem you have been working on. You will also build an action plan that defines how you will go about implementing your project. What you wish to do may be very clear in your own mind at this point, but the action plan is a vital document that helps keep you and everyone working with you honest, focused, and on task. Thus, you will be using what you have learned and the new knowledge you have created to create a blueprint for improving instruction in your school. There are many potential distractions on the path from original conception of the problem, challenge, or gap you may wish to address to actually doing something about it. A well-written action plan serves as an anchor, as a means to avoiding distraction. Quite often, the work of leading school improvement seems to stall once an action plan is written. But as we will discuss in Chapter 10, the point of all your hard work is to implement something, not just to plan it. Consideration of issues relating to implementation and evaluation of your work is critical to your success and to promoting a culture of continuous improvement.

BIG IDEAS: TURNING IDEAS INTO ACTIONS

1. Best practices aren't always...

2. Leaders must articulate a persuasive logic of action that accounts for the fact that solutions must eliminate the *causes* of achievement gaps to be effective.

3. Solutions must be considered within the immediate school context and also in terms of the broader consequences of implementation.

4. Action plans are living documents; flexibility is important.

5. An ounce of prevention goes a long way—predict potential barriers to implementation through consequence analysis.

6. "Success" isn't always meeting your objectives—change takes time, and learning occurs along the way (if you are open to it).

7. Continuous learning requires a sound evaluation plan.

Your work ends with a single, culminating performance: The School Improvement Project Proposal. The proposal is built from the work you have done already, which is extended through your careful consideration of how you will turn ideas into actions that you will implement in your school. The document that you produce should *literally* be suitable for presentation to those leaders in your school (or department) whose approval and support you need to enact your plan, and it will serve as a guide to your work. The plan that you create embodies the potential that you possess as a leader to improve the lives of your students through more effective instruction. When you finish Part IV, it is our hope that you will have a School Improvement Project Proposal that makes you proud, that engenders enthusiasm from your colleagues and administration, that you will implement as a leader in your school with your collaborative team, and that will serve as a vehicle for promoting the creation of a learning organization.

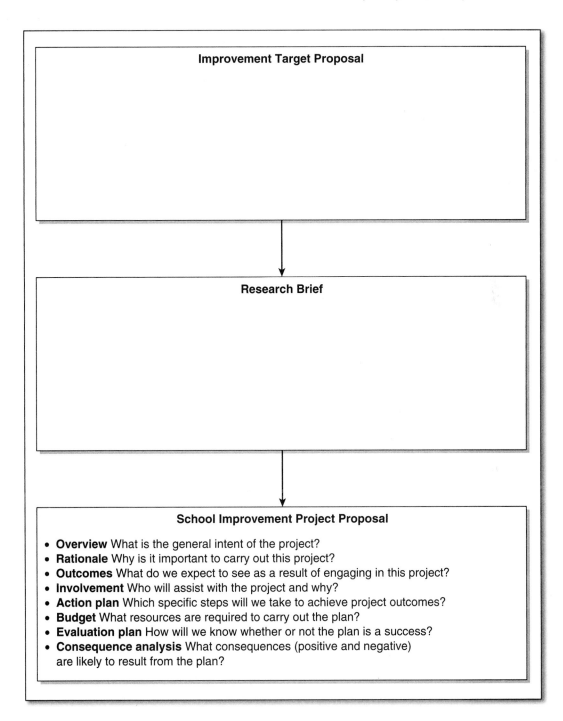

Improvement Target Proposal

Research Brief

School Improvement Project Proposal

- **Overview** What is the general intent of the project?
- **Rationale** Why is it important to carry out this project?
- **Outcomes** What do we expect to see as a result of engaging in this project?
- **Involvement** Who will assist with the project and why?
- **Action plan** Which specific steps will we take to achieve project outcomes?
- **Budget** What resources are required to carry out the plan?
- **Evaluation plan** How will we know whether or not the plan is a success?
- **Consequence analysis** What consequences (positive and negative) are likely to result from the plan?

School Improvement Project Proposal Description and Rubric

Overview

School leaders are increasingly expected to engage in short-term action research projects to demonstrate the efficacy of school programs and practices. Building on your work thus far, you will create a School Improvement Project (SIP) that addresses the problem or "achievement gap" identified through research on your school. Your proposal will describe a specific improvement project that you will *design, implement,* and *evaluate* over the next year. The expectation is that you will lead a team in implementation of this project.

Tasks

1. *Overview:* The proposal should start with a concise and well-thought-out description of the achievement gap you have identified through your assessment of student performance and achievement data, followed by a clear *statement of purpose* that generally demonstrates how you intend to address the performance gap. After stating this purpose, include an *overview* of the project that provides a brief description of what you intend to do to implement your proposal.

2. *Rationale:* Include a concise and well-thought-out *rationale* that describes why it is important to address the performance gap you identified and your espoused theory of action that suggests why taking the proposed action will lead to improvement in the targeted area. Be sure to describe how your SIP connects to or reinforces your school's vision and objectives. Use the research literature to support your strategy for addressing the achievement gap you identified.

3. *Outcomes:* Provide a short description of the *specific outcomes* you believe you will achieve by successfully implementing your project. Be specific; identify the performance indicators you intend to track in order to measure the educational outcomes that are important in your improvement area.

4. *Involvement:* The expectation is that you will be engaging members of your school community in designing and enacting your improvement project. Provide a short summary of who you involved in the creation of this proposal and which stakeholders you envision involving in the enactment and assessment of the SIP. Describe how you plan to enlist their support and build your team, including means you will use to maintain effective communication throughout the project.

5. *Action Plan:* The proposal must include a clear, step-by-step *action plan* that defines the objective of the project (i.e., restates your purpose as an action objective) and delineates each of the major tasks that need to be completed during the project, when each task will be completed, who is responsible for each task,

the resources needed to complete each task, and specific "success signals" that serve as indicators of the completion of major steps in the project. This should be presented as a table—use the action planning format in Chapter 9 to prepare the action plan.

6. *Budget:* Following the action plan, a clear, well-thought-out *budget summary* should be presented. This can be a short narrative presentation (you do not need budget codes, etc.). The narrative should include a synopsis of the funding needed to complete the project, a description of any existing resources that will be devoted to the project, and a discussion of how authority to use these resources has been (or will be) procured (if necessary).

7. *Evaluation Plan:* Include a narrative explanation of how you plan to *evaluate your project,* which includes (a) the specific indicators you will be examining to determine impact of the project on student performance or on the learning environment, (b) a description of how and when you plan to collect data about these indicators, and (c) a brief description of the analysis you plan to conduct to examine these data in order to ascertain the impact of the project on your intended outcomes.

8. *Consequence Analysis:* In closing, briefly discuss the advantages and the potential limitations of the project. In particular, conduct a *consequence analysis* to predict any issues that might arise during implementation or any limitations you might face in terms of using the evaluation design to draw trustworthy inferences about the effectiveness of the project. If possible, include reference to issues raised in the literature.

Note: The proposal is not an essay, per se; it can be written using each of the sections listed above, and some information can be presented in bullets (e.g., a listing of outcomes measured) or in tables (e.g., the action plan). There is a fair amount of redundancy in this proposal—for instance, the description of the project should provide a brief narrative explanation that matches the project delineated in the action plan, and the list of outcomes measured should relate to the evaluation plan (which describes how you will go about collecting these data and what you will look at to know if you were successful). The audience for this proposal is your principal (or other administrator who has authority to approve implementation)—imagine that you are presenting this document to him or her and lobbying for adoption of this project (which you will lead).

Your research proposal should be no more than twelve (12) pages and should include citations and a reference list in APA format.

(Continued)

School Improvement Project Proposal Assessment Rubric

Criteria	Exceeds Expectations	Meets Expectations	Approaching Expectations	Falls Below Expectations
Statement of purpose and overview of project: Use of data to identify SIP topic that relates to and supports the school's vision and objectives (ELCC 1.2) Weight: 10%	The proposal begins with a clear statement of purpose, which relates specifically to an improvement area identified using assessment results, demographic data, and analysis of school and community needs. A concise but thorough description of the proposed project is provided that spells out the actions proposed to reduce the identified performance gap.	The proposal begins with a statement of purpose, which relates generally to an improvement area identified using assessment data. A brief description of the proposed project is provided.	The statement of purpose and/or description of the project is evident but is vaguely worded or poorly spelled out. It is difficult to discern a clear focus of the project.	The statement of purpose and/or project description is missing or wholly inadequate.
Rationale: Use of best practice research strategies to promote improvement (ELCC 2.3) Weight: 10%	The proposal includes a concise and well-supported rationale that describes the nature of the problem being addressed, why the problem is important, and how taking the proposed action is intended to lead to improvement. Specific, current research is presented in support of the strategy selected to address the identified performance gap.	The proposal includes a rationale that describes the nature of the problem being addressed and why the problem is important to the attainment of the school's objectives but is somewhat unclear about how taking the proposed action is intended to lead to improvement. Research support is referenced.	The proposal includes a rationale but only generally connects the proposed action to the reduction of the identified performance gap. Research supporting the proposed action is weakly presented or not evident.	The rationale is weak or wholly inadequate. It is not clear how enacting the proposed project relates to reducing the identified performance gap.

Criteria	Exceeds Expectations	Meets Expectations	Approaching Expectations	Falls Below Expectations
Outcomes: Identification of specific outcomes that will be used to monitor and evaluate the project (ELCC 1.4) Weight: 10%	Specific indicators are identified and described that will be used to monitor and evaluate the implementation and impact of the project. Each indicator is well connected to either monitoring implementation fidelity of the project or promoting the desired outcome(s).	Specific outcome indicators are identified and described that could be used to monitor and evaluate the impact of the project. Indicators used to monitor implementation fidelity are unclear.	The proposal makes general reference to the kinds of outcomes sought, but specific measurable indicators of implementation fidelity and/or project outcomes are not clearly identified.	The outcomes associated with the project are not specified, or outcomes that do not relate to the identified performance gap are proposed.
Involvement: Identification and formation of team to enact project (ELCC 1.3) Weight: 5%	The proposal clearly describes which stakeholders will be involved in enactment, monitoring, and evaluation of the SIP. All stakeholders who are important to the success of the project are involved. Team member roles and responsibilities are outlined, as are means that will be used to maintain effective communication among team members.	The proposal describes the primary stakeholders who will be involved in enactment of the SIP. One or more groups whose involvement may be important are omitted. Attributes of team organization are described in general terms.	The proposal is unclear about stakeholders' involvement in enactment of the SIP or fails to mention groups who are obviously important to the success of the project. Attributes of team organization are referenced in general terms.	Stakeholder involvement in planning and/or implementation is not evident.

(Continued)

(Continued)

Criteria	Exceeds Expectations	Meets Expectations	Approaching Expectations	Falls Below Expectations
Action Plan: Development of action plan to guide the implementation of SIP (ELCC 3.1) Weight: 20%	The proposal includes a clear and well-thought-out action plan that focuses on effective deployment of human, fiscal, and material resources to guide the implementation of the SIP. The plan thoroughly delineates each of the major tasks to be accomplished in enacting the project, when each task will be completed, who is involved in accomplishing each task, the resources needed to complete each task, and specific "success signals" or process indicators that will be tracked to monitor completion of each stage of the project, including evaluation of the project.	The proposal includes an action plan that describes how human, fiscal, and material resources will be used to implement the SIP. The plan delineates most of the major tasks needed to enact the project, when various tasks will be completed, who is involved in accomplishing each task, the resources needed to complete each task, and specific "success signals" or process indicators that will be tracked to monitor completion of each stage of the project. Some necessary tasks or implementation details are vague or missing.	The included action plan details tasks, timelines, persons responsible, resources, and success indicators but does so in a fashion that is unlikely to result in successful deployment of human, fiscal, and material resources to accomplish the stated purpose. Significant tasks are inadequately spelled out or are missing entirely.	The action plan is poorly organized, severely lacking in detail, or wholly missing. It is entirely unclear how any proposed actions can result in successful implementation of the project.

Criteria	Exceeds Expectations	Meets Expectations	Approaching Expectations	Falls Below Expectations
Budget: Use of new and existing resources to facilitate SIP (ELCC 3.3) Weight: 5%	The proposal includes a budget summary that demonstrates the ability to identify, seek, and procure new and existing resources to facilitate the implementation of the SIP. The budget includes a synopsis of the funding needed to accomplish the project, a description of any existing resources that will be devoted to the project, and a discussion of how authority to use these resources has been or will be procured.	The proposal includes a budget summary that spells out in general terms how resources will be identified and procured to facilitate the implementation of the SIP. Funding needed to accomplish the project is identified, a description of any existing resources that will be devoted to the project is outlined, and a discussion of how authority to use these resources has been or will be procured is described.	A budget summary is presented, but it is lacking in sufficient detail or is missing necessary components. The use of existing resources is not well thought out, and/or procedures for leveraging these resources are undeveloped or missing.	The budget is poorly organized, severely lacking in detail, or wholly inadequate to support the objective and action plan described.

(Continued)

(Continued)

Criteria	Exceeds Expectations	Meets Expectations	Approaching Expectations	Falls Below Expectations
Evaluation: Plan to monitor and evaluate the project (ELCC 1.4) Weight: 15%	A clear, well-developed plan to monitor and evaluate the project is presented, which specifies how data related to each educational indicator will be collected, when these data will be collected, and how they will be analyzed. The evaluation plan includes steps that will be taken to examine and adjust the project during enactment (i.e., monitor implementation) and to summatively assess the efficacy of the project in terms of reducing the identified performance gap.	A plan to monitor and evaluate the project is presented, which specifies how data related to most of the identified educational indicators will be collected, when these data will be collected, and how they will be analyzed. The evaluation plan includes general steps that will be taken to monitor implementation and to summatively assess the efficacy of the project.	A plan to monitor and evaluate the project is presented, but it lacks specificity and/or is not clearly connected to the espoused objectives of the SIP. Steps that will be taken to collect and analyze various data are unclear, as are methods that will be used to monitor implementation and to summatively assess the efficacy of the project.	The evaluation plan is poorly organized, lacks sufficient detail, or is wholly inadequate to support the evaluation of the project.

Criteria	Exceeds Expectations	Meets Expectations	Approaching Expectations	Falls Below Expectations
Consequence analysis: Identification of potential issues related to enactment of plan within the school and school community (ELCC 4.2) Weight: 10%	The proposal concludes with a detailed analysis of the benefits and limitations of the proposed project design, highlighting possible issues relating to enactment of the plan within the school and school community. Advantages and disadvantages of the project and evaluation design are highlighted, including an assessment of issues relating to the involvement and support of important stakeholders within the school community. Issues relating to implementation fidelity and the trustworthiness of the evaluation research design are clearly spelled out.	The proposal concludes with a general analysis of the benefits and limitations of the proposed project design, including issues relating to the support and involvement of important stakeholders. Obvious advantages and disadvantages of the project and evaluation design are identified. Select issues related to implementation fidelity and trustworthiness of the research evaluation design are explored, though some important potential issues are not identified.	The proposal concludes with a cursory analysis of the advantages and disadvantages of the proposed design. Issues of stakeholder involvement, implementation fidelity, and trustworthiness are only superficially addressed.	The proposal concludes with a general restatement of the project's purpose and/or description but lacks any reasonable reflection on the strengths or weaknesses of the proposed design. A consequence analysis is not evident.

(Continued)

(Continued)

Criteria	Exceeds Expectations	Meets Expectations	Approaching Expectations	Falls Below Expectations
Support: Informed consumer of educational theory and concepts (ELCC 6.1) Weight: 5%	Specific, developed ideas and/or evidence from research is used to support the selection of the achievement gap and the strategy identified for addressing it.	Supporting research used for the project lacks specificity or is loosely developed.	General supporting ideas or evidence is presented.	Few to no solid supporting ideas or evidence from research is included.
Organization of proposal Weight: 5%	Proposal is powerfully organized and fully developed.	Proposal includes logical progression of ideas aided by clear transitions.	Proposal includes brief skeleton (i.e., introduction, body, conclusion) but lacks effective transitions.	Proposal lacks logical progression of ideas.
Mechanics Weight: 5%	Proposal is nearly error-free, which reflects clear understanding and thorough proofreading.	Proposal includes occasional grammatical errors and questionable word choice.	Proposal includes errors in grammar and punctuation, but spelling has been proofread.	Proposal includes frequent errors in spelling, grammar, and punctuation.

CHAPTER 9

IDENTIFYING SOLUTIONS AND ACTION PLANNING FOR SCHOOL IMPROVEMENT

LEARNING OUTCOMES

Readers who grasp the most important ideas from this chapter will be able to

- select a promising solution (or set of solutions) that addresses root causes of the problem, challenge, or gap they have identified and
- create a step-by-step action plan to implement and evaluate the identified solution.

All the hard work you and your collaborative team have done to think about the instructional gap you wish to address is brought together in this chapter as you consider planning a course of action. You have been working on a logic of action that goes something like this: "Our primary instructional challenge is [ ] that affects [ ] students in a number of ways. The most critical root causes of this problem that we can influence at school are [ ]." Having done all the previous work, now is the time to review the proposed solutions you found in literature, through investigations in your school, and with your collaborative team to choose a course of action that you believe will reduce the root causes of your problem and thus promote improvement in your target area. This chapter is about selecting a solution or course of action and about the processes that go into creating an action plan that defines how you will successfully implement your strategy.

FINDING THE PREFERRED SOLUTION

Throughout the previous chapters, we have suggested that it is best to stay away from locking into a solution until you and those on your collaborative team thoroughly understand the problem you are addressing. Despite these warnings, unless you are exceptionally rare, you have been tempted by several "obvious" courses of action, either because you have networked with leaders in other schools or in your school system office who have recommended actions they know to be successful or because you have run across literature touting a program that works, or both. Even as you were building your knowledge about the nature of the problem and its likely causes, you have no doubt been tempted to lock onto a course of action. After all, you're human.

You and your collaborative team may indeed find that choosing a solution is obvious because of the natural course of your discussions about the problem, the target student group, the literature that informs the problem, and the root causes you have identified. Our research suggests that a well-functioning team is able to arrive at a solution relatively easily and quickly when they focus first on the problem and when a common perspective has been developed over time (Brazer, Rich, & Ross, 2010). The more difficult task is being persuasive that the solution you have chosen will actually reduce or eliminate root causes—a task often neglected by teams pleased with their agreement about a solution.

Just as some teams arrive at solutions easily, others struggle to agree. Settling on a particular solution is a big commitment. The team is stating that this is the way to make a potentially long-standing problem better and to improve student achievement. Very strong implications about change are embedded in the proposed solution. As we learned in Chapter 2, making change is difficult because people get frozen into a specific way of doing things. For a leader to help others change how they do things, she or he must find ways for them to "unfreeze" from their current thinking (Lewin, 1947). You may be feeling good about the extent to which your team has become unfrozen during the processes you have gone through up to this point. Do not be surprised, however, if some refreezing occurs before the group actually moves to a solution. Making changes in the ways in which instruction is carried out will make teachers nervous because it may undercut their influence as their old ways of teaching go into decline and because moving to a new teaching strategy or means of delivering a portion of the curriculum carries teachers into an untried and unknown professional reality. Some resistance under these circumstances is natural.

Your search for a solution is complicated, as well, by the broader policy environment. As we discussed earlier, federal policy stresses the adoption of evidence-informed change strategies based on scientifically based research. Although there has been a fair degree of debate over what kinds of research are credentialed under this definition, as we discussed in Chapter 8, experimental research is touted as the "gold standard" for supporting cause-and-effect claims (i.e., instituting this program for these groups will produce the following improvements in student learning). The What Works Clearinghouse is available as a repository of information about the evidence supporting various change strategies.

ACTIVITY 9.1   Exploring the What Works Clearinghouse

In the initial Reading Research activities, we suggested that you first access secondary research sources that would typically be available in easily read journals such as *Phi Delta Kappan* and next identify and read primary sources from academic, peer-reviewed journals. For the most part, these initial activities were directed at developing a deep understanding of the causes of your instructional target area.

As we turn our attention to solutions, we suggest you familiarize yourself with one of the websites designed by the U.S. Department of Education to provide broad access to research knowledge about "what works" (i.e., potential research-based solutions of educational problems). To complete this activity, access the What Works Clearinghouse at http://ies.ed.gov/ncee/wwc and peruse the site. (Start by locating *Using the WWC: A Practitioner's Guide* to gain basic familiarity with the site.) Next, search the Clearinghouse for programs that appear to connect well to your identified problem and its causes. Select one such program, and review material available on the site concerning the efficacy of the program.

Using Worksheet 9.1, summarize the evidence you glean from the What Works Clearinghouse entry for this program. With one or two partners, exchange your bibliographic entries and provide some constructive criticism of each other's work.

- What did each of you think of the program and its applicability to your school improvement work? What criteria did you use to assess this?

- What did you find useful about the site?

- How useful is the material you accessed for researchers and practitioners seeking to find ways to improve schools?

To debrief, discuss your collective reactions to the material you found and to the Clearinghouse. Also discuss how members of your group decided what was important to access, what was important to share, and what conclusions (if any) you were able to make based on examination of these materials. What did you learn? How, or in what ways, might you consider the material to be trustworthy? Why? What questions do you have about the Clearinghouse itself?

(Continued)

(Continued)

Addendum

The U.S. Department of Education provides a companion site designed to assist educators to learn how to implement the kinds of strategies featured as effective in the WWC. The Doing What Works Clearinghouse can be accessed at http://dww.ed.gov.

Certain types of methodologies are obviously stronger than others and allow greater confidence in the inference that taking an action will produce a particular result. However, we have encouraged you throughout to concentrate on building a thorough understanding of the problem you are working on in your school and to triangulate the evidence you have about the problem and its possible causes. Similarly, your inquiry en route to selecting a preferred solution needs to be guided by amassing credible information from a variety of sources, systematically weighing the worth of available evidence, and incorporating your craft knowledge about your school, its staff, and your students to develop a defensible rationale for what will work for you.

Goldring and Berends (2009) provide an excellent discussion of the kinds of criteria you might bring to bear on this decision. In noting that many educators consider "promising practices" that they learn about from observation and discussion with colleagues at other schools, they write,

> It is important to articulate specifically what the purpose, goal, and outcomes of the practices are. Not all fads should be considered promising practices. What makes this practice promising? How widespread is the evidence about the effect of the practice under consideration, in the absence of high-quality scientific research? (p. 175)

They go on to suggest that additional considerations might include whether the setting and circumstances existing in other schools are similar to your own, whether the staff and other participants are similar (e.g., do they have similar skills and abilities?), whether existing programs and practices in other settings "fit" with the proposed practice in a fashion that would be similar in your school, and whether the level of support in other settings would be similar in your own school.

You and your team should consider the strength of the evidence that a promising practice is indeed promising, whether it is appropriate for your school, and if adoption of the strategy has a high probability of success. Worksheet 9.1 provides a tool for synthesizing this information using a format that is similar to the one you used as you examined the literature to learn about causes (found in Worksheet 6.1).

Assembling your evidence systematically using this tool will help foster comparison and promote dialogue among members of your collaborative team.

Matching Proposed Solutions to Root Causes

Using the data you have amassed about potential solutions, the team can now turn to the process of selecting what they perceive to be the best solution, or set of solutions, to address the specific learning problem, challenge, or gap on which the team has agreed. Criteria for selection must be understood by everyone on the team in order for the process to work well and for the ultimate solution to be as effective as possible. In the process of attaching potential solutions as the last link in the chain that is the logic of action of your school improvement project, your team will test how well the solutions fit by applying the agreed-on criteria. In short, you and your team will be asking, "Can we persuade others that our solution will achieve the outcomes we seek?" Answering this question provides the core of the rationale that will become a critical element in your School Improvement Project Proposal.

Worksheet 9.2 provides a format for the initial team discussion of potential solutions. Essentially, we recommend that team members share their analysis of potential solutions and that the group outline on butcher paper your analysis of these solutions in terms of the cause(s) they may eliminate, the outcomes you would expect, and the strength of the evidence you have amassed suggesting that implementing the solution(s) will work in schools like yours. The goal of this discussion is to work toward a consensus decision on a solution, which will yield a coherent logic of action connecting all your work to a proposal for change.

We have used the term *logic of action* throughout the book as a fancy way of explaining why a particular solution makes sense. Essentially, your goal all along has been the formulation of a coherent and persuasive logic of action that explains your proposal for change. The general pattern of a logic of action statement follows:

> Problem A exists for Student Population B because of Root Causes X, Y, and Z that we control or influence. The best way to reduce or eliminate the root causes is through Action(s) D (E and F).

Clearly articulating the logic of action of your school improvement effort in this manner allows you and your team to consider specific solutions in terms of their effectiveness in addressing root causes, rather than on the basis of internal politics, power, or personal influence. The problem, the student population, and the root causes become important criteria for considering proposed solutions. Consider the example in the following box.

LINKING ROOT CAUSES AND SOLUTIONS

Natalie and her team determined that they wanted to improve math achievement for sixth-grade limited-English-proficient (LEP) students. They started to develop their logic of action based on the following:

- Sixth-grade LEP students are achieving substantially below state standards because...

- They lack vocabulary necessary to understand instruction and solve word problems.

- Additional root causes identified by Natalie's team include poor attendance, instruction that does not accommodate second-language learners, and inadequate understanding of basic math facts.

The team considered the following solutions derived from their reading of published literature and their discussions about their local situation:

1. An after-school tutorial program to help build LEP students' vocabulary

2. Collaboration among math and language arts teachers and those who teach English to speakers of other languages to help build math vocabulary in multiple settings

3. Professional development for math teachers focused on creating culturally responsive classrooms that help meet the needs of LEP students

4. Working with feeder elementary schools to learn how LEP students are responding to math instruction and what happens when basic math facts are not mastered

5. Enlisting the help of a central office math specialist to work with feeder elementary schools and the middle school to create common assessments for LEP students that help track their progress over time

6. Engaging parents in a culturally appropriate parent education program intended to help parents support their children more effectively at home, including requiring them to attend school unless they are ill

Each of the listed solutions can be considered based on the root-cause criteria. We would reject Solution 1 immediately, because the idea of after-school tutoring contradicts the poor-attendance root cause. If these students are having difficulty attending school at all, they are not likely to participate in after-school tutoring, and there are logistical problems with this alternative. Solution 2 seems attractive because it directly addresses the root cause of weak math vocabulary. It has the added benefit of tapping into school-site expertise—both about vocabulary and about the children involved—to help reduce or eliminate the root cause. Similar to Solution 2, Solution 3 could be implemented and have an effect in the current school year. More important, it is a clear response to the root cause of instruction not accommodating the needs of LEP students. More culturally responsive classrooms might also mitigate the attendance problem, but this outcome seems less assured. Solutions 4 and 5 are potentially helpful, but they appear to be longer term efforts that would not bear fruit for a few years. These might be put aside to be considered later in favor of implementing solutions that will have a more immediate effect on student achievement. Solution 6 might be appealing to the team, because enlisting parent support would reinforce efforts made from within the school and because it could address the attendance root cause.

Specific Objectives

Note from the box that an overall goal is heavily implied by articulation of the challenge area and its root causes. The goal in this case would be to improve LEP students' math achievement. Specific objectives are implied in the proposed solutions. Solution 2 suggests the objective of enhancing math vocabulary through specific activities taking place in English for speakers of other languages and language arts instruction. The objective associated with Solution 3 is to enhance math teacher effectiveness by improving the cultural responsiveness of their classrooms and teaching. Solution 6 carries with it the objective of helping parents become closer partners in the schooling process of their children. All these objectives could be more specifically stated in terms of benchmarks or standards, such as 40% of LEP parents will attend at least one parent education event. The point we wish to emphasize is that goals and objectives that are implicit in our development of a logic of action should be made explicit in the School Improvement Project Proposal so that others who have not been on the collaborative team can understand the team's intentions.

Solutions 2, 3, and 6 might appear the most attractive to Natalie's team because of their logical links to the identified root causes and because of their potential for near-term impact (a criterion we added as we considered the example). These are merely our perceptions, however. Natalie's hypothetical team would be far more informed than we are about the problem, the student population, and the school context. Nevertheless, the exercise we have engaged in demonstrates how each of the major pieces of problem identification and solution searching might contribute to the creation of a clear logic of action that would support an action plan. We encourage you to use Worksheet 9.3 to engage your own team in the creation of a logic of action for your School Improvement Project Proposal.

Additional Criteria

Up to this point in our discussion, we have been considering the logic of action of your proposal within the very narrow perspective of your collaborative team. To make your ultimate action plan truly persuasive to your administrative team and others, you need to use a broader point of view. Place yourself in your principal's chair for a few minutes. Every proposal for change that is brought to you for approval carries with it consequences, even if the rosy predictions of the proposer come true. Teachers, parents, students, central office administrators, and school board members individually and collectively could be upset by the proposed change for a wide variety of reasons. Every change represents an exponential increase for you (the principal) in time and effort spent on your job because of the multiple constituencies that must be communicated with and placated. Then there are practical considerations such as whether or not the school can tolerate one more initiative, whether the proposal is consistent with board policy and procedures, and whether the necessary resources are available.

Moving back to your own chair, it is your job to lead your team through a process of matching preferred solutions to criteria beyond the root causes of the problem you have identified. The best solution in the world cannot succeed in the face of a principal's reluctance. You and your team will need to articulate persuasive arguments that use multiple criteria as their foundation. Consider the questions presented in Figure 9.1 as guidelines for your thinking; these were constructed to span the four analytic frames derived from Bolman and Deal (2008) introduced in Chapter 2 and, thus, to promote consideration of a variety of perspectives.

No single solution is likely to satisfy all the above criteria equally well, but at least some will need to be met in order for your proposal to have a good chance of being accepted. For example, a principal who agrees that the solution will make him or her look good in the eyes of the central office and the community is more likely to work hard to find resources to support the proposal.

Whatever criteria you use to assess the quality of your proposed solution—root causes and others—you must be able to provide clear evidence to support your arguments about how your solutions address the criteria. Doing so could be as simple as pulling out key language from the vision, mission, or goals; as direct as using a quotation from a board member that appeared in a local newspaper; or as subtle as tapping into one of the principal's core values. The more criteria that can be satisfied by the solutions you and your team select,

Figure 9.1   Evaluating Solutions Through Bolman and Deal's (2008) Four Frames

Structural Frame	Human Resource Frame
1. Does the proposal support the stated mission and/or strategic goals of the school?	1. What are participants' needs as they implement the proposal?
2. Does the proposal address a priority? (Do multiple constituencies agree that the problem addressed by the proposal is a priority?)	2. How will you motivate people before, during, and after implementation?
3. Do rules, roles, and relationships support the changes you intend? (Have you involved people with the roles and relationships that are most needed to support the proposal?)	3. Do leaders and followers have the skills and knowledge they require to support proposal implementation?
Political Frame	**Symbolic Frame**
1. How will implementers be involved in decision making?	1. Is the proposal consistent with "the way we do things around here"?
2. Whose authority is needed in order to boost the likelihood of widespread implementation?	2. Does the proposal contradict or reinforce any cherished myths or stories?
3. Have significant stakeholders who might be affected by the change been consulted?	3. What are the "sacred cows" the proposal challenges? (How are people likely to react?)
4. What are the significant interest groups associated with proposal implementation? (What do they want? What power do they have to influence the change? Where does their power come from?)	4. How will you help constituents interpret the meaning of the changes embedded in the proposal?
	5. Does the proposal honor the past, anticipate the future, or both?

the more effective your choice is likely to be. The process of linking solutions to multiple effectiveness criteria leads to the creation of an overall rationale for implementing your school improvement project.

The rationale for your school improvement project can be stated by answering the question that may be on many people's minds but is likely not to be asked directly: "Why should we change what we are doing to do what you recommend?" You have come to the point in the planning process where

Common Questions Stakeholders Have About Proposed School Improvement Projects

1. What larger goal am I accomplishing by participating in this proposal?

2. How does the proposal benefit me directly? What problem is it solving for me?

3. How does the proposal benefit me indirectly?

4. In what ways will the proposal make my work more effective? How do you know?

5. In what ways will the proposal make my work easier to accomplish?

6. In what ways will the proposal make my work more gratifying to me?

7. How does the proposal give me a brighter future?

8. What benefits will the school community see as a result of implementing this proposal?

what you say is no longer just about your target population of students. Your school improvement project must be seen by those who are charged with implementing it as beneficial to them, or they are likely to ignore you—or worse. In the next chapter, we will discuss issues related to implementation, including the benefit of exploring potential barriers that may come up as you announce and begin to implement your work. For now, suffice it to say that as you arrive at your preferred solution, you are working to establish a rationale that incorporates the ideas and concerns of multiple stakeholders in your school and in the school's community, including students, teachers, parents, school and district administrators, and potentially members of the community at large. Exploring their likely questions and interests (see sidebar) will help you and your team develop a rationale that speaks to their concerns.

A Case of Organizational Learning

Clearly articulating your logic of action and presenting a strong rationale to your school community are two processes that engage those who work and learn in your school in the process of organizational learning. However, organizational learning tends to be nonlinear, and much of it began long before you got to this stage. All the work you did with respect to problem identification and root-cause analysis is based on the concept of comparing espoused theories with theories in use. Depending on how public you have been in your work and how widespread your involvement of others has been, you are likely to have opened up many undiscussables, some of which are probably painful to members of the school community. To fully engage in organizational learning will require you to change the governing variables that have allowed the problem you have identified to persist for so long (Argyris, 1999). Taking action to eliminate root causes and improve student and school performance will eliminate some governing variables and institute others. In short, action planning and ultimate implementation are, at the core, results of organizational learning.

In Chapter 2, we borrowed from Schlechty (2001) to explain that most changes in schools have little meaning, because they are too shallow. Part of the action planning process needs to address this question: "How can we plan and communicate in a manner such that this action plan will be in place long enough to see results?" Bringing the whole school along with you in the process of organizational learning goes a long way in changing perceptions of your project from trivial to vital.

Conclusion

We conclude our discussion of identifying and selecting solutions with two cautions. Much of decision theory—and by extension, much of our thinking about practical decision making—is dominated by the concept of optimization. Optimization defines the best solution as that which provides the greatest value at the least cost. Certainly, this is a fine criterion when all variables are known. It is difficult to apply in educational settings, however, because there are numerous variables impacting learning problems that we either do not understand or cannot influence. Think about the common challenge of different teachers handling the same curriculum and instructional strategies with very different outcomes. Under conditions of ambiguity and uncertainty—characteristics that are prevalent, if not dominant, in schools—decision makers are more likely to choose solutions that appear to be "good enough" to address specific needs. March and Simon (1993) call this process *satisficing*. It is no better or worse than optimizing. It may simply be the best we can do under certain circumstances. The concept of satisficing suggests that selecting the "best" solution is relative, among other things, to the opportunities you and your collaborative team have to implement what you select.

Second, organizational theory teaches us that organizations such as schools are subject to a great deal of pressure from the environment to adopt change strategies that are popular at the time. DiMaggio and Powell (1983) talk about these forces as an "iron cage," powerful because they reward adoption of practices more because they are readily accepted and associated with "effective schools" than because they produce lasting results. We are all subject to such forces; they come in the form of central offices supporting favored programs with resources, the popular and trade press touting certain solutions as preferred, and so on. (Of course, to borrow wisdom from a different context, just because a strategy is heavily touted doesn't mean it won't be effective in your school, for your issue.) At this point, you and your team have built an evidence-based argument and articulated a logic of action that spells out quite clearly why you believe the action you endorse will work, and in endorsing this course of action, you have also expressed willingness to be leaders in implementation and accountable for assessing the efficacy of your actions. Now, it is time to plan how you will enact this project.

ACTIVITY 9.2   Some Questions to Ask About Solutions

At this juncture, you and members of your collaborative team are likely convinced that the actions you are proposing are compelling. In preparation for moving from concept to action plan and in preparation for the need to "sell" your idea to colleagues, spend some time with one or more critical friends discussing the following:

- What evidence suggests that taking this action will help us achieve our goal?

- What more do we need to know about this course of action—about the efficacy of the strategy, the resources needed to successfully implement it, the connection between this strategy and other things we are doing at school and so on?

- What *evidence* do we have that suggests that this strategy is "high leverage"— that is, that it will *affect student learning and/or alter teacher behavior*? How do we know that it is the most effective and efficient means to reach our goal?

CREATING YOUR ACTION PLAN

As important as it is to develop the arguments that link your team's proposed solutions to addressing the larger goal of your project and specific root causes of the problem, you will need to take specific steps to move from choosing a solution into implementation. Quite literally, you will need to create an action plan that spells out how you and your team will lead others to make your change project a reality and how you will determine if the project was a success. You will be formulating a work plan that you can use to communicate to others and to track the fidelity of implementation at each stage of the project. Creating the action plan will also help you clarify whose support you need, including whose permission or authority you will need to procure to enact the project and the resources you will need to amass to be successful.

Virtually everyone in the education business has experience as an action planner. A lesson plan, for instance, is a type of action plan: It specifies clearly and simply how a teacher intends to facilitate learning to meet well-defined learning objectives, a timeline for implementation, and a means for assessing learning. In a similar fashion, the action plan you and your team will create will communicate clearly the tasks that need to take place to enact your plan, who will be responsible and accountable for leading each task, the resources you will need, a timeline for completing various tasks, and success signals that will allow you and your team to conduct an ongoing, formative evaluation of your implementation and adjust your actions along the way.

Before laying out the steps to create your action plan, we want to emphasize that an action plan is truly a living document. The plan you create now is a hypothesis about what you will need to do to implement your project successfully. However, in the real-world context in which you will work, an awful lot can happen to require adjustment to your plan along the way. As some examples, staff included in your plan may be reassigned, resources you believed to be available might not be as plentiful as you had hoped, or the district might announce adoption of a new program that affects how your work will proceed. Along the way, you might learn based on your ongoing assessment of the action plan that some assumptions you had at the outset need to be reconsidered.

The point here is exceedingly important. A well-developed and thought-through action plan is like the blueprint of a building: It provides you guidance and a "big-picture" view of your work. But just as an architect needs to revise the blueprint when the building code changes or it is discovered that the ground under one wing is ill suited to bear the weight of the building or needed material is in short supply, so too will you need to adjust your action plan as you implement your project to adjust for events and circumstances you could not predict beforehand. We recall an instance when we were working with a high school principal who had major parts of his building unexpectedly shut down during the school year and who commented that the only thing that kept him sane during that time was a comprehensive action plan guiding his school's improvement activity. Even amid a great deal of chaos and even though the action plan required substantial revision at the time as a result of this chaos, it also provided a touchstone that showed where the school was and what still needed to be done. Perhaps more important, it was also shared by the entire school community, who then also had a common point of conversation.

You cannot plan for all eventualities; indeed, to attempt to do so would be paralyzing. So you do the very best you can ahead of time creating your plan; you communicate the plan widely as a means of gaining consensus on your goal and course of action; and you understand up front that while enacting the project, you will also be assessing your plan and revising it as needed based on evidence you collect as you work.

Formulating Your Plan

Just as there are many different formats for creating a lesson plan, there are many different formats for action planning; no doubt, your school system or state education agency has endorsed a preferred format. These plans typically require context-specific information such as a reference linking the proposed action to state or district instructional standards or school board goals, may require the inclusion of district-specific budget categories for the expenditure of funds or purchase of equipment, and so on. The core of an effective action plan includes a very well-defined set of information, though, and the simplified format, presented in Figure 9.2, requires you to think through enactment of your project quite thoroughly.

Figure 9.2   Simplified Action Planning Format

Objective:				
Tasks	Who's Responsible	By When	Resources Needed	Success Signals

As an initial step, write a one-sentence statement that describes what you intend to do as an action objective. Ideally, your objective will state the circumstance you will reach, the time in which you will reach it, and the measure you will use to prove you have reached it. For instance, returning to the example presented earlier in this chapter, Natalie and her team might adopt the objective, *Increase the percentage of LEP students passing the 2009–2010 state-mandated, end-of-course assessment by 25% by engaging parents in a culturally appropriate parent education program intended to help them support their children more effectively at home.*

The heart of your action plan is the delineation of tasks necessary to complete the project. There is no magic we can offer to complete this step; it requires thinking through how the project needs to be implemented, engaging in conversation with your team and other stakeholders who may be affected or who have knowledge and expertise needed to complete the project, and learning about existing policies and procedures that may affect implementation. This is an iterative process, often initiated as a brainstorming exercise with your team and/or others whose expertise would contribute to the planning effort. First, make a list of the tasks that need to be completed to reach your objective. Try to strike a balance here by focusing on significant steps in enacting your plan, trying not to omit anything that represents an important component necessary to your success but also not getting bogged down with minutiae. Once you have identified these tasks, put them into a logical sequence—which tasks must come first, which follow, and so on. Once this is completed, go over the entire sequence again to see if there are missing pieces, and revise as necessary.

Once the various tasks are drafted, work across the table to fill in the specifics for each and every task: Who will be responsible for ensuring that the task is done? What is the target date for completion of the task? What material, financial, and human resources are needed to complete the task?

Most of the School Improvement Project Proposals we have reviewed over the years have had multiple components, and they often include some aspect of curriculum development for the targeted population and complementary professional development to help teachers adapt their instructional techniques to the identified problem. Each of those major strands may require some amount of research and articulation of what is intended. These major components can be approached as mini action plans, or plans within the overall plan; the task of completing drafts of these component plans may be effectively distributed to subteams. Each component may be quite involved. For example, professional development requires considerations of instructional strategies appropriate for working with adults who are teachers, timing of the professional development experience so that it is most useful to teachers, and follow-up to engage in timely reflection and problem solving as teachers attempt to use what they learned in the professional development experience.

The work involved in your school improvement project will likely seem daunting at times. Nevertheless, figuring out the details involved in that work prior to committing to a specific course of action will help you understand the implications of your project more deeply and address the concerns of others. Figuring out the work ahead of time will also help you spread the work more evenly among team members and others, rather than taking on all the surprise tasks by yourself because everyone else is already too busy. Worksheet 9.4 may be used to help you and your team brainstorm necessary components of the action plan. The sections that follow explore some of the issues that often come up as teams complete various sections of their plans.

Assigning Tasks

Figuring out the tasks is likely to be a highly collaborative effort, because different members of your team with their varied perspectives will think about and emphasize different aspects of the work. You will also probably involve other stakeholders in your school, whose knowledge and skills will help you do a good job laying out tasks needed to complete your plan. Task assignment may not work the same way. It is difficult for a group to divide tasks in a manner that both is fair and matches skill and expertise to tasks well. This is where your "decision about how to decide" (refer back to Activity 3.3) becomes important, because you do not want your team to be bogged down in bickering or silence if no one volunteers for the apparently less desirable tasks.

You may prefer bringing a completed plan to your team for assigned tasks and taking feedback on your plan (i.e., a Type 2 decision, as discussed in Chapter 3). It might be desirable to use a table similar to that in Worksheet 9.4 to allow people to suggest their own roles, but you will need to be more specific about exactly what will be accomplished by whom. It would be best, to the extent possible, for you to give every team member a mixture of "grunt work" and more engaging tasks that require expertise and/or talent. It is often wise to give individuals responsibility for entire sections of the plan (e.g., all tasks associated with needed professional development or summative evaluation).

As you present the plan, you will explain your rationale behind task assignments so that others can understand your effort to be fair. Thinking back to the kinds of factors you considered when you selected your team (see Worksheet 3.2), when suggesting task assignments, it seems prudent to consider team members' skills, motivations, and habits of mind. Who is best able to do various tasks? Who will be most motivated? Who is most likely to embrace the challenge, involve others, maintain good records, accept direction, and so on?

At the same time, it will be important for you to be open to group feedback so that others can have influence in the final outcome. It is important for you to listen for that kind of expression of multiple perspectives and help sort through it. The result of such a discussion may be that your plan is the "least bad" alternative on which the team can agree. On the other hand, team members may have ideas that are stronger than yours in certain ways and should be incorporated into the plan. Finally, we have found that it is usually best to receive the feedback in one session, consider it away from the group, and return at a later time with a response that demonstrates how you did and did not use feedback you received. Whatever your approach, remember that as team leader, you are modeling effective group process and setting a tone for your team.

Timeline

One of the great struggles involved in making school improvements is that everyone is locked into a relentless schedule governed by bells or electronic tones, weekly and monthly standing meetings, quarterly grades, and holiday breaks. It is difficult to get everyone's attention to a sufficient degree to complete the necessary work. We have found that one of the most effective ways to get work completed is to create a realistic set of deadlines and stick to them. The same is true for your collaborative team. You will want to create a timeline for task completion that accounts for three important factors: (a) task order (i.e., what comes first, second, and third), (b) when the work must be completed so that the project can move forward, and (c) roadblocks in the regular school calendar that are likely to delay your team's task completion. Setting deadlines that are achievable and monitoring progress at regular intervals will reduce disappointment from periods of inactivity or low productivity.

Resources

One of the most common pieces of feedback we give our students on their School Improvement Project Proposals is that they have not fully considered the resources necessary to support their projects. This tendency is understandable because budgets are generally tight and teacher leaders are reluctant to ask for money. It would be better to consider three possibilities: (a) Resources can be allocated away from other uses, (b) outside funding sources (grants) can be helpful for getting a new project started, and (c) nonmonetary resources have high value.

One reason schools often have difficulty changing is that budget allocations become frozen. Taking money away from one use and giving it to another is a challenging leadership activity. It is quite natural for teachers who have worked in an area for a number of years to be devoted to it. They are bound to be unhappy if their funding is reduced or cut, despite the fact that not all educational efforts are worthy of funding in perpetuity. Understand, therefore, that your principal is likely to weigh the political consequences of cutting someone else's funding in order to provide resources to your very worthwhile project. It is possible that you will be persuasive enough to get at least some reallocation, but do not be too disappointed if you discover that funding something new is more difficult than funding an established program. Other sources may be easier to obtain, and some are at your fingertips.

Many school districts have local foundations that provide small- to medium-sized grants to teachers and administrators. The application process for such grants is typically straightforward, and the foundations are often eager to fund innovative ideas intended to boost student learning. Check application guidelines and talk with your principal and/or central office staff about what the foundation is interested in funding to see if there is a match with your project. Even if the foundation is unable to give you everything you need for your project, it may get you started with money that can be combined with other sources.

Our students, with the exception of those working in special education, tend to be unaware of state and federal categorical funding that may be available to them, because this money is often allocated and monitored by central office administrators. If your project focuses on special education students, LEP students, students in poverty, or students in vocational or technical education, there may be categorical money that could be allocated toward your project. If you inform yourself about the funding rules for categorical money, you can work with district personnel to bring some of that money into your project. Check federal and state websites for specific information about the rules governing categorical funds.

The U.S. Department of Education (and very likely your state department of education) also offers competitive grants directly to schools and districts. Although federal websites can seem a bit intimidating, the Department of Education website lists numerous grants for efforts from advanced placement incentive programs to elementary and secondary school counseling to the Striving Readers program, intended to boost literacy for middle and high school students. Websites from both not-for-profit and private for-profit companies may also make grants available. Some vendors in the field provide funding information because they are hoping that you will use grant money to buy some of their published materials. For example, the website maintained by Pearson Education offers information about federal grants and how they work. Pearson also offers a free grant-reviewing process to enhance the quality of your grant before it is submitted. Although applying for a grant can seem like a great deal of work in a busy schedule, you need not do it alone. Your school district may have personnel who specialize in grant applications who can help you.

As helpful as a grant may be, not all resources come in the form of money. Larger school districts include central office personnel whose job it is to assist with curriculum development and/or professional development (recall the discussion from Chapter 3 about involving central office personnel). If you include such people in your project, they can provide expertise and learning opportunities to your faculty at no cost to your school site. They might also be aware of books and materials that could be purchased from budgets that they control or that are currently available in the school district. Productive partners at the central office can help you span all three types of resources for your project—budget reallocation, outside funding, and nonmonetary resources.

One last consideration about the "resource" column is worth highlighting: While many resource considerations reduce to asking for financial or material support, an entirely different resource question is, "Whose authority do we need to complete this project?" Principals we work with often have line authority to make the decisions needed to enact a project, but teacher leaders seldom have the authority needed and instead must seek permission of the person with legitimate authority to approve the project, an expenditure of funds, or even access to needed information. As you build your plan, it is worth asking whether the team has the authority to enact the task and, if not, whose authority is required. Part of the plan needs to include gaining this authority.

Success Signals

We will deal more with evaluation in the next chapter, but an important part of your action plan is defining success signals for each and every task. How will you know each task has been completed and you are ready to move on to the next portion of your plan? This column defines the formative evaluation of the plan, which enables you as a leader to monitor implementation fidelity. By being diligent conducting this formative assessment as you enact your plan, you will be amassing evidence you will need to fully explain your success and will be enabling the kind of organizational learning needed to fuel continuous improvement.

Consider an example: Suppose at the end of the 2009–2010 school year, Natalie's team learned that their plan did not achieve its stated objective. In fact, the percentage of LEP students passing the math exam increased by only about 6%, rather than the 25% they had hoped. Why? Assuming Natalie and her team had a well-specified action plan and had been diligently "working the plan," including conducting a formative evaluation along the way, we might already know that parent involvement in the project was limited, and we may know something about the reasons for this. For instance, we might have learned along the way that there are serious problems with contact information for parents who are new to the district, or we might know that two training sessions had to be cancelled because of funding issues. We might already know, also, that children whose parents participated in the program passed the exam. Armed with just the post hoc, summative data about efficacy of the program, we would be poorly equipped to advocate for continuing; with the more detailed, in-process evidence, we would be able to argue for the program's promise.

This may be the most difficult part of planning. We are eager to plan and develop ideas. We are reluctant to decide ahead of time how we will measure achievement. With all that you are putting into your school improvement project and considering the fact that you are leading a dedicated team of teachers and administrators, you will want to know if your project is succeeding as you engage in the action plan. If you have clearly stated goals and objectives, then achieving the processes and outcomes embedded in specific objectives can serve as important success signals. Measures of your success range from regular and productive meetings of your collaborative team (an important process goal documented through meeting minutes) to the development of new teaching strategies for the content at the core of your project to improved common assessments at a specific grade level. These benchmarks of success help you and your team understand whether or not your project is on track and which course corrections you may need to make. Identifying incremental success may also boost the morale of your team and others in your school community as they see your project beginning to bear fruit.

CONCLUSION

This chapter has helped you think through the logic of action for your school improvement project from start to finish. Understanding the logic of action behind your project helps make your work more systematic and transparent. Being explicit about how we move from Step A to Step B to Step C forces us to operate from evidence rather than a hunch or myth. Transparency is about explaining our choices and actions to others. The two characteristics combine to improve the likelihood that we will understand what we have done and be able to communicate it more articulately to others.

Action planning is fundamentally about visualizing, creating a road map for how you will improve students' performance and their academic and lifelong opportunities. The work may seem irritatingly detailed and mundane, but being meticulous is an important ingredient in your ultimate success. The action plan keeps you and your team honest. It lays out what you have committed to deliver and how you will deliver it. You are far more likely to achieve your goal if you are clear in your own mind and publicly about how you intend to get there.

Our experience and research suggests that schools and districts often get only to the planning stage in their thinking. The tacit belief seems to be that if a plan for improvement is published, everyone will follow it and performance will improve. In contrast, we advocate for careful planning of implementation and evaluation so that the entire school improvement process is understood. We have known for a generation or more (Berman & McLaughlin, 1976; Tyack & Cuban, 1995) that implementation varies from what planners expect. Sometimes the variation improves the plan and sometimes it doesn't. We focus in the next chapter on implementation of your team's ideas and the specifics of evaluating the outcomes so that your school improvement project has a greater likelihood of achieving what you intend.

REVIEW QUESTIONS

1. How will you know if your potential solutions have high potential to resolve the problem, challenge, or gap you identified?

2. What are some useful strategies for assigning duties in a manner that you are not required to carry the entire load of your project?

3. What is the logic of action for your school improvement project?

WORKSHEET 9.1   Format for Recording Information About Potential Solutions

Full bibliographic citation:
What is the proposed solution?
Why is it believed that this action will work? What causes of the problem will it eliminate?
What are the "boundary assumptions" (i.e., conditions under which the cause-effect relationship is thought to hold)?
What are your thoughts about the trustworthiness of this claim? Any limitations?

WORKSHEET 9.2   Format for Discussion of Solutions

Taking this action . . .	will eliminate these causes . . .	producing the following outcome(s):	Evidence to support this claim:

WORKSHEET 9.3   Articulating Your Logic of Action

In Activity 4.1, we asked you to reflect on past efforts to improve student achievement by asking a series of questions. In this worksheet, we ask you to work with your collaborative team to respond to similar prompts but with a twist toward creating your logic of action. Your responses to these prompts should be based on the work you did to create your Improvement Target Proposal and your Research Brief.

1. Our target student population is [be specific about which students you intend to help] . . .

2. Because [state the needs of this population that warrant being addressed] . . .

3. Evidence of these needs includes [explain how you know this particular student population requires an action plan] . . .

4. Root causes of the needs are [use your local knowledge and library research to explain] . . .

5. Our team believes the best way to address the root causes of this problem is [list your preferred solutions here] . . .

6. Because [complete the logic of action with your specific rationale for adopting *these* specific solutions] . . .

WORKSHEET 9.4   Figuring Out the Work and Appropriate Roles

Use or modify the table below to spell out the general work and specific roles you believe are required to take your school improvement project from a proposal into action. (Not all roles are required for each work strand, but some may require multiple roles.) After you and your team have figured out the nature of the work, determine who is likely to play which role and place those names in the appropriate cells. This last step brings you closer to assigning tasks.

| Roles | Work Strands | | | |
	Curriculum Development	Professional Development	Logistics/ Support	Communications/ PR
Design				
Staffing				
Scheduling				
Resource procurement				
Enlisting support				
Participant recruitment				
Follow-up				

CHAPTER 10

CONSIDERING IMPLEMENTATION AND EVALUATION

LEARNING OUTCOMES

Readers who grasp the most important ideas from this chapter will be able to

- understand how to implement the action plans they have developed;
- avoid some of the pitfalls of implementation;
- recognize implementation as a process, not an event; and
- evaluate the results of their implementation.

As we said at the close of the previous chapter, our experience and research suggests that many change projects are well planned. In fact, it would not be an exaggeration to say that the emphasis of school change activities in many settings is on creating an annual action plan that communicates a commitment to specific problem areas and a course of action to remedy them. Cuban (1990), among others, notes that schools are full of reform efforts, but "most get implemented in word rather than deed, especially in classrooms" (p. 9). Similarly, Pankake (1998) observes that the "history of educational change initiatives is crowded, while the history of successful implementation of these initiatives is less so" (p. 2).

Consider your own experience with changes that have been announced and adopted in your school. How many of these changes "stick"? How many become part of the "way we do things around here"? We have said from the outset of this book that one of the reasons school improvement projects fail is that there is a faulty or incomplete logic of action embedded in the change effort itself—solutions are adopted without a clear understanding of how the action connects to valued outcomes, the root causes of the problem are not well articulated, teachers and other stakeholders who are critical to implementation are not involved or made aware of the change ahead of time, resources needed to institutionalize change are not forthcoming, and so on.

In the previous chapter, you articulated a complete logic of action for your school improvement project, including your commitment to a specific course of action. This logic of action is based on a thorough understanding of the problem, its root causes, and evidence that suggests that the proposed solution will help reduce its causes and thus remedy the problem. Then, you and your collaborative team spelled out in detail how you planned to implement your improvement project, including the tasks that would be required, who would be involved and accountable for each task, the resources you would need, and success signals you would use to monitor how well the project was going as you implement it. Understanding the logic of action behind your project helps make your work more systematic and transparent; having an action plan provides a coherent road map that lays out what you and your team have committed to do and how you will deliver it. As leaders of change, you and your collaborative team have already done a great deal to overcome many of the most predictable barriers to change.

But the point of your work is not to create plans; it is to produce tangible changes in practice that lead to enhancements in student learning. Reaching your objectives depends on *doing something* with your plan. Consequently, in this chapter, we turn to the issues of the implementation and evaluation of your work so that your school improvement project has a greater likelihood of achieving what you intend.

A NOTE ON "SUCCESS"

Before we move on to our discussion of implementation and evaluation, it is worthwhile to revisit some of our assumptions about the change process itself and about the notion of "success" in your work as a leader of change. Your effort up to this point has been built on a solid foundation of what we know about change: You have involved stakeholders in the process, created a vision that is tempered by a keen understanding of the current reality, and established a careful plan that considers the path you hypothesize will enable your school to reach your objectives. Building on what Lewin taught us about the change process (Weisbord, 2004), first discussed in Chapter 2, you have engaged in a process that helps stakeholders "unfreeze" from the current reality, created a blueprint for "moving" in the desired direction, and are now poised to consider what it will take to institutionalize the change you seek to make.

Success would seem to be a simple matter here, correct? On the surface, this much is true: Success means meeting stated objectives. In practice, though, the matter is seldom so clear-cut, and even if it were, explaining success simply in terms of meeting objectives misses an important point. The inquiry cycle you have engaged in is a microcosm of a broader process, not an end in itself. It is not a "thing we do" periodically. Your use of research in evidence-based decision making is not an isolated set of tasks; it is a way of leading, and when distributed appropriately, it becomes a part of the culture of your school as an organization. (This point is akin to our belief about professional learning communities. We cringe when someone tells us that their school "does professional learning community"—a professional learning community is something your school *becomes*, not something you or a few people on a team *do*.) Your success as a change leader cannot, and should not, be defined in terms of meeting the objectives of one plan or another but, rather, in terms of the culture of learning and continuous improvement you instill through your leadership practice.

In this sense, when we work with in-service leaders or students in our leadership preparation program, we stress the fact that while it is important to know if you reach the outcomes you seek, it is equally vital to consider during implementation and through evaluation of your work what you are learning yourself and the learning you are prompting in others through the change process you are leading. Therefore, in the sections that follow, we will stress formative evaluation as much as or more than summative evaluation. To be sure, you want to make progress in terms of the instructional problem you identified. But you also want to seize the opportunities you have to learn through the change process itself—through both your successes and troubles—and help yourself and others develop as leaders.

This is especially important because change takes place over long periods of time and may not be linear. You do not stop gaining knowledge about the process you crafted once your plan is done; you continue to learn along the way. This learning may result in changes to the current plan of action; it may also breed new ideas about how to improve. For instance, the instructional problems you are tackling have multiple causes, as your own analysis demonstrated, and as you implement your plan, you may learn a great deal that prompts you to revisit and refine your logic of action and adjust your plan. As you make progress, you may also discover opportunities to go back to your causal analysis and consider making further gains in your problem area by creating or refining plans to tackle additional causes. As you can see, the process of using research and the inquiry cycle to promote continuous improvement is both to promote specific gain and to help your school become a learning organization.

CONSIDERING IMPLEMENTATION

In her book titled *Implementation: Making Things Happen*, Pankake (1998) notes that implementation has a range of synonyms in the context of leadership, including "making things happen," facilitating and coordinating, and taking action. She makes the point, as well, that implementation may refer to routine or everyday activities or new (nonroutine) efforts to promote change. Your work fits the latter definition; we may consider implementation in your context to refer to the process of enacting your school improvement proposal and monitoring these efforts as you "work your plan."

Pankake (1998, pp. 16–22) provides an excellent review of what is known about the characteristics of successful implementation in a change context. Briefly, the following attributes are thought to contribute to successful implementation:

- The effort has clear *purposes* and identifiable *outcomes*.

- The *resources* needed to support implementation are consistently available.

- Project leaders see the project as *feasible*.

- *Training* and *opportunities* for skill development are ongoing, as needed.

- *Progress checks* are done on an ongoing basis: Data are gathered about implementation itself, and "success signals" are monitored along the way.

- *Feedback* based on these progress checks is supplied to leaders responsible for implementation.

- Somebody serves as a *coach* and/or *cheerleader* for the project during implementation.

A key point, Pankake (1998) emphasizes, involves "viewing implementation as a process and not an event, and seeing it as an unfolding process to be coached, rather than directed" (pp. 24–25). This is consistent with the perspective we have applied from the beginning. You and your collaborative team have already dealt effectively with many of these attributes and are poised to lead the change effort as it unfolds. So what can you do beforehand to strengthen implementation?

CONSEQUENCE ANALYSIS: PREDICTING THE FUTURE

Niels Bohr, the Danish physicist, is said to have observed, "Prediction is very difficult, especially about the future." What will happen as you implement your project? It is easy to see the future only in terms of the goals and objectives you have set. Naturally, these are your aspirations, and some or all of them may be achieved. Making a meaningful change in your school will also have results you didn't intend, however. The now common reform of extending class periods to 90 minutes or more at the secondary level provides an illustrative example. Working at the high school level, we believed that longer class periods would provide opportunities for deeper and more meaningful instruction. Indeed, we could point to numerous early successes in this area. However, we also found that by reducing the number of times students changed classes during the block schedule, attendance and tardiness improved and disciplinary incidents declined. We never anticipated that with less unstructured time on their hands (i.e., passing time between classes), students would have fewer opportunities and incentives to violate school rules. A more negative unintended consequence is that some teachers attempted to do what they always did in shorter class periods, only do more of it. Some showed entire movies instead of breaking them up into two parts, while others handed out twice as many worksheets.

Anticipating consequences—both intended and unintended—helps you and your team strengthen implementation by refining your plan ahead of time to deal with as many outcomes of the plan as you can. When you understand that there are individuals and programs that may be negatively impacted by your project, through no intention of yours, then it is possible to mitigate the negative effects by structural and human resources means. For example, outdated efforts to boost student achievement that may be overshadowed by your project can be phased out gradually if your success signals look positive. Likewise, teachers involved in other initiatives that are becoming obsolete can be invited to work with your team on this new effort. Shifting the emphasis on "how things are done around here" may send an unintended message to some teachers that what they have been doing is unimportant because it is outdated. Oftentimes, personal contact is an effective salve for bruised egos. To reduce the negative effects of the changes you are initiating, you must be able to see future consequences of your actions.

ACTIVITY 10.1   Guaranteed to Fail

In preparation for your discussion of implementation, working with one or more critical friends (or members of your collaborative team), brainstorm answers to the following questions about your school improvement project:

- What can you do to make sure that the project is a total failure?

- What types of attitudes or dispositions would ensure that the project is a waste of time and that you accomplish nothing?

- In what ways might you interact with others to ensure that they do not cooperate?

Be frank—consider playing the role of the most curmudgeonly, reluctant, recalcitrant, or unabashedly negative person on your school's faculty. (Chances are one or more names are running through your head already.)

To debrief, answer the questions, "What have you learned about the most important attributes of your role as a leader of change?" and "In what ways can you avoid guaranteed failure?"

Figure 10.1 uses Bolman and Deal's (2008) four-frame analytic scheme to derive four separate sets of questions that you and your collaborative team can use to conduct a consequence analysis for your proposed project. You can work through these as a team in a brainstorming and debriefing format, or to strengthen the process and build greater trustworthiness into your data collection, you could conceive of involving others in considering the possible consequences of your actions. For example, we have worked with teams that adjust the symbolic exercise dealing with naysayers' complaints by literally handing out index cards to a room full of teachers. After explaining the proposed project, they invite each person to write down their complaints or problems they can envision with the plan. These data, assembled before casting the action plan in stone and well before beginning to put the plan into action, allow you and your team to consider how you might adjust implementation to deal with some of the potential negative consequences, communicate with affected stakeholders ahead of time to enlist their support, or devise a way to deal with the situation if a consequence seems unavoidable.

Figure 10.1   Consequence Analysis: Predicting Barriers to Success

Structural	Human Resources

• Ask the question, "What's potentially unchangeable in our school that might serve as a barrier to success for our plan?"
 	
• Focus on Rules, Roles, and Relationships—do structures generally support the change?
 	
• Based on the insights revealed through the answers to this question, see if you adjust your plan, see alternative implementation paths, or seek an exception to the rule!
	• List the stakeholder groups who might be affected by the change, who might not feel they had a voice in the decision. Ask:
	   o "How will this affect each stakeholder group?"
	   o "Is there an unanticipated consequence that might impact these groups?"
	
	• How can you deal with each group's needs? (Consider both skill and will—how will you help them gain competence to participate in the plan, and what would motivate them to engage fully?)

Political	**Symbolic**
• Brainstorm the payoffs and risks associated with implementation of your action plan in your school. • Who stands to benefit, and who might experience costs? What are these costs? In what ways can you help participants deal with these costs? • How might power shift as a result of your project's implementation?	• Imagine the stakeholders in your school who most embrace "the way we do things around here." What will their complaints be about the changes you're trying to implement? (What will addressing their concerns convey, symbolically, about your team's efforts?) • What ways of doing things—"sacred cows"—will they need to abandon in order for the change to work? • How can you help them negotiate the adoption of these changes?

Source: Several of these exercises were inspired by examples from Kaner (2007).

MONITORING AND EVALUATING YOUR PROJECT

Imagine teaching a diverse group of youngsters for an entire year without taking stock of their learning. With curriculum, pacing guide, and lesson plans in hand, you boldly go where no teacher has gone before—no assessment before the state-mandated, end-of-year, high-stakes test. Is this apt to result in powerful learning for all your students? It would be hard to imagine an educator buying into this exercise in futility. Formal and informal assessments provide feedback to both teacher and learner that are critical to the success of the entire enterprise. The student gains an awareness of his or her mastery of the material and important information about how he or she is approaching the tasks associated with learning. The teacher, as well, gains both summative and formative information that can be translated into knowledge to guide the process of facilitating learning most effectively for all learners.

Yet one of our consistent observations in working with school improvement teams is that evaluation gets short shrift. In the planning process itself, for instance, many district and state school improvement planning formats require schools to specify outcome measures but say precious little more about the evaluation. School leadership teams seem to run out of time before being able to prepare monitoring or evaluation procedures for action plans. Furthermore, once plans are enacted, participants are generally swamped with business as usual. Monitoring the action plan and considering ongoing data about implementation to adjust the plan takes a back seat to working the plan. At the beginning of the next year's planning cycle, state-mandated testing data becomes the focus of attention, with any evidence collected during implementation of last year's plans seeming to vanish into the ether.

Perhaps we're being a bit dramatic; this view may be more extreme than the reality you experience in your school. But we are well aware of the pressures that exist in your school to "move on" and the fact that the current environment in education credentials testing data above all else as evidence that should be used to craft school improvement plans. Nevertheless, from our perspective, the heart of the learning organization is the use of feedback to guide and refine action. Building on the seminal work of Argyris and Schön (1974), we believe that your efforts to collect and use evidence related to implementation and outcomes to guide your work can help you reconceptualize the problem, challenge assumptions that guide practice, and refine your actions to provide you with much more than just a barometer that answers the question, "How well did we do?" Considering the evidence of success that flows from implementation of your project affords you the possibility of learning how and why your efforts produce the outcomes you observe and, thus, the possibility of learning more about the improvement process itself (Argyris & Schön, 1978). Learning is central to the notion of continuous improvement and becomes the engine that enables your school to truly become a professional learning community.

EVALUATING OUTCOMES

Suppose, for the moment, that a central feature of your school improvement plan was to implement an after-school tutoring program for fourth-grade students who are at risk of failing in reading. Articulating success signals and figuring out positive and negative consequences resulting from your project points you in the direction of evaluation. It is in the best interests of your students, those working with you to improve student performance, and the school in general to know whether or not your project is successful. You would naturally seek to devise an evaluation plan that includes tracking specific indicators associated with the achievement gap you identified initially. In other words, you will try to answer the summative question,

> "What impact did our school improvement project have on outcomes associated with the instructional problem we identified at the beginning of our analysis?"

In the after-school tutoring case, you would certainly evaluate your project in terms of some measure of reading achievement, perhaps using pre- and post-measures of performance on a state-mandated test or a benchmark assessment that is aligned with learning standards.

The process of evaluation takes you back in many ways to earlier chapters in which we discussed data collection and analysis of evidence. Your assessments of local data, library research, and root-cause analysis were all grounded in finding evidence of the problem on which you have chosen to focus and enhanced by identifying solutions that would reduce or eliminate root causes. Summative evaluation of your project essentially asks two questions: (a) "Have we reduced or eliminated the causes of the problem we seek to solve?" and (b) "How do we know?" It is up to you and your team to identify the evidence that will help you answer these questions. You will need to know which data you should collect and how you will analyze it. Returning to your literature may prove helpful at this point, because you may wish to emulate some of the methodology found there.

To avoid becoming overwhelmed and possibly abandoning the evaluation process, we recommend that you keep the measures and analysis basic. You are not setting out to publish a peer-reviewed article about the results of your school improvement effort (though that might be a happy outcome). Instead, your intent should be to demonstrate with a reasonable measure of trustworthiness what happened and the effect it seems to have had on students. You will naturally find multiple factors at work simultaneously, some of which you were able to control and some of which you weren't. All this can be reasonably discussed from a professional perspective that takes an honest look at what your team has accomplished. The evaluation process helps your team figure out what should be kept in the project, modified, or eliminated and therefore provides a vehicle for reflection and learning. In the process, you will set a strong, positive example for the rest of the school community. Overall, the evaluation process answers the question, "Was our logic of action valid?" The answer is important to your students' futures, as well as to the learning you and your colleagues experience as leaders in the school improvement process.

Sanders and Sullins (2006) provide a useful framework for creating an evaluation plan, which we have adapted for your use as Worksheet 10.1. They suggest that your consideration of evaluation start with posing a series of questions that probe the strengths and weaknesses of your proposed project. You and your collaborative team might begin with the logic of action you articulated. At this point, focus on the summative evaluation questions: What do you need to know to determine if your project worked? Using the worksheet provided, you and your team can pose questions related to the intended outcomes of the project and describe why each question is important, what data you will need to answer the question, when and how you will collect these data, and how you will analyze this information. In the next section, we will expand our consideration to formative evaluation questions.

MONITORING IMPLEMENTATION

The summative evaluation questions provide you with critical evidence regarding the outcome of your project. But to be able to understand *why* your actions produced the observed results, whatever they might be, you will also need to collect a variety of process-oriented evidence relating to the implementation of your project. You will need to know exactly what happened during enactment of your action plan. Thus, your evaluation should also involve monitoring your work to provide data to answer the question,

"Why did our school improvement project produce these results?"

MONITORING IMPLEMENTATION AND EVALUATION

Your evaluation plan should include tracking specific indicators associated with the achievement gap you are trying to reduce. It should empower you to answer the question,

"What impact did our school improvement project have on our target area?"

This is the *summative* assessment of your plan.

(Continued)

(Continued)

To understand why your actions produced the observed outcome, you need to know what happened during the enactment of your plan. Your evaluation must also allow you to answer the *formative* question,

"Why did our school improvement project produce these results?"

For instance, if your plan involved implementing a tutoring program for at-risk students to improve performance on a math test, to understand *why* your project achieved specific results, you might need to consider data about *implementation fidelity* (i.e., how well your *treatment* was implemented), including the following:

- Student attendance and persistence data: Your plan has no chance of impacting test scores if students did not participate in the tutoring process.

- Data on tutoring processes: To understand the impact of tutoring, you will need to understand what tutors did with students, how they taught them, what materials they used, and so on.

- Data on student attitudes toward tutoring: How did students feel about tutoring? Students who feel "singled out" or "labeled" are likely to experience different outcomes than those who feel "special" or "helped."

The box above provides just a few samples of the kinds of data that may be useful to understand implementation fidelity (i.e., whether the project you envisioned is carried out as you planned). It us up to you and your team to monitor implementation in terms of some of its in-process consequences.

Pankake (1998) makes the point that "feedback helps differentiate between efforts and accomplishments, between assuming and knowing, and between busyness and productivity. Feedback is essential in ensuring the progress of implementation; it should be frequent and provided at critical decision points" (pp. 119–120). She then suggests that we consider the following in order to develop assessment plans that allow us to monitor implementation as they are put into action:

- Identify periodic checkpoints for monitoring (p. 108). For the plans you established, these are defined in terms of the "success signals" you specified for each task in your plan.

- Secure resources (including time, personnel, and access) needed to monitor progress (pp. 108–109). This is also defined in your action plan as the "resources needed."

- Define who will be responsible for monitoring, what will be monitored, when monitoring will be done, and what information will be collected when monitoring (p. 109). Some of this information is already specified in your action plan, but it seems likely that as you think through your monitoring needs, some elaboration will be required.

- Include "probing" as needed (pp. 113–114). Seek to include in your monitoring activities opportunities to probe why implementation is progressing as it is, and seek opportunities to adjust the action plan as needed.

The goal, then, of refining your action plan to include ongoing monitoring activity is to provide useful feedback about the fidelity of implementation and any unanticipated consequences of your actions so that you and your collaborative team can either maintain, alter, or adjust your implementation to ensure optimal results. Remember, your action plan is a living document; you should feel free to add to it, omit steps, or change the implementation process as you learn through the process of enacting your school improvement project. For this to happen, quite simply, you must incorporate into your leadership the notion of systematically amassing evidence through the process of monitoring implementation.

Return now to Worksheet 10.1, and work with your collaborative team to craft evaluation questions that focus on understanding implementation fidelity and the process of enacting your plan. What do you need to know, in process, that will help you understand if the plan is being enacted as you envisioned? Using the Sanders and Sullins (2006) framework is especially helpful for completing this exercise. Examine your action plan and timeline for implementation, and look not only for what you need to know but especially why these data may be of use to you. Careful consideration of these questions before enactment can enable you and your team to incorporate into your action plan specific checkpoints, and then you can affirm or change your plan based on the feedback you have collected.

CONCLUSION

In this chapter, we asked you to focus your attention on predicting the future, on anticipating the consequences of the actions you will lead to improve teaching and learning in your school, and then to create a thoughtful plan for evaluating your work both in terms of outcomes and in terms of the implementation process itself. In doing this work, you refined your action plan to account for likely consequences and you incorporated the steps you and your team will need to take to monitor implementation. As you begin to implement the plan, it will be important to document your decisions as you engage in formative assessment of your work so that at a later date, you and your team can reflect competently on the actions you took and the rationale you had for making these changes. We recommend that team leaders literally keep a journal throughout implementation to keep a record of the evidence collected and decisions made and to reflect on various decision points along the way (see box).

KEEPING A REFLECTIVE JOURNAL

A deceptively simple means to ensure that you track implementation well is to keep a *reflective journal*. This is one of the most powerful means at your disposal to promote continuous learning as you lead the implementation of your plan. But it requires vigilance—the utility of your journal is very much dependent on recording entries often, at least weekly.

Organize your journal according to the major tasks included in your action plan, along with the "success signals" you defined for each task. Keep in mind important evidence you want to collect along the way related to implementation (e.g., student attendance, instructional quality). And to ensure that your journal is more than just a recounting of "what happened," make sure each entry includes reflection on questions such as the following:

- Why did events unfold the way they did this week?

- What can we learn from these events? What might we do differently next time?

- How might we alter what we are doing to improve?

Militello, Rallis, and Goldring (2009) suggest that school principals who are successful at leading a collaborative inquiry cycle that prompts change in instructional practice both facilitate and focus activity in their school. Specifically, they suggest that principals focus on the following to lead the inquiry process:

- Motivating teacher will

- Building teacher capacity

- Establishing collaborative and participatory decision-making processes

- Making research-based, information-rich decisions

- Monitoring, recognizing, and rewarding practice and learning (pp. 108–109)

This list is consistent with the leadership attributes stressed by Fullan (2001) in his book *Leading in a Culture of Change*, discussed in Chapter 2, as well as our discussion of the attributes of effective team leaders in Chapter 3. Looking back on the journey you are now completing, we would argue that you have led in a fashion that is highly consistent with these visions of effective change leadership.

In particular, Fullan (2001) reminds us that knowledge creation and sharing is an integral part of change leadership. We believe that the investment you and your team made by carefully considering implementation and evaluation can promote a degree of personal and organizational learning that is rarely seen as a result of participation in school improvement activities.

REVIEW QUESTIONS

1. What are the roadblocks or pitfalls you are most likely to encounter during the implementation phase of your school improvement project?

2. Which success signals are most important to indicate whether or not your school improvement project is on track?

3. To what degree do you anticipate distributing leadership as a result of planning and implementing your school improvement project?

4. How will you know whether or not your school improvement project is "good enough" to sustain over time?

WORKSHEET 10.1　Evaluation Plan

Evaluation questions	Why is this question important?	What information will you need to answer the question?	When and how will you collect this information?	How will you analyze this information?

Source: Adapted from Sanders and Sullins (2006).

EPILOGUE

Why put so much effort into a school improvement project? Some might argue that unless the fundamental ways in which education is practiced change, we will not see lasting differences in teaching and learning. This book is a testament to our more optimistic, and possibly pragmatic, view. Change happens at the school-site level, one classroom at a time. There are roadblocks and pitfalls along the way, to be sure, but if teachers and administrators can understand more deeply why some students learn while others don't and take action to help those who are struggling under present circumstances, then, we believe, teaching and learning will improve. It may not improve in the same ways and to the same degree in any given school or district, but if improvement happens, students learn more and have brighter academic futures. Isn't that what really matters?

At the outset of this book, we used the metaphor of a journey to describe the process readers were going to experience by actively engaging in the school improvement planning described in this book. But we were less clear about the nature of this journey, what the destination might be, and why we believe it is so important. If you have engaged with this book and, consequently, with other leaders in your school in the process of applying research to school improvement in the fashion we have recommended, the journey you started is one of continuous improvement—as a leader, personally, and for your school as an organization.

As an instructional leader, you have learned a systematic process of planning and decision making that employs various kinds of research to improve your school. You used evidence to identify an instructional problem worth working on in your school, you employed published research and the results of your own action research to develop a deep understanding of the sources of this problem and ways to approach reducing its causes, and you developed a plan for enacting this solution and evaluating it so that your school can improve in the short term and learn over time how best to tackle this instructional challenge. In enacting this process, you have had an opportunity to apply various lenses associated with organizational theory and you have distributed leadership to others—first informally and later by purposefully creating a collaborative team.

The journey is not yet complete, however. To promote the improvement you envision and, indeed, to prompt organizational learning around this issue in your school, you need to continue to lead during implementation and assessment of your project. Planning is not a destination; it is a means to ensuring your primary goal of making an impact on student learning in your school. The process of planning, implementing, and evaluating projects that are research-informed and tailored to the specific needs of your school and its student population generates learning on the part of the professionals charged with educating children. As this learning is absorbed by large numbers of adults in the school, "the way we do things around here" begins to change. School improvement is a manifestation of organizational learning.

Carrying out your project is important, but the truth of the matter is that the destination for your journey should not be a thing you do, simply your project; rather, it should be a learning process of instructional leadership that incorporates disciplined inquiry that you can apply to various puzzles as you grow into the leader you will become. The creation, implementation, and evaluation of your school improvement project is a case in point, not the point itself.

REFERENCES

Argyris, C. (1999). *On organizational learning* (2nd ed.). Malden, MA: Blackwell Business.

Argyris, C., & Schön, D. (1974). *Theory in practice: Increasing professional effectiveness.* San Francisco: Jossey-Bass.

Argyris, C., & Schön, D. (1978). *Organizational learning: A theory of action perspective.* Reading, MA: Addison-Wesley.

Baker, S. (1977). *The practical stylist* (4th ed.). New York: Thomas Y. Crowell.

Barlow, L. (2004). *The spider's apprentice: How search engines work.* Retrieved December 5, 2010, from http://www.monash.com/spidap4.html

Berman, P., & McLaughlin, M. (1976). Implementation of educational innovation. *Educational Forum, 40,* 344–370.

Bernhardt, V. (1998). *Data analysis for comprehensive schoolwide improvement.* Larchmont, NY: Eye on Education.

Bolman, L., & Deal, T. (2008). *Reframing organizations: Artistry, choice, and leadership* (4th ed.). San Francisco: Jossey-Bass.

Bonstingl, J. (1992). *Schools of quality: An introduction to total quality management in education.* Alexandria, VA: Association for Supervision and Curriculum Development.

Brazer, S., Rich, W., & Ross, S. (2010). Collaborative strategic decision making in school districts. *Journal of Educational Administration, 48*(2), 196–217.

Bryk, A., & Scheider, B. (2002). *Trust in schools: A core resource for improvement.* New York: Russell Sage Foundation.

City, E., Elmore, R., Fiarman, S., & Teitel, L. (2009). *Instructional rounds in education: A network approach to improving teaching and learning.* Cambridge, MA: Harvard Education Press.

Cohen, M. D., March, J. G., & Olsen, J. P. (1972). A garbage can model of organizational choice. *Administrative Science Quarterly, 17*(1), 1–25.

Collins, J. (2001). *Good to great: Why some companies make the leap . . . and others don't.* New York: HarperBusiness.

Conley, S., Fauske, J., & Pounder, D. (2004). Teacher work group effectiveness. *Educational Administration Quarterly, 40*(5), 663–703.

Covey, S. (1992). *Principle-centered leadership.* New York: Simon & Schuster.

Creighton, T. (2007). *Schools and data: The educator's guide for using data to improve decision making* (2nd ed.). Thousand Oaks, CA: Corwin.

Creswell, J. (2005). *Educational research: Planning, conducting, and evaluating quantitative and qualitative research* (2nd ed.). Upper Saddle River, NJ: Prentice Hall.

Creswell, J. (2008). *Educational research: Planning, conducting, and evaluating quantitative and qualitative research* (3rd ed.). Upper Saddle River, NJ: Pearson Education.

Creswell, J. W. (2009). *Research design: Qualitative, quantitative, and mixed methods approaches* (3rd ed.). Thousand Oaks, CA: Sage.

Critical evaluation of resources. (2009). UC-Berkeley Library. Retrieved December 5, 2010, from http://www.lib.berkeley.edu/instruct/guides/evaluation.html

Cuban, L. (1988). *The managerial imperative and the practice of leadership in schools.* Albany: State University of New York Press.

Cuban, L. (1990). Reforming again, again, and again. *Educational Researcher, 19*(3), 3–13.

Cuban, L. (1993). *How teachers taught: Constancy and change in American classrooms: 1890–1990* (2nd ed.). New York: Teachers College Press.

DiMaggio, P., & Powell, W. (1983). The iron cage revisited: Institutional isomorphism and collective rationality in organizational fields. *American Sociological Review, 48,* 147–160.

Distinguishing scholarly journals from other periodicals. (2009). Olin and Uris Libraries, Cornell University. Retrieved December 5, 2010, from http://www.library.cornell.edu/olinuris/ref/research/skill20.html

Educational Research Service. (2003). *K–12 principals guide to No Child Left Behind.* Arlington, VA: Author.

Engle, M., & Cosgrave, T. (2009). *Critically analyzing information sources.* Olin and Uris Libraries, Cornell University. Retrieved December 5, 2010, from http://www.library.cornell.edu/olinuris/ref/research/skill26.htm

Evaluating sources. (2010). Campus Library, University of Washington-Bothell and Cascadia Community College. Retrieved December 5, 2010, from http://library.uwb.edu/guides/eval.html

Evaluating web pages: Techniques to apply and questions to ask. (2010). UC-Berkeley Library. Retrieved December 5, 2010, from http://www.lib.berkeley.edu/TeachingLib/Guides/Internet/Evaluate.html

Fisher, R., Ury, W., & Patton, B. (1991). *Getting to yes: Negotiating agreement without giving in.* New York: Penguin Books.

Frankl, V. (1984). *Man's search for meaning.* New York: Washington Square Press/Pocket Books.

Fullan, M. (2001). *Leading in a culture of change.* San Francisco: Jossey-Bass.

Gersick, C. (1989). Marking time: Predictable transitions in task groups. *Academy of Management Journal, 32*(2), 274–309.

Glaser, B. G., & Strauss, A. L. (1999). *The discovery of grounded theory: Strategies for qualitative research.* New Brunswick, NJ: Aldine Transaction.

Goldring, E., & Berends, M. (2009). *Leading with data: Pathways to improve your school.* Thousand Oaks, CA: Corwin.

Hackman, R. J., & Walton, R. E. (1986). Leading groups in organizations. In P. S. Goodman (Ed.), *Designing effective work groups* (pp. 72–119). San Francisco: Jossey-Bass.

Holcomb, E. (2004). *Getting excited about data* (2nd ed.). Thousand Oaks, CA: Corwin.

How search engines work. (2007, March 14). Retrieved April 18, 2009, from http://searchenginewatch.com/2168031

Hoy, W. (2010). *Quantitative research in education: A primer.* Thousand Oaks, CA: Sage.

Ishikawa, K. (1985). *What is total quality control? The Japanese way.* Englewood Cliffs, NJ: Prentice Hall.

Janis, I. L. (1971). Groupthink. *Psychology Today, 5,* 84–90.

Juran, J. (1992). *Juran on quality by design: The new steps for planning quality into goods and services.* New York: Free Press.

Kaner, S. (with Lind, L., Toldi, C., Fisk, S., & Berger, D.). (2007). *Facilitator's guide to participatory decision making* (2nd ed.). San Francisco: Jossey-Bass.

Katzenbach, J., & Smith, D. (2003). *The wisdom of teams: Creating the high-performance organization.* New York: HarperCollins.

Kenny, D. (1979). *Correlation and causality.* New York: John Wiley & Sons.

Kirk, E. (1996). *Evaluating information found on the Internet.* Retrieved March 10, 2009, from http://www.library.jhu.edu/researchhelp/general/evaluating

Kochan, F., Jackson, B., & Duke, D. (1999). *Voices from the firing line: A study of educational leaders' perceptions of their job, the challenges they face, and their preparation.* Columbia, MO: UCEA Press.

Larson, C., & LaFasto, F. (1989). *Teamwork: What must go right/what can go wrong.* Newbury Park, CA: Sage.

Leithwood, K., & Riehl, C. (2003). *What we know about successful school leadership.* Paper prepared for the American Educational

Research Association Division, a Task Force on Developing Research in Educational Leadership.

Leithwood, K., Seashore-Louis, K. A., Anderson, S., & Wahlstrom, K. (2004). *How leadership influences student learning.* New York: Wallace Foundation.

Leithwood, K., & Steinbach, R. (2004, April). *Successful leadership for especially challenging schools.* Paper presented at the annual meeting of the American Educational Research Association, San Diego, CA.

Levine, A. (2005). *Educating school leaders.* Washington, DC: Education Schools Project.

Lewin, K. (1947). Frontiers in group dynamics, Part 1: Concept, method, and reality in social sciences: Social equilibria and social change. *Human Relations, 1,* 5–41.

Making sense of the literature. (n.d.). University of Queensland, Australia. Retrieved December 5, 2010, from http://www.uq.edu.au/student-services/phdwriting/phlink17.html

March, J. G. (1994). *A primer on decision making: How decisions happen.* New York: Free Press.

March, J. G., & Simon, H. A. (1993). *Organizations* (2nd ed.). Oxford, UK: Blackwell.

Maxwell, J. (2005). *Qualitative research design: An interactive approach* (2nd ed.). Thousand Oaks, CA: Sage.

Maxwell, J. (2006). Literature reviews of, and for, educational research: A response to Boote and Beile. *Educational Researcher, 35*(9), 28–31.

McGregor, D. (1960). *The human side of enterprise.* New York: McGraw-Hill.

McGregor, D. (2006). *The human side of enterprise: Annotated edition.* New York: McGraw-Hill.

Merriam, S. B. (2009). *Qualitative research: A guide to design and implementation.* San Francisco: Jossey-Bass.

Miles, M., & Huberman, A. (1994). *Qualitative data analysis: A sourcebook for new methods* (2nd ed.). Thousand Oaks, CA: Sage.

Militello, M., Rallis, S., & Goldring, E. (2009). *Leading with inquiry and action: How principals improve teaching and learning.* Thousand Oaks, CA: Corwin.

Osterman, K., & Kottkamp, R. (2004). *Reflective practice for educators* (2nd ed.). Thousand Oaks, CA: Corwin.

Pankake, A. (1998). *Implementation: Making things happen.* Larchmont, NY: Eye on Education.

Peters, T., & Waterman, R. (1982). *In search of excellence: Lessons from America's best-run companies.* New York: Harper & Row.

Phelan, P., Davidson, A., & Yu, H. (1998). *Adolescents' worlds: Negotiating family, peers, and school.* New York: Teachers College Press.

Preuss, P. (2003). *School leader's guide to root-cause analysis: Using data to dissolve problems.* Larchmont, NY: Eye on Education.

Preuss, P. (2007). *School leader's guide to root cause analysis: Using data to dissolve problems.* Larchmont, NY: Eye on Education.

Primary and secondary sources. (2010). Ithaca College Library. Retrieved December 5, 2010, from http://www.ithacalibrary.com/sp/subjects/primary

Robinson, V. M., Lloyd, C. A., & Rowe, K. J. (2008). The impact of leadership on student outcomes: An analysis of the differential effects of leadership styles. *Educational Administration Quarterly, 44,* 635–674.

Rogers, E. (1995). *Diffusion of innovations* (4th ed.). New York: Free Press.

Rothstein, R. (2004). *Class and schools: Using social, economic, and educational reform to close the Black-White achievement gap.* Washington, DC: Economic Policy Institute.

Sanders, J., & Sullins, C. (2006). *Evaluating school programs: An educator's guide* (3rd ed.). Thousand Oaks, CA: Corwin.

Schlechty, P. (2001). *Shaking up the schoolhouse.* San Francisco: Jossey-Bass.

Schneider, B., Carnoy, M., Kilpatrick, J., Schmidt, W., & Shavelson, R. (2007). *Estimating causal effects using experimental and observational designs.* Washington, DC: American Educational Research Association.

Simon, H. A. (1993). Decision making: Rational, nonrational, and irrational. *Educational Administration Quarterly, 29,* 392–411.

Slavin, R. E. (2007). *Educational research in the age of accountability.* Boston: Allyn & Bacon.

Southern Regional Education Board. (2006). *Schools can't wait: Accelerating the redesign of university principal preparation programs.* Atlanta, GA: Author.

Steiner, P. (1993, July 5). On the Internet, nobody knows you're a dog [Editorial cartoon]. *The New Yorker, 69,* 61.

Strickland, J. (n.d.). *Why is the Google algorithm so important?* Retrieved April 19, 2009, from http://computer.howstuffworks.com/google-algorithm1.html

Trochim, W. (2001). *The research methods knowledge base* (2nd ed.). Cincinnati, OH: Atomic Dog.

Tyack, D., & Cuban, L. (1995). *Tinkering toward utopia: A century of public school reform.* Cambridge, MA: Harvard University Press.

Ury, W. (1993). *Getting past no: Negotiations in difficult situations.* New York: Bantam Dell.

U.S. Department of Education. (2003). *Identifying and implementing educational practices supported by rigorous evidence: A user-friendly guide.* Washington, DC: U.S. Department of Education, Institute for Education Sciences, National Center for Education Evaluation and Regional Assistance.

Vroom, V., & Jago, A. (1978). On the validity of the Vroom/Yetton model. *Journal of Applied Psychology, 63,* 151–162.

Vroom, V., & Yetton, P. (1973). *Leadership and decision making.* Pittsburgh, PA: University of Pittsburgh Press.

Wahlstrom, K., Seashore-Louis, K., Leithwood, K., & Anderson, S. (2010). *Investigating the links to improved student learning: Executive summary of research findings.* New York: Wallace Foundation.

Waters, T., Marzano, R., & McNulty, B. (2003). *Balanced leadership: What 30 years of research tells us about the effect of leadership on student achievement.* Denver, CO: Mid-Continent Research for Education and Learning.

Weick, K. E. (1976). Educational organizations as loosely coupled systems. *Administrative Science Quarterly, 21*(1), 1–19.

Weick, K. E. (1989). Theory construction as disciplined imagination. *Academy of Management Review, 14*(4), 516–531.

Weisbord, M. (2004). *Productive workplaces revisited: Dignity, meaning, and community in the 21st century.* San Francisco: Jossey-Bass.

What is the literature? (n.d.). Wesleyan University Library. Retrieved December 5, 2010, from http://www.wesleyan.edu/libr/guides/litrev/thelit.html

Wolcott, H. (2003). *The man in the principal's office* (updated ed.). Lanham, MD: AltaMira.

Writing a research paper. (2010). Owl Online Writing Lab, Purdue University. Retrieved December 5, 2010, from http://owl.english.purdue.edu/owl/resource/658/01

Yin, R. (2009). *Case study research: Design and methods* (4th ed.). Thousand Oaks, CA: Sage.

Index

ABOUT THE AUTHORS

Scott C. Bauer, PhD (Cornell University), is an associate professor in the Education Leadership Program at George Mason University. Prior to coming to Mason, he served on the faculty at the University of New Orleans and as research director at the School Leadership Center of Greater New Orleans (SLC-GNO). Bauer's research interests involve the application of organizational theory and design to the improvement of schools and the efficacy of various strategies used to develop school leaders at all levels. He is a steering committee member at the Northern Virginia School Leadership Center, a member of the Board of Directors of the SLC-GNO, a steward of the International Network of Leadership Centers, and serves on the editorial boards of *Educational Administration Quarterly* and the *Journal of School Leadership*.

S. David Brazer is associate professor and coordinator of the Education Leadership Program at George Mason University. After receiving his PhD from Stanford University in 1988, Dr. Brazer pursued a career in high school administration, serving as the principal of Los Altos High School for 6 years. During his 11 years at Mason, he has taught most of the courses in the EDLE licensure sequence and several PhD courses in the Education Leadership specialization. Dr. Brazer's research interests include strategic decision making in educational contexts, the effects of leadership preparation programs on graduates, and principal isolation.